A LITTLE

HISTORY OF SNODLAND

ANDREW ASHBEE

© Andrew Ashbee 1994

ISBN 0 9507207 6 3

Printed by Quill Graphics, 6 Cross Street,
Padstow, Cornwall PL28 8AT

Published by Andrew Ashbee
          214, Malling Road,
          Snodland,
          Kent
          ME6 5EQ

CONTENTS

Introduction	v
Acknowledgements	vi
Beginnings	1
Romans	2
A Saxon Cemetery	4
Early Charters	5
After 1086	7
Thirteenth Century	11
1300 - 1400	12
1400 - 1450	14
Some Fifteenth Century Parishioners	14
The Palmer Family	17
Holloway Court	19
The Tilghman Family in Snodland	21
The Sixteenth Century	27
The Seventeenth Century	31
The Eighteenth Century	35
The May Family	47
The Nineteenth Century - A General View	48
The Paper Mill: Early History	52
The Lime and Cement Industry	56
The National Schools	58
The British Schools	61
Henry Dampier Phelps	63
The Toll Road	65
Thomas Fletcher Waghorn	67
The Ferry	71
The Hook Family	72
The Paper Mill Fire of 1906	74
A Chronology of More Recent Events	82

AROUND THE VILLAGE: PLACES AND PEOPLE

All Saints Church	88
Christ Church, Lower Birling	90
The Non-Conformist Churches	93
The Church of the New Jerusalem	95
The Catholic Church	96
The Salvation Army	96
C. of E. Mission Church, Holborough	96

Around the Village: Holborough	99
Holborough Road	109
High Street, North Side	111
High Street, South Side	113
East of the Railway Line	114
Some Lost Alehouse	114
The Upper High Street and Birling Road	115
The Paddlesworth Road	116
Snodland Charities	118
Road Names in 1994	120
Extracts from the 1891 Snodland Census	123
Bibliography, Sources and Further Reading	148

Diagrams, Lists, Genealogical Tables and Maps within the Text

Snodland Householders: 1438 - 1500	18
Alisander family	20
Tilghman family	23
Oswald Tilghman	26
Assessment of Snodland Parishioners: 1524	27
Giles family	31
Hearth Tax returns for Snodland: 1662-1664	33-4
Four Inventories	36-41
Population of Snodland: 1801-1901	49
Population of Snodland and District: 1821	49
A List of Papermakers at Snodland: 1748-1833	54
Lee and Roberts families	57
Thomas Fletcher Waghorn and family	67
Hook family	72
Map of Holborough: 1842	98
Map of Snodland, East Side: 1842	107
Map of Snodland, West Side: 1842	108
1891 Census extracts	121-148

ILLUSTRATIONS

Plate 1:   Holborough Knob, 1930
           Early Tracks

Plate 2:   Plan of Roman Villa

Plate 3:   838 Charter
           Ferry: 1924

Plate 4:   Courtlodge
           All Saints church and the foundations of Snodland Courtlodge. 1881?

Plate 5:   Bischoptre and Tilghman brasses

Plate 6:   All Saint's church interior, about 1900.
           Snodland Brook with 'Blackbrook Bridge', about 1900.

Plate 7:   Charles Townsend Hook (1831-1877)
           The first Independent Chapel in Mill Row.

Plate 8:   At the Paper Mill fire, 12th August 1906.
           Salvaged belongings in the station yard after the Paper Mill fire.

Plate 9:   'The Veles', home of the Hook family.
           High Street, 1864; site of New Jerusalem church on left; Gorham's cottages on right.

Plate 10: 'Mulberry Cottage' before restoration in 1933.
           Woodlands farm before rebuilding and enlarging in 1880.

Plate 11: John May (1732-1805)
           William Lee; his daughter Ann Roberts; her son William Henry Roberts; his son William Lee Henry Roberts. 1878.

Plate 12: Covey Hall farm, probably painted by Agnes Hook in the 1860s
           Holborough Road in 1926, before it was widened.

FOR GERALD EDGELER

INTRODUCTION

1994 sees not only the centenary of Snodland Parish Council, but also the centenary of the first historical account of the place: Woolmer's *Historical Jottings of the Parish of Snodland* which he printed and published from his premises in Bramley Road. A new account of Snodland and its past seems timely. Woolmer packed a good deal into his 47 pages, but its chief value to us today is not so much his sketchy historical account, but rather the information on nineteenth-century Snodland, and particularly the memories he includes by those who were old at the end of the century. Some years later Charles de Rocfort Wall, Rector of Snodland from 1909 to 1930, incorporated more historical notes into his parish magazines, eventually gathering them together (1928) into *Snodland and its History: A.D. 55 to 1928*. At the time, of course, Wall had many of the village's precious historical documents in his care, and he was able to select items from them in compiling his book. He also took account of information gleaned from experts like F. C. Eeles, the church historian, and from some old books of Kentish history like John Thorpe's *Registrum Roffense* (1769) and John Wever's book on Funeral Monuments (1631) - although he must have mistakenly turned over too many pages in the latter because many of the memorials he cites were in Northfleet church and elsewhere, not at Snodland.

With the establishment of the Centre for Kentish Studies (formerly the Kent Archives Office) at Maidstone and, more recently, the archives room in the Council Offices at Strood, we who enjoy researching the past are now presented with something of an embarrassment of riches regarding Snodland's history. To write it down requires careful selection if the main story is not to be swamped with too much detail, but it would be wrong to exclude the vivid stories of former parishioners which bring the tale to life. On the other hand, there will always be frustrating gaps in our knowledge, but then an unfinished jigsaw remains a challenge; one hopes to add further pieces in time. So this is deliberately a 'little' history: one which I hope will tell of Snodland's past more fully than Woolmer or Wall, because the material searched was not all available to them, but which leaves room for more detailed exploration of particular times or subjects elsewhere. That being so, I have avoided duplicating much of what has already been published in my other books (all of which remain available and which it is hoped will be reprinted as necessary): *A History of the Parish Church of All Saints Snodland* (1980), *Snodland 1865-1882: A Selection of Newspaper Cuttings* (1991), and *Notes from Snodland Rectory 1865-1882, compiled by Rev. Carey and Rev. Bingley* (1992). Future plans include similar books on the history of Paddlesworth and perhaps one on Holborough. So there is no mention of Paddlesworth here, except in passing; although small, it was originally a separate parish with its own institutions.

I have avoided using footnotes. Instead I have tried to give a comprehensive list of sources in the Bibliography, at least indicating the group, if not the precise document within the group, from which information is taken.

To those of us who have lived here for many years, it is difficult to come to terms with calling Snodland a 'town', although this is clearly the right term for a community of the present size. I make no apologies for retaining 'village' in this account, for that is what Snodland was for all except a few lines of my narrative. The parish, as defined in the old documents, excludes all the area to the south of Rocfort Road and Chapel Road, which was part of Birling. For a history of that part (which until the late nineteenth century was largely fields anyway) the reader is referred to Margaret Collins, *Birling - A Backward Glance* (Birling, 1981). In any case parish boundaries were no barrier to inhabitants or estates and one of the fascinations of reading histories of nearby parishes is to discover both people and places linked to one's own community.

ACKNOWLEDGEMENTS

I thank the following for permission to reproduce illustrations: Albert Daniels and the Maidstone Area Archaeological Group for their diagram of the Snodland Roman Villa; the British Library for the Snodland charter; The British Museum (Dept. of Prints and Drawings) for William Twopeny's drawing of Snodland Court Lodge; Snodland Town Council for the painting of John May. I am very grateful to Reg. Hunt for making new prints of many of the remaining illustrations, some of which come from my own collection and some from that of Gerald Edgeler.

The bulk of the research on which the book is based was actually done in the 1970s and early 1980s, although I have tried to keep up-to-date with new discoveries as time has permitted. My special thanks go to the staff at the Centre for Kentish Studies (formerly the Kent Archives Office) at Maidstone and also at the 'branch' in the Council Offices of Rochester-upon-Medway (who now hold the Snodland parish records) for help freely given over many years. I am greatly indebted to many local people who have shared their memories of the place: to my late mother for collecting and recording much of Snodland's past, and to living relations of past parishioners whose own research has filled some gaps in my knowledge. The spurt of interest in tracing one's ancestors has led many to discover the fascination of research for themselves. I thank in particular Hyacinth O'Connor, descendant of the Palmer family, and Robin Handley and Vicky Beer, both descendants of sisters of Thomas Fletcher Waghorn, who are currently and fruitfully pursuing their respective ancestors. Miss Elizabeth Tillman has been extraordinarily diligent in tracing the history of the Tilghman family and again she has been enthusiastically keeping me abreast of her findings. Most of all I thank Gerald Edgeler, whose fascination in Snodland's history has lasted a long lifetime. His memory is prodigious, his attention to detail is amazing, and his collection of pictures is unique. We have shared many happy hours of study and reminiscence and I warmly dedicate this book to him.

BEGINNINGS

Water is the key to Snodland's beginnings. Water to drink, from the two streams at either end of the parish: the one at the north serving the community at Holborough, and the other at the south supplying the needs of the first villagers. Water as a natural barrier, in the form of the river Medway, but which at this particular point could be forded at certain times. Water, moreover, which eased communication with other river-side dwellers in higher or lower reaches. But one could have too much water at times of flood and the parish is sited at the point where the river cuts through the North Downs and where gentle slopes keep flooding at bay.

The Medway valley has been inhabited since prehistoric times and Snodland is surrounded by memorials of Early Man. Most striking of these are the Neolithic burial chambers of Kit's Coty and the Countless Stones at Aylesford, and the Coldrum Stones by the Pilgrim's Way near Trottiscliffe. In August 1912 in the neighbouring parish of Halling workmen found the skeleton of a man dating from about 2000 BC.

It was not until 1952, however, that evidence of prehistoric man in the parish itself came to light. Old photographs of the hill at Holborough [PLATE Ia] show both its summit - a little over 200 feet high - and, further down the slope towards the river, the raised hump of a well-recorded Roman tumulus. To villagers of recent times the hill was known as 'Holborough Knob', although in earlier centuries it was more generally called 'Barrow Hill'. One part of the area, at the highest point, was curiously named 'Monk's tippet'. Since a tippet is a collar, this probably referred to the collar of trees and shrubs surrounding the summit. All has now been eaten away by chalk excavation. Indeed it was just these excavations which cut into a hitherto unknown Saxon cemetery and which simultaneously revealed a prehistoric ring ditch. The outside diameter of this ditch was about 100 feet and it is thought that it may have been part of the construction of a round barrow, which formerly incorporated a mound or bank. No trace of a burial was discovered at the centre of the circle, but this may originally have been laid directly on to the chalk at ground level and have been dispersed later as the ground was ploughed and re-ploughed. Some bones found in the ditch may be human, suggesting that there was a secondary burial. The uppermost layers of the ditch contained various types of pottery fragments ranging from the Late Bronze Age to Roman times.

'Holanbeorge' is mentioned in the earliest surviving charter relating to the parish, dating from 838 [Plate III]. The Old English *beorg* denotes a hill or mound, especially a burial mound, while *Hol* correspondingly refers to a hollow. It is no accident, therefore, that among the earliest families of the parish whose names are recorded is that of Holloway, living in the valley at Holborough (as it became) at the foot of the hill. Clearly the two barrows - one prehistoric and one Roman - would have been major landmarks in the area and would attract a special name like 'Holanbeorge'.

The barrows were sited beside an ancient trackway. This had run along the foot of the escarpment at the spring-line, through Trottiscliffe and Paddlesworth, but it deviated here to run down to the river, crossing at Holborough to run south-east past the numerous megalithic monuments towards Boxley [PLATE Ib]. Higher up, the track now called the Pilgrim's Way ran on through Cuxton to cross the river at Rochester. On the hills above Paddlesworth it was once joined by an even higher route which ran along the summit of the Downs. It seems likely that these ways were used by Early Man to move himself and his animals - much as still occurs in some primitive parts of Europe today. Shepherds and sheep would keep to the highest routes, while the cattle would need the water-bearing springs at the lower level. Both would be able to move more easily in these less-densely wooded areas above the heavy Gault Clay and Greensand levels.

There has been much speculation about the river crossings. It is clear from geological studies that the valley floor has changed radically since prehistoric times. With the ending of the Ice Age the sea level rose, forcing the Medway to slow down and deposit much gravel in its own channel instead of in the sea as formerly. From about 10,000 years ago the influence of tides was first felt at the mouth of the Medway and they gradually penetrated further and further inland. This in turn caused further deposits of alluvium over the gravel and formed the salt-marshes which are present today. However, the evidence from borings suggests that the alluvium layer was not formed until after the river crossings had come into use.

It has always been assumed that Rochester stood at about the limit of tides and that a prehistoric crossing existed there. Holborough may have been too difficult for sheep, but two tracks converge to cross the river here: the one past the two barrows and the other, slightly further to the North, descending straight from the hills. The latter forms part of the Halling-Snodland boundary and may be a route made or improved by the Romans to connect (eventually) with Watling Street towards the west. Perhaps in time, as tides continued their advance, the Holborough crossing became unreliable. At any rate a further route was later opened up, for tracks branching off both of those to Holborough make instead for Snodland. Here, even today, is a feature in the river bed known as the 'Snodland Rocks' - 'a bar of iron-cemented conglomorate, with large and small flints and pebbly material visible at low tide'. It has been suggested that this feature, which does not seem to be a natural formation, is what remains of the track between Snodland and Burham. The great S-shaped meander in the river, if it existed at all, would have been further upstream; it is more likely that the river flowed past this point in a number of different streams until the alluvium was laid down.

We may assume that such an important location would encourage settlement nearby, especially since the meeting of the hills and river valley afforded a wide variety of soil and terrain. It is likely that a few round huts were scattered along the valley during the Iron Age, each the home of a farming family. Traces of such settlements are rare, however, and it is only exceptional discoveries like those of Halling Man and the Bronze Age circle which point to their existence.

ROMANS

In 43 A.D. the Roman army invaded Kent in force, advancing swiftly to Rochester, already the most important town in West Kent. The Medway proved a barrier, however, and a two-day battle ensued. Specialist troops forded the river unseen by the Britons - and in an unexpected place - giving the Romans victory. The importance of

Rochester as a military and economic centre, and its position as a crossing-point of the Medway, encouraged Romans to settle along the valley nearby. The quality of life for some Britons in the area may have improved with the introduction of better building techniques, but for others life is likely to have gone on much as before.

Evidence of Roman settlement is found in most of the villages in the Medway Gap today. In Snodland, such evidence has been coming to light for centuries. William Lambarde, in the second edition of his *Perambulation of Kent* (1596), writes:

> 'As touching that Holboroe (or rather Holanbergh) it lieth in Snodland...and tooke the name of Beorgh, or the Hill of buriall, standing over it; in throwing downe a part whereof (for the use of the chalke) my late Neighbour, Maister Tylghman discovered in the very Centre thereof, *Urnam cineribus plenam*, an earthen pot filled with ashes, an assured token of a Romane Monument...'

A lease dated 3 February 1806, concerning the lands by the river belonging to Snodland Court Lodge, records 4 acres called 'Stone Grave Mead', clear evidence that a Roman burial (since re-discovered) was known by that time. There are - or were - two major Roman sites in Snodland, together with a few smaller remains. One was the barrow quarried by William Tilghman, the other was a villa by the river. Both have suffered much through later developments: the barrow site, following a full excavation, was eaten up by chalk quarrying, while the villa remains were subjected to great disturbance by the foundations of modern factory buildings. Recent excavation of the latter has been possible, however, following closure of the works and clearing of the ground.

It was reported to the archaeologist Thomas Wright that around 1815 a Roman bath was discovered at the villa site. which had been covered up again. In 1845 Charles Roach Smith noted that he had seen foundations of a building in Church Field, together with walls and flooring of a small room exposed in the bank of the river. Occasional finds had been made since then, but the first serious excavation took place in the mid-1920s during alterations to the Gas Works occupying the site. A terra cotta mask and a rare bronze buckle-plate were found, together with pottery and five coins. More recent excavations in 1964 and 1971 have now been capped by extensive work over several years made by the Maidstone Area Archaeological Group.

Such a villa would have been owned and occupied by some high-ranking person in Roman society, although this one takes second place to the major house at Eccles, some two kilometres to the south-east. The excavation of ditches indicates that the site was occupied even before construction of the Roman building. In time an extensive house was built, forming three sides of a quadrangle facing east towards the Medway [Plate II]. To the south-west was an aisled barn, measuring some 40 metres by 25 metres, which was apparently built in the mid-second century and demolished in the late fourth. The bath house (presumably the one mentioned by Wright) seems to have stood separate from the main villa. Here a furnace at the eastern extremity led to the hot room (*caldarium*) and warmer room (*tepidarium*), both of which were hypocausted. The cold room (*frigidarium*) adjoined to the west and the whole was served by a separate water-tank to the south, probably connected by wooden piping. In time this bath-house seems to have been abandoned, for by the fourth century two rooms at the south-west of the villa were heated, one with an elaborate channeled hypocaust and the other with the normal pillored hypocaust. It is possible that these rooms were by then being used as a bath-house. With so much destroyed by later developments, the number of finds has been more limited than would otherwise be expected. Nevertheless, discoveries of coins, pottery and small domestic items all point to the villa having been occupied from the first to the fourth centuries.

A stone sarcophagus was found adjacent to the buildings in 1933. A small cremation cemetery was also discovered in 1923 in the garden at the back of "Holboro' Garage" (now "Willowside"), a mile to the west, and another materialized at Ham Hill. But it was the barrow at Holborough which was reserved for the most prestigious burial. The site chosen was close to the prehistoric ring-barrow. The body of a man, probably about 40 years old - possibly an important official of Rochester - was carried here. A funeral pyre was set up just to the south of the burial site and he was cremated, possibly sitting on a bronze-mounted folding stool with a metal-fringed cushion, which was later buried in the barrow. Some glass vessels were also put in the fire and these fused in the great heat. Also placed on the pyre was an old coin, appropriately showing a cremation on its reverse side. A grave was dug and a temporary wooden hut was built over the spot, perhaps to afford shelter during the funeral ceremony. This included the ritual smashing of a group of five jars (*amphorae*). The man's ashes were placed in a wooden coffin together with some of the chalk which had been removed to make the grave itself. A libation of wine or oil was offered and a feast (which included a fowl) was held. Later the remains were collected and buried, mostly in special pits. A dome of chalk and turf was erected above the grave and a larger mound covered the whole, rising to 11 feet above the original surface. The barrow was surrounded by an oval ditch and bank. The pottery remains suggest that all this occurred in the first quarter of the third century A.D. Before long, however, the mound was partially re-opened at its southern extremity to receive the burial of a small child, aged about one, in a fine lead sarcophagus (now in Maidstone Museum). Presumably this was a relative - perhaps a child or grandchild - of the man for whom the barrow was made. Within the sarcophagus with the body, which had not been cremated, was the remains of a purse - a luxury item suggesting the child had come from a wealthy family. This sarcophagus has been described as the most interesting found at any Romano-British site, because of its decoration of scallop shells and Dionysiac figures, which were symbolic representations of the after-life in Roman Mediterranean art. It seems likely that the maker was relatively local, but used a 'pattern-book' imported from abroad for the design. The use of such figures was widespread in Roman times and does not necessarily imply that the Snodland family were especially devoted to the worship of Dionysius.

A SAXON CEMETERY

If Roman rule declined in the area after the fourth century, and the villa was abandoned, what happened to the land? There is surprisingly little evidence of settlement along the Medway in the centuries after Roman occupation and it is quite possible that previously cultivated areas became overgrown. Yet the river crossing would continue to bring people to Holborough and Snodland, so there was always a likelihood that some would take up residence, however temporary, close by.

In 1952, continued chalk quarrying revealed a series of 39 graves between the prehistoric and Roman barrows. Some others had already been lost to the diggers, but a full investigation of those remaining was carried out. Apart from one infant grave, all were lying with the head to the west. As occurs in other locations, it seems likely that the Bronze Age barrow was deliberately chosen as the site for these burials. The cemetery gradually spread from the first graves, dug into the prehistoric barrow, south and east down the slope. Again this is a practice known elsewhere. Some burials were in lidless wooden coffins and some had grave goods buried with them: buckles, shields, spears, swords, knives, bowls and other utensils, and pottery. It has been suggested that some of the finds, especially two buckles, indicate a Christian connection for these people. One buckle has a cross similar to known Christian forms of the time, the other has a bird motif which compares with another from Faversham with a fish - also a Christian symbol. In 604 Justus had been ordained as the first Bishop of Rochester by Augustine and a small church dedicated to St. Andrew was built in the city - later enlarged to become the cathedral - so Christianity was already established in the area.

The cemetery was begun in the seventh century and continued into the next, to serve a group of settlers living by the stream at Holborough. It cannot have continued for too long, judging by its relatively small extent. The finds can all be dated to a span of some fifty years, but the later burials had no grave-goods in them.

EARLY CHARTERS

By the ninth century, when the first documents appear, Snodland had gained its name in the form 'Snoddingland'. Since nearly all the -ingland names are derived from personal names, it is thought probable that a man called Snodda lived here and gave the place its identity. All land was held by the King, but he would freely present parcels of it to favoured noblemen and others. So it is that the earliest Snodland charter reads as follows [Plate III]:

> 'In the name of our Lord Jesus Christ, saviour of the world, A.D. 838, I King Egbert, with the consent of my dearest son King Ethelwulf, give to my bishop Beornmodo all that land of mine: four ploughlands in the place called Snoddingland and Holanbeorge, granting that they should be free from all service...And a mill on the stream called Holanbeorges burna, and on the King's hill fifty loads of wood, and also four denberries [in the Weald]: Hwetonstede, Heahden, Hese, Helmanhyrst.'

Two examples of extraordinary continuity are supplied by this charter. Although it is no longer working, the mill at Holborough is likely to be on or near the site of its predecessor more than 1100 years earlier. The fact that the gift of land was made to the Bishop of Rochester, enabling it to descend through his successors and not be dependent on the fortunes of a family line, seems to have preserved its identity for almost as long. At any rate, among the last of the manorial documents for this area, dating from the 1820s and 1830s, are lists of the Bishop's tenants and the rents paid by each. These all relate to Snodland, Holborough and Halling, except for a final group, headed 'Wild Rents in the Borough of Wested [Whetsted] & Tudely'. Here, it seems, are the remnants - if not more - of those four 'denberries' in the Weald.

All the earliest records mentioning our village were copied into one of the most famous of early English manuscripts: the *Textus Roffensis*. This great book was compiled at Rochester during the bishopric of Ernulf [1115-1124]. It includes a register of royal charters and grants to the cathedral including those, like the one above, of which independent copies survive.

In 841 Ethelwulf (who was King of the West Saxons) added two ploughlands at Holanbeorge to the gift and many other small bequests from lesser men increased the Bishop's holdings in the parish in later centuries. It is thanks to some shifty dealings in the 10th century that Snodland again comes to notice. The will of a couple from Meopham in A.D.950 shows that one Aelfere bequeathed his holdings of land at Bromley, Fawkham and Snodland to St. Andrew's at Rochester, a gift confirmed by his wife Aescwyn. However, priests stole the charters of Snodland from the Bishop and sold them secretly to Aelfere's son Aelfric. (Perhaps he was annoyed that he had been excluded from enjoying rights of the property in his turn). The Bishop, of course, demanded the return of the charters. In the meantime Aelfric died, so the Bishop then demanded them from Aelfric's widow Byrhtwaru. It was her son, Byrhtic, with his wife Aelfswith, who made the Meopham will, bequeathing Snodland to St. Andrew's, Rochester, 'after Byrhtwaru's day'. In any case, a court in London had decreed that the stolen charters should be returned to Rochester and to the Bishop, with compensation to be made for the theft.

Some time before 1011 another court, held at Canterbury, deliberated for a long time concerning a further tussle for land at Snodland - this time between the Bishop of Rochester and the 'shiresman' Leofwine [of Ditton] (who had an abbot, Aelfun, to support him). Eventually the Bishop was asked to grant the land to Leofwine for his lifetime, and he agreed. For his part Leofwine pledged that the land would then revert to the Bishop without argument 'and gave up the titles that he had to the land which had before been alienated from the place, and all the messuages which he had west of the church, to the holy place [Rochester].' This last sentence is particularly interesting, for it confirms that there was a church in Snodland before the Norman Conquest and that there were also houses lining the High Street leading to the west.

For military help the village would have looked to Rochester, where the fortifications had been developed by the Romans. The maintenance of Rochester Bridge was the responsibility of the whole district. The bridge was made of wood and had nine piers and a tower (used for defence and as a gate) near the east end. Around 975 A.D. we read:

> Then is the ninth pier the Archbishop's, which is the land pier at the west end, belonging to Flyote and to his Clive and to Hehham and to Denetune and to Melatune and to Hludesdune and to Meapeham and to Snodilande and to Berlingam and to Peadleswyrthe and all the men of the dens, and four rods to plank and three supports to place....These

shall repair the bridge at Rochester whenever it is broken, and let it be noticed that all the beams which are placed in this bridge ought to be of large dimensions, that they may well support the planks, and the great weight of all those things that pass over them.'

AFTER 1086

It has been proposed that the boundaries of some English villages match the estates of Roman villas. It seems quite likely that Snodland would be one of these, serving the substantial villa by the river. Some of the parish boundaries have always been clearly defined. The river to the east and the stream to the south, bounding on the parishes of East Malling and Birling, and the border with the (once) separate parish of Paddlesworth to the west: all these seem to have been well established from earliest times. But the boundary with Halling was at first not so precise, perhaps because both Holborough and Halling were part of the same manor held by the Bishop of Rochester. Early residents living beside this boundary are sometimes listed in one parish and sometimes in the other. Ecclesiastical boundaries defined the extent to which each church was responsible not only for the cure of souls, but also for help (via the parish officers) for those needing social care of any kind.

Domesday Book, a detailed survey of the country made in 1086, sets out the answers to a series of questions from William the Conqueror. He sent commissioners to each place to ask:

1) the name of the place. Who held it (a) before 1066 (b) now?
2) How many hides? [a unit of about 120 acres]. How many ploughs, both those in lordship and the men's?
3) How many villagers, cottagers and slaves, how many free men and Freemen?
4) How much woodland, meadow and pasture? How many mills and fishponds?
5) How much has been added or taken away? What the total value was and is?
6) How much each free man or Freeman had or has? (a) before 1066; (b) when King William gave it, (c) now; and if more can be had than at present.

The answers for Snodland were:

'The Bishop of Rochester holds Esnoiland. In the time of King Edward the Confessor [before 1066], it was taxed at six sulings, and now at three. The arable land is six ploughs. In lordship there are two ploughs and ten villagers, with six smallholders, having six ploughs. There is a church and five slaves, and three mills of forty shillings, and thirty acres of meadow, wood for the pannage of four hogs. In the time of King Edward and afterwards it was worth six pounds, and now nine pounds.'

Though King William gave his own followers possession of vast tracts of land in England, he took over both the organization of English society and the way the land was cultivated from the Anglo Saxon era - what we call the feudal system. At the head of the system was the lord of the manor - here the Bishop of Rochester. All villagers were subservient to him, being bound to their tenancy - with some forced to move at his command, forced to grind their corn at his mill, forced to till his fields on certain days of the year, forced to give him military service, and requiring his permission when giving their children in marriage. One remnant of this service in Snodland is probably the great earth rampart, formerly known as 'the wall', built to separate fresh water pasture from the salt marshes by the river. We can imagine the villagers toiling with their simple tools for many days to form this impressive earthwork for the Bishop.

Each manor was divided into its 'demesne' land - intended to provide for the particular needs of the lord's own household - and the remainder, which was usually sub-let to tenant farmers for rent. All villagers needed land of their own to raise food for the families and this was distributed in individual strips scattered through one or two great 'open fields'. Here was the fairest means of sharing out good and bad land to all alike. (The lord was always likely to have acquired some of the very best land - like 'Bishop's Reed', a very fine field in the south of our parish.)

It is becoming increasingly clear that the Domesday description is but the most impressive example of a number of early documents showing that those who governed the land, whether noblemen or clergy from the great cathedrals, monasteries or abbeys, had a detailed knowledge of their holdings and of those who lived on their estates. The amounts of land which the tenants farmed for themselves were used to assess them for taxes. So the Domesday entry for Snodland records that the Bishop himself had land for 2 plough teams, there was arable land for 6 plough teams, and the villagers themselves (in the common fields) had lands for another six. This area probably matches that of a Roman villa estate, so again we are led back to the villa by the river as the key for the extent of our parish. Here were ten 'villagers' - the highest class of peasantry - who, although required to serve the lord on his land, might also hold between 30 and 100 acres each in the common fields. The six smallholders were of lesser standing in the community, but higher than the five slaves - treated as chattels of the lord in every respect. With wives and children that suggests a total population of nearly 100 people.

Can we discover how this land was distributed? Yes, to a limited extent. Evidence can be deduced from surviving deeds and maps, even as late as the eighteenth century, for these show the last remnants of the strips of land tilled for centuries before that. Then there are a number of early mediaeval tax assessments which are also helpful. But perhaps most important of all is the evidence which can be superimposed on information from the documents: evidence now fast vanishing but available at least within living memory to anyone walking round the parish. It is the farms, and the sites of farms, which are the key to unlocking the secrets of the Domesday entry.

A seventeenth century map of the Bishop's 'Manor of Halling' - to which both Holborough and Cuxton belonged - shows that his fields lay largely at that end of the parish, together with his mill at Holborough. Tenant farmers would have occupied his farm or farms by the mill. By the late 13th century one of these tenant families was that of Holloway, whose members lived on there until around 1500 and who gave their name to the property. Other early residents of Holborough and Halling, and who held land in both, were called Canon, Herring and Usher. All were well established there for several hundred years.

In addition to the Bishop's manor, at least two others formed part of the parish of Snodland. One was the manor of Veles and the other was the manor of Potyns. Both seem to have been named after the families who owned and/or lived in them. The manor house of Veles was sited by the church and river-crossing (now part of the paper mill car park) and a large part of its land bordered on the river, taking in the villa site, but also extending into the parishes of Birling and East Malling. We may surmise that once the Roman villa fell into decay it was succeeded by this farm. It probably included another of the mills mentioned in the Domesday survey, served by the adjacent stream, and developed hundreds of years later into the paper mill. (Where, one wonders, was the third mill mentioned by Domesday?) The Vele family, or their predecessors, would certainly have been counted among the chief inhabitants of their time. They are mentioned in documents between 1242 and 1346.

The other manor, of Potyns, has a different pedigree. It always seems to have belonged to the lords of the adjacent manor of Paddlesworth. At the time of King Edward this was Godric. In 1086 Hugh of Port held Paddlesworth from Odo, Bishop of Bayeux. Later it passed to the lords of Linton and Saye. The manor may have taken its name from 'William Potin, Thurstan of Strood', clerk of the works in building a new ditch and wall round the city of Rochester in 1225. By a legal settlement in Canterbury on 21 September 1227, Robert le Kempe was granted the tenancy of 5 acres of land at Holborough at a yearly rent of 12d., having acknowledged that the land belonged to William Potyn. A similar settlement in Rochester on 8 July 1271 showed the tenant of a house and (presumably the same) 5 acres of land now to be Robert, son of Benedict Hemer, and his wife Eleanor. The landlord was still a William Potyn, perhaps son or grandson of the other man of this name. A John Potyn was bailiff of the city of Rochester with William de Snodeland in 1271-2. Maybe this William was called Potyn too, for surnames were not yet well established. A person might be called after his profession, such as Miller or Baker, or, more commonly he might be named after his home parish or some identifiable place within it. Eventually the reverse happened, as here, with property being named after its owner or occupier. The principal farmhouse for this manor may have been the predecessor to what is now called 'Cox's Farm', or 'Woodlands'. Its sixteenth century name of 'Newhouse' implies that the present building replaced an earlier one. But the manor house might equally have been Mark farm - so called because of its position near the boundary of the parish - which is also very ancient. Members of a family called 'de Merke' can be traced around 1300 and after.

Two other families from the 13th century can also be associated with Snodland farms. Lad and Povenesse gave their names to Lad's farm and Punish farm respectively. What others remain? Presumably those farms which by their size, position and known history were the equal of those above. One would be Grove farm whose site so close to Birling led to a legal ruling in the seventeenth century that it belonged to Snodland, although it still appears in the Birling censuses of the nineteenth century! Another would be 'Home' or Covey Hall farm on the Holborough Road, while a third would be centred on the timbered house in the High Street now known as 'Mulberry Cottage'. All these had substantial amounts of land attached to them as one would expect for the property of a mediaeval 'villein' or 'villager'. The 'borderers' or small holders would occupy smaller units.

Again we can pick out certain properties as of ancient lineage and with a more limited area of associated land. The Bull, where the High Street and road to Rochester met, and 'Benet's Place', formerly at the junction of the Paddlesworth and Birling roads, are two examples. Others are the buildings called 'Prospect Cottage' on the east side of Holborough Road, which seem to have developed from a single 'hall house' of the 15th century, and at least one more called 'Acacia Cottage', demolished by Charles Townsend Hook to make way for his imposing nineteenth century house in the High Street - which he confusingly called 'Veles'. There was at least one more small holding at Holborough, later known as 'Gilder's Farm'.

In Snodland it seems that the common field devoted to arable land extended from the village westwards as far as the Pilgrim's Way, with the Bishop's lands on the north side. The 1844 tithe commutation map shows 'Islands' as the great field at the west end, but this is a corruption of 'Highlands'. The common arable land for Potyns seems to have been located in the valley behind Lad's farm. Each year part of the common land would be kept fallow while the other part was cultivated. Chalk does not favour trees, so the woodland tended to be cultivated as narrow 'shaws' around the edges of fields - which also served as wind-breaks. Larger wooded areas (where the soil allowed it) were confined to the downs where opportunity for cultivation was limited and where the game could roam freely. These were nevertheless an important feature of the environment, for they supplied both material for buildings and implements and fuel for heating. A third element was pasture land to provide food for the livestock and on which animals could graze when not working. Naturally it was the land near the river which best served this purpose and Snodland's common pasture, part of which still survives, has always been known as 'The Brook' or 'Blackbrookes'. More common pasture, probably for the Holborough manor, was next to the Medway near Halling. A final part of the 'jigsaw' was the glebe land granted to the rector of the parish for his own use. We have detailed descriptions of the glebe land from 1634 to 1848 and there is no reason to doubt that these would also be valid as far back as mediaeval times. They give a good idea of what was deemed necessary for his subsistence (considerably more than the 4 acres which seems generally to have been reckoned a feasible amount):

1) Half an acre of arable land (later reduced to a quarter) 'lying in the South East end of Upper Mill Field' [behind 'Prospect Cottage' in Holborough Road, now part of Willowside].
2) A quarter of an acre of meadow land 'in the South-West corner of Parsonage Meadow' [near the Brook].
3) An acre of salt marsh 'in the Common Salts' [near the Medway at Holborough]
4) Two and a half acres of arable land [near 'Highlands'].
5) Three acres of arable land [near (4)] 'in the Comon fields belonging to Holborrowe'.
6) An acre of arable land 'in a common field called Lad's'.
7) An acre of arable land in a field called 'The hanging hill'.
8) Around 11 acres of arable and pasture land (on which the rectory itself was built after the Reformation) [now the cricket meadow and adjoining land to the south.]

The three centuries after the Domesday Book was compiled are thinly documented. Three main sources of information are available: the registers of the bishops of Rochester, books from the monastery of St. Andrew's, Rochester, and a series of legal agreements known as 'fines'. They record the comings and goings of the earliest known rectors, grants of land, and a varied crop of disputes and misdemeanours. From them we cannot glean much of the life of the village beyond the names of the chief inhabitants and they are perhaps best presented as a calendar (to which other items may be added by future research).

THIRTEENTH CENTURY

In 1193 Gilbert de Glanville freely paid the salary of a priest from the tithes of his own knights in Halling, Holborough and Cuxton for the support of the poor staying there.

The earliest known grant of land by ordinary parishioners here was made at Bermondsey on 9 February 1219. Philip de Allingg and his wife Emelina granted the tenancy of 3½ acres of their land at Snodland to Gilbert Pistor [latin for 'Baker'] and his heirs at a yearly rent of 1d., although he was required to undertake any service due to the lords of the manor.

In an undated document Robert Vitulus [Vele], with the agreement of his wife Emme and his brother Seunfredi gave to the monks of St. Andrew's, Rochester, two acres of his own land in Snodland, held by his tenant William Enif at a yearly rent of 12d. He wrote that this was done 'for the good of my soul and of the souls of the ancestors of me and my wife, and of my own free will.'

In an undated document Robert Vituli [Vele] releases to John and William, sons of Richard of Snodland, clerk, one virgate and four day-works of land placed between the land of the lord bishop towards the East, the King's highway leading from Snodland to Rochester towards the West, a headland belonging to his messuage towards the North and lands of the bishop [of Rochester] towards the South. Witnesses: Phillipo de Powenesse, Ricardo le Veel Alexandro Harange, Johanne le Lad, Thoma de Kyngesmelle, Nicholas Godesgrace, Ada Syward, Willelmo de Merke, Nicholas his brother, Adam de Swanscompe, Johanne atte Penre and others. [Bishop's registers]

In 1242 the villagers wealthy enough to be taxed (according to the amount of land they held) were Philippus de Povenesse [half a fee], Johannes le Vel [half a fee] and Walterus le Ladd [half a fee]. Between them they paid ten shillings.

In 1254 Reginaldus Harynge held a 10th part of the Fee in Snodilonde of the Bishop of Rochester; Henricus de Pevenseye held two parts [...]; Anselinus Lad held a quarter part [...]; Ricardus le Veel held a sixth part [...].

[1299] 27th Edward III. Deed of Johannis le Usser: five dayworks of land. Witnesses: Philippo de Povenesse, Johannes le Veel, Johanne Lad, Alexandro Herynge, Johanne de Langeriche, Ada Lylye, Radulfo le Canoun, and others. [Bishop's registers]

20 March Ed. III. Surrender by Johannes le Usser of three virgates and 2 day-works of demesne land in Colemannsfeld in longitude from the North by the lane called Broclane to the Bishop's lands. Witnesses: Philippo de Povenesse, Alexandro Harange, Roberto de la

Chambre, Johanne de Langeriche, Johannes le Lad, Ada Lylye, Willelmo de Holeweye, Henrico le Vitele. [John Thorpe, *Registrum Roffense*, p.602]

At the end of the century a Judge, Solomon de Rochester, was living in Snodland. But he was fined and imprisoned for corruption. Soon after he was poisoned by Wynand de Dryland, parson of Snodland. Wynand was charged with the murder, but the Bishop confirmed that he was a clerk in holy orders, and after a period of penance at Greenwich he was freed.

1300 - 1400

On 21 July 1303 Bishop Thomas of Wouldham ordered the vicars of Hallyng and Berlyng and the parish priests of Padeleswrthe, Snodlonde, Cuclestan, and Luddeston to admonish the persons who have broken his park of Halling, cut and carried off oaks and other trees, and taken his deer. They were to make restitution before St. Bartholomew's Day, on pain of excommunication. The Bishop's park, heavily wooded, is clearly shown on the 1634 map of his manor and even today a large part of it survives as 'Greatpark Wood'.

1312. A dispute between Nicholas de Estmallyng with Roger, son of Hugh de Boxstede and Andrew de Lenn with Alice his wife concerning lands at Leyburn, Hallyng, Snodelond, Berlyng and Est Mallyng.

1314. Ralph Canoun of Snodelonde and Alice his wife are acknowledged as the owners of a house, 26 acres of land and 1 acre of meadow in Snodelonde

1316. In an agreement between Geoffrey, son of Adam de Gillingham, and John, son of John le Lad of Snodylonde, Geoffrey is granted the title to a house, 54 acres of land, 5 acres of wood, 4s. 8d. rent and rent of 1 goose, in Snodilonde. John is granted the tenancy for his life, which then passes to Alice, the daughter of Geoffrey, and after her death reverts to the heirs of John.

15 June 1322. Hamo, Bishop of Rochester, lets to farm to William de Herdefelde and his heirs, 7 acres of land in a field called 'Rifshet' in Snodelonde at an annual rent of 7 quarters of barley, worth 4d. a quarter. William also has 16 acres in Snodelonde and 16 acres in East Malling which are to come under the jurisdiction of the Bishop.

1322. The mill of Holbergh at the same time was new made of timber from Perstede [Bearsted] and cost £10. [Life of Hamo of Hythe]

1326. The parishioners of Snodland and Halling were given permission by the Bishop to mix blackberry juice with their grape wine. Tithes had to be paid on the vines. [Life of Hamo of Hythe]

1330. At the death of Hamo, Bishop of Rochester, an inventory of Holebergh was taken: 16 cows, 4 oxen, each valued at 10s, 1 horse valued at 20s., 2 swans, seed from the goods of the deceased. 4 caructate and 1 from the goods of the deceased; forge and iron implements. [British Library, MS Faustina B.V, f.101v-102r]

1330. In an agreement between John de Melford with Katherine his wife, and William le Ussher of Snodelond, William is acknowledged as the owner of 2 houses, 41½ acres of land, 1 acre of meadow, 1 acre of wood, and 20s. rent, in Hallyng and Snodelond. He grants all this to John and Katherine and to her heirs.

25 June 1330. Document of Hamo, Bishop of Rochester. Johannis le Melforde and Johannis Herynge. Wynando le Veel, Henrico de Ponesshe, Johanne Lad, Willemo de Chelesham, Willelmo Ussher, Willelmo Holloweye, Thome Canoun, Johanne Bakere, Roberto Noble. [John Thorpe, *Registrum Roffense*, p. 603]

31 August 1330. Wynand le Veel confesses an assault on John Pyr in the churchyard of Snodland. His penance is to procure the reconciliation of the churchyard, polluted by the drawing of blood. This affair dragged on and involved others. Wynand failed to appear before the Bishop's Court and was pronounced "contumacious" [a wilful breaker of the law]. Eventually, however, on 30 March 1331, the Bishop granted the absolution of Wynand le Vel from excommunication, and Thomas Canon, Ricardus Lusk, Johannes le Meller, and Walterus Holeweye of Snodland from suspension upon Wynand's undertaking to pay the procuration demanded at Midsummer and the others were to see that he did so. The rector of Snodland was guarantor for them all.

[Undated]: Let for rent: Johanne le Ushher/ Radulfo Canonn:
    Ricardi Lulke: 5 acres in the same field
    Galfridi Lylie: 2 acres in the same field
    Johannes Herynge: 1 acre in the same field
    Willelmi Pyr: 1 acre in the same field
    Johanne Pyr: 1 acre in the same field
    Johannis Wedone: 1 acre in the same field
    Nicholai Lulke: 1 acre in the same field
    Thome Duntefrenche: 1 acre in the same field
[John Thorpe, *Registrum Roffense*, p. 603]

11 December 1330. The rector of Snodland is admonished to make good all defects in the books, vestments and chancel of his church before Easter under a penalty of 20 shillings.

21 February 1342. In the valuation of Strood hospital is a meadow at Snodland, valued at 6 shillings.

1346. Ricardo de Povenasshe, Johanne de Melforde, Johannis Lad and Ricardi le Veel are assessed for the half fee which Philippus de Povenasshe, Johannes Harang, and Walterus Lad held in Snodelond of the Bishop of Rochester. Johannes de Melford holds an eighth part and all are to pay 20 shillings.

1364. Henry de Scortneye was appointed to the Chaplaincy of St. Andrew, Holboro', but no church or chapel appears ever to have been built.

10 June 1387. Grant of a property in 'Holberghe' by Thomas Brynton, Bishop of Rochester, to Peter Parker, which property came to the bishop on the death of Thomas Rokherst.

23 April 1391. An agreement between Peter Hattere, and Thomas Pole with Christina his wife. For 100 marks [£66. 13s. 4d.] Hattere buys from them a house with 120 acres of land (rent value 20s) in Hallyng, Snotheland and Cokklestan.

1400 - 1450

2 February 1403. Command that the Bishop of Rochester attend Chancery to give reason why there should not be a postponment of the hearing against Roger Punyarde and Agnes Piers of Snodelande, excommunicated for contumacy. They have appealed to the court of Canterbury. William Usher, Thomas Brewere, John Reynolde, each of London [?] 'shipwright' are mainprise for them. [Calendar of Close Rolls]

St. Matthew/ 1 Hen. VI [1433]. Grant of a croft to Peter Fyscher of Snodland by John Marchaunt and John Essex, both of Birling. Croft lying at 'Sharnale' in Birling. [Arch. Cant. X]

SOME FIFTEENTH CENTURY PARISHIONERS

From the middle of the fifteenth century, a wealth of documentary material becomes available - in particular a steady stream of wills which introduces us to the principal parishioners. These wills are supported by a number of deeds concerning property and land. One of the latter, made on 24 September 1460, is especially illuminating. It says (in Latin):

> Know all men by these presents that we Thomas Benett of the parish of Snodland, Edward Pekerynge, gentleman, and John Dobbys of Cobham, grant to John Beauley all our tenement in the said parish of Snodland, with all its associated buildings, land, croft and garden adjoining, called Benetysplace, situated between the tenement of John Sevare towards the west, the tenement of Richard Palmer towards the east, the King's highway towards the south and the land of the said Thomas towards the north; giving to the said John Beauley 30 acres of land etc. in the said parish; and also 2½ acres of the said land lying on the north side of the said tenement, between the land of Simon Spayn towards the east, the land of John Sevare towards the west and abutting on the land of Roger Stalworth towards the north; and another part of the said 2½ acres lying between the land lately belonging to Thomas Permanter towards the north and abutting on the land of the said Roger and land of John Herynge and Thomas Permanter towards the north; and 2½ acres of the aforesaid land lying towards Boghtmere between the land of John Holwey towards the west, abutting on the land of the said Roger towards the north and east and to the king's highway towards the south; three rods of the said land lying towards Longdowne between the land lately belonging to Nicholas Smyth towards the south, abutting on the land of Roger Stalworth towards the west, the land of Thomas Brooke and Simon Spayn towards the north and the land of Thomas Dalby towards the east; three yards of the said land lying

towards Dalefeldhegge between the land of Roger Stalworth towards the east, land lately belonging to Thomas Permanter towards the west and abutting on Dalefeld towards the south; two acres of the said land lying towards Lompcoupe between the land of Roger Stalworth towards the west, land of Richard Canon towards the north and land of Thomas Ussher, Thomas Dalby, clerk, and Richard Canon towards the east; three acres of the said land lying towards Wodecockdowne between the land of John Berman, Richard Canon and Walter Andrewe towards the north and land of Simon Spayn and the heirs of Nicholas Smyth towards the west, land of the heirs of John Fen towards the east and land of Thomas Dalby, clerk, towards the south; 1½ acres of the said three acres lying between the land of Roger Stalworth towards the north, land lately belonging to John Fen towards the east, land of Walter Andrewe towards the west and land of Thomas Dalby, clerk, towards the east; seven day-works of the said land lying towards Wodecockdowne between the land of Thomas Dalby, clerk towards the north, land of John Butler towards the east and land lately belonging to John Fen towards the south and west; seven day-works of the said land lying towards Wodecockdowne between land of the heirs of Nicholas Smyth towards the south, and land of Thomas Dalby, clerk, towards the north; 2½ acres of the said land lying in a croft towards Moltland beside the king's highway called Riedstrete west of the said highway; 1½ acres of the said land lying in a croft to the west of the Parson's Field of Snodland, between the land of John Butler senior towards the east and the King's highway there called Riedstrete towards the west; 6½ acres of the said land lying towards Weelesrede also called Benetysrede; ½ acre of the said land lying towards Litill Pightyll between the land of John Butler and the King's highway towards the south and land of Nicholas Wotton towards the west; 2½ acres of the said land called Whetcroft lying between the land of the Bishop of Rochester towards the north, land of John Coton towards the east and land of Stephen Browne towards the south and west; three acres of the said land lying towards Stonecroft and Longcroft between the land of the Bishop of Rochester towards the north, land of Stephen Browne towards the east and south and land of the heirs of Henry Canon towards the west; three rods of the said land called Litill Mede beside Molthill lying between the land of Nicholas Wotton towards the north and east, land of John Canon towards the south and land lately belonging to Thomas Permanter towards the west. John Beauley is to pay 34 marks in instalments and the document is witnessed by Thomas Dalby, [Rector of Snodland], Roger Stalworth, John Butler, Simon Spayn, Thomas Ussher 'and many others' at Snodland.

By a fortunate chance surviving deeds show that 'Benet's Place' was a large house sited at the junction of the Paddlesworth and Birling roads (immediately east of the "Monk's Head"). In 1817 this was bought and turned into a group of separate cottages for farm labourers by Thomas Stevens, farmer of Paddlesworth; in more recent times they were known as 'Dodnor' Cottages. From this we can further deduce that John Sevare is likely to have lived at 'Woodland's Farm' and Richard Palmer at the 'Bull'.

Who were these men? We can learn a little from their wills. Thomas Parmenter had died in 1459. Like many others, his will included a bequest of money for repairs to the bridge of 'Blakebroke'. Maintenance of parish roads and buildings was entirely the responsibility of the inhabitants and it was imperative that the wealthier inhabitants saw to it that money, material and labour was available for such work. In his turn, in 1461, Thomas Benet asked to be buried 'att ye Westdorr of ye Chyrch of Snodland', adding 'I bequeth to ye makyng of ye same porch 4 mark of mony' [about £1.35]. Simon Spayn's will of March 1467 specified: 'I give to repairing the King's highway between Jolyff's Crosse and the 'mansion' which was lately Thomas Goseler's, where most need is, 12s. [60p.] And to repairing the ways between the back cross and the church of Snodelond, 12d. [10p.]'. Spayn's house was at 'Burgate Cross', perhaps the old house (now demolished) on the corner of the High Street [once 'Burgate Street'] and Holborough Road, and he owned another house called 'Fynderus' together with other property in Snodland, Birling and Paddlesworth. In 1457 John French gave some virge-stones to mend 'the highway leading towards Mallyng' and 'between my house and the house of Roger Stalworth'.

But it was not only the well-being of their fellow men which concerned them, nor the disposing of their worldy goods to their kinsfolk and friends. Their spiritual life was strong and the well-being of their souls too needed appropriate consideration. Money for the burning of candles before the many images in the church is a common feature of many wills, whether to 'Our Lady in the North Chapel', 'Mary Magdalene', 'Our Lady of Piety', 'St. Stephen', 'St. James', 'The High Altar', or to others. John Pole (1487) gave 6s. 8d. towards the

> 'Chapell of our lady in the north side of ye church of Snodland ... Also I bequeyth to a tabell of alabastr for ye autor in ye seid chapell a 40s for to pray for John Haw, Christopher Haw and for the soulis of John Pole and John Cotton. Also I will that myne executors by a stone to ley on my grave wtin a yere of my decease. Also I will yt ye best crosse in Snodland Church be amendyd on my cost. Also I bequeyth 10s. to bye a pyx for the blyssyd sacrament in the sayd church.

In particular there are innumerable bequests to 'ye croslytt', no doubt illuminating the marvellous incised crucifix on the pillar. In 1457 John French gave a considerable sum, 13s. 4d. [67p.], 'to provide oil to burn in the lamp before the image of the Holy Cross for ever'. Donations were given to the Augustinian Friars in London (but why them especially is not known) and to the Carmelite Friars at Aylesford. It was customary to pay a priest to say masses for one's soul, particularly one month after death and on anniversary days, and some goods, bread and drink might be allocated to the poor 'for the good of my soul'. Money for 'the making and mending of the shrine of the figure of the Blessed Virgin Mary', the donation of a cloth to cover the image of Mary Magdalene to protect it from becoming defiled and unclean', 'a beautiful book of pleas and diriges', and 'a chased gilt cup' are among other bequests to the church at Snodland, together with more mundane offerings to repair the churchyard wall and the like.

In his will of 20 November 1472, Thomas Usher asked to be buried in the churchyard of Snodland next to his father. Most unusually for the time, he specified that a commemorative stone be installed:

> 'I will that myn executors by a stone to Cowvyr my fadeys grave & myn & that my fadyrs name & myn be wryttyn ther uppon for a p[er]petual remambrance & memory that all men & women that rede or se it pray by in way of Charyte.'

After all these years, no trace of it remains.

Although the names of about 100 Snodland men are known from this period, scarcely one has a named occupation. All of them worked principally as farmers or small-holders, of course, but the skills of carpenters, masons, millers, blacksmiths and other trades would also have been available to the community. William Boteler, of Norwich, describes himself as a 'barbour', but his will is concerned with the disposal of the land he owned in Snodland. He remembered to bequeath 33s. 4d. 'to the church where I was born'. Henry Scryvener (d.1477), was a miller, but his own property was in Wateringbury.

The Palmer Family

Old books on Kentish history make much of the association of the Palmer family with Snodland. Foremost among these (and drawn upon by later historians) was Thomas Philipott who, in his *Villare Cantianum* (1659), wrote:

> 'The Courtlodge by the Church, was, as high as I can by the Guide and Direction of Evidence trace out, the Palmers, as appears by very ancient deeds, sealed with a Cheveron between three Palmer's Scrips. William le Palmer, who was Owner both of this and Rye-House in Otford, flourished here in the reign of Edward the third [i.e.1327-1377], and stood depicted in the Church-Window, with the above-recited Arms on his Tabard or Surcoat, untill some rude hand defaced the Signature.'

It would be nice to find some of these ancient deeds with their seals, but they have disappeared and we have to take Philipott's information on trust. Even the church memorials have gone. John Weaver [1631] set down an epitaph, missing even then from the gravestone in the chancel:

> Palmers al owr faders were,
> I, a Palmer, livyd here
> And travyld still, till worne wyth age,
> I endyd this worlds pylgramage,
> On the blylst Assention day
> In the cherful month of May;
> A thowsand wyth foure hundryd seven,
>   And took my jorney hense to Heven.

SNODLAND HOUSEHOLDERS : 1438 - 1500

The list derives from surviving wills and administrations and does not include family members. The date is the year of death. Some people owned property in Snodland, but lived elsewhere. The poorest parishioners would not have troubled to make a will and are not represented here

Robert Wedyngton of London	1438	William Speryn	1471
John Boteler	1440	Margery Spayn (Crossroads)	1472
William Bereman	1442	Thomas Ussher	1472
Walter Canon of Halling	1442	Thomas Dalby (Rector)	1472
John Halman	1443	Thomas Broke	1473
William Usscher, senior	1444	John Goldhawke (Holborough Rd)	1474
Peter Fyssher	1444	Thomas Rowe	1474
Robert Dowle	1445	William Kent (High St)	1477
John Parmenter	1448	Henry Scryvener, miller	1477
Margaret Renolds	1448	Walter Andrewe (High St)	1478
John Bamburgh of Wouldham	1449	John Holway	1478
John Sherreve	1451	John Beauley (Wouldham Hall)	1480
John Fenne	1452	John Sevare	1480
William Coumbys of London	1452	Stephen Hickmott	1480
John Aston (Rector)	1453	Thomas Haylok	1481
Robert Hokynge	1453	Isabella Ussher	1481
Robert Mawner	1453	Walter Canon	1485
Thomas Sevare of Halling	1453	William Holdernesse	1485
Henry Canon	1454	John Kyng	1485
Margery Hokyng	1455	Richard Stokke	1485
William Andrew of Halling	1456	Margaret Bischoptre	1487
Alice Canon	1457	Edward Bischoptre	1487
John Frenche	1457	John Pole ('Botelers')	1487
Nicholas Smyth *alias* Benet	1457	Joan Stalworth	1487
William Canon	1459	Margaret Stok	1487
Thomas Parmenter	1459	William Wode	1487
--- Frenssh	1459	John Goldhawke	1487
John Boteller, senior	1460	John Coton	1489
John Phelipp	1460	John Parmenter	1489
William Smyth	1460	Richard Canon of Holborough	1490
William Andrew	1460	John Taylor	1490
Elizabeth Canon	1460	John Andrew of Halling	1491
Thomas Benet	1461	Roger Canon	1492
John Berneman	1462	John Godeale	1492
Elizabeth Ussher	1462	Nicholas Hilles	1493
John Pechin	1462	Dionesia Swetyng	1493
John Andrew	1463	John Dalley	1494
Isabella Goseler	1463	John Edward	1497
Thomas Cowper	1464	Thomas Stalworth (High St)	1497
--- Bocher	1464	Ralph Alderson	1499
--- Crelemok	1464	Robert Canon	1499
Alice Tiler	1465	John a Fever	1499
Cecilia Andrew	1466	William Joye	1499
Simon Spayn	1466	Richard Arnolde	1500
William Boteler of Norwich	1466	William Hammonde of Birling	1500
William Alisander	1469	Margery Harper	1500
Robert Grene	1470	Isabella Myhett	1500
Geoffrey Alisander & Richard Palmer	1471	Robert Smyth	1500

John Thorpe, in his book *Registrum Roffense* [1769], noted that in the chancel 'on a gravestone (the inscription lost) are these arms, viz. on brass:

I. A chevron between three palmers scrips, with strings and tassels. [These are the PALMER arms.]
II. the same arms impaling three inescutcheons, a crescent for difference.'

Just once, in the 1390s, these impaled arms (implying husband and wife) are attributed to a Richard Fitz-Symond: Thomas Palmer, whose epitaph appears above, married the daughter of Richard Fitz-Symond, so here undoubtedly was his tomb. For all we know it may still lie beneath the present chancel floor (which was raised during the Victorian renovations). John Philipot drew the Palmer arms when he visited the church in the seventeenth century.

The so-called 'Palmer' window, formerly at the east end of the north aisle, has also had a very chequered history. The original one may not have survived being defaced by 'rude hands' and what we now call the 'Palmer' window may have been an early replacement. By the 1840s, when Charles Winston drew it, very little old glass remained. The two figures are said to be St James the Great (hence the allusion to Palmers as pilgrims, with their sign of a scallop shell) and a bishop, but perhaps one of them was intended to represent William (or more likely Thomas) Palmer. Later glass was added from time to time, but the whole was blown to pieces by a land mine in 1942. Remnants were painstakingly put together and re-installed in the west window next to the tower after the war, but these seem to bear little resemblance to Winston's faithful paintings which are now in the British Library.

The family's association with Snodland Court Lodge has yet to be confirmed. But the Richard Palmer (d.1471) who seems to have lived in a house on the site of the Bull may have been a member. Unfortunately his will tells us little beyond the fact that his 'mansion' and land were bequeathed to his son Thomas. Neither man features in any other Snodland document of the time, so they seem rather isolated from village life in general.

HOLLOWAY COURT

Among the families known to have lived in Snodland in early times, that called 'Holloway' is prominent. It presumably took its name from 'Hollow Way' and must, at least at some time, have owned the property at Holborough latterly called 'Holloway Court'. This was a house situated near the mill, slightly to the north-west, and separated from it by the road leading up to the Pilgrim's Way. (In later years this was closed off and replaced by 'New Road', now called 'Ladd's Lane'.) There are recorded:

Thomas Holeweye and John Holeweye, brothers (1288);
William de Holoway (active 1302-1305);
Walter Holeweye (active 1330-1338);
William Holeway (active 1327-1352); his wife Joan died in 1348;
Richard Holeweye (active 1327-1349), a priest, instituted to Halling vicarage in 1349;
John (the elder), (active from 1442) died 1478. Wife: Dionisia; son: John;
   grandchildren: Thomas, Walter, Joan, Alison.

By the 1460s this John Holway owned 'Newhouse' (which we know as 'Woodlands Farm') and other properties. A seventeenth century list of deeds records this and notes the transfer of ownership of his houses and lands between 1468 and 1522. Meanwhile the farm called 'Holloway' had passed to William Alisander by 1469.

William Alisander was clearly a man of substance - and of piety. By his will, dated 15 January 1470, he asked to be buried in the porch of Snodland church. The large stone in front of the inner door may be his grave and it is likely that the brass indent on the east wall above is also his. He left money to pay the rectors of Snodland and Northfleet for a year's supply each of consecrated bread and wine; for a priest to say daily services for two years; for the Augustinian Friars, the Minorites and Carmelites in London, the Carmelites at Aylesford, and the monks at Canterbury each to say 100 masses for the souls of his father and mother, himself and his wife, and of John Lowe, late Bishop of Rochester. The Prior at Canterbury received from him a gold ring with a sapphire set in it, and silver cups were presented to Canterbury, Malling Abbey, and Higham Priory. The rector at Stone received a cup of maple covered with gem-stones with silver and gilt, weighing 16½ ounces, and the Archdeacon at Rochester some books. Curiously, there is no mention in his will of his charity (still announced on the charity board in the church) providing a weekly portion of bread to the poor 'for ever'. The Alisander family may have moved to Snodland from the Northfleet area, but records of them are very sparse. The wills of William and his son Geoffrey enable us to construct a family tree:

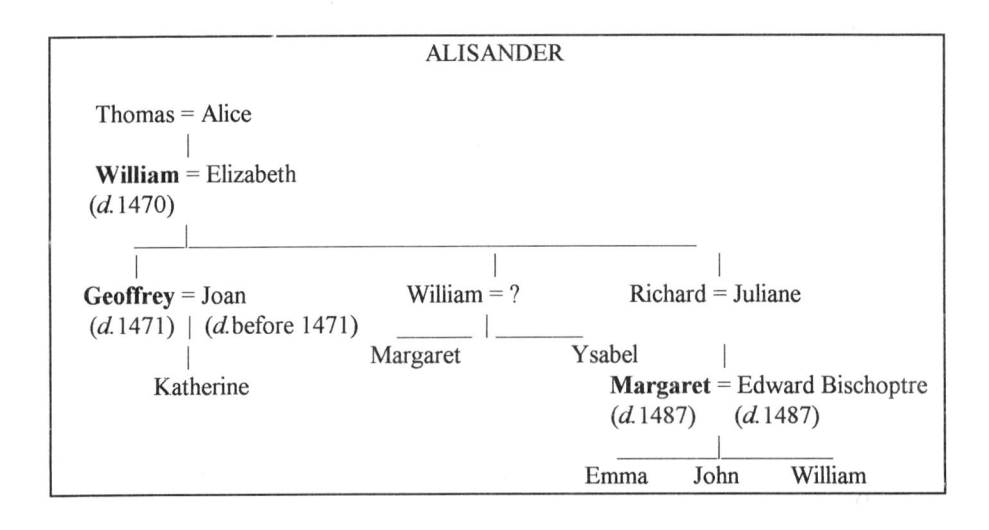

```
                              ALISANDER

        Thomas = Alice
                 |
        William = Elizabeth
        (d.1470)
        _____|_____
        |                        |                       |
        Geoffrey = Joan        William = ?           Richard = Juliane
        (d.1471) | (d.before 1471)    |                       |
                 |                 Margaret    Ysabel          |
              Katherine                                 Margaret = Edward Bischoptre
                                                       (d.1487)   (d.1487)
                                                       _____|_____
                                                       Emma    John    William
```

This is useful in determining what happened to 'Holloways' and to the adjacent farm called 'Nasshenden'. William bequeathed 'to Geoffrey my son all household goods, beds and bedlinnen, etc., which I have in my tenements of holweys and nasshynden, with all ironwork and other instruments which I have in the forge of Robert Parmenter' (who clearly was the blacksmith). His son William received 'my entire white bed (in

Nasshynden) dyed with flowers.'; Juliane had 'a dress of red russet decorated with silver and gilt'; her daughter Margaret acquired silver spoons and a bed.

Geoffrey did not long survive his father. He made his will on 19 September 1471, describing himself as 'gentleman'. His property in Snodland, Halling, Paddlesworth and Hadlow was to go to his daughter Katherine once she reached the age of fourteen; in the meantime his brother William was to receive the rents. Katherine was also to receive all his moveable goods, cattle and jewels. Sadly, it seems likely that she died before her fourteenth birthday, for, in the event of her death, the will made provision for the property to descend to others who can be shown to have owned it. If Katherine died, wrote Geoffrey, Margaret Bischoptre 'shall have my tenement ... at Holbergh ... called Nasshinden' (with about 25 acres of land), while brother William 'shall have my tenement at Holbergh which was formerly John Olwey's [= Holoway's]', its land and another cottage. Of William Alisander the younger we hear nothing more, but Margaret Bischoptre made a will on 13 November 1487, three days before her death. She was then living at Addington. (Her husband Edward had died on 1 September and both are commemorated in a marvellous brass in the north aisle of All Saints church. - Plate) Her son William was to inherit the Snodland property at the age of 22 years, but in the event of his death, her executors were authorised to sell it. Again, this seems to have come to pass and we next hear of Holloway and Nasshenden as belonging to the Tilghman family, whom we shall meet next.

THE TILGHMAN FAMILY IN SNODLAND

In recent years Snodland has welcomed many members of the Tilghman family, which believes its roots are here. The Tilghmans have a remarkable genealogical record: a book compiled by one of its members, Stephen Frederick Tillman, entitled *'Spes Alit Agricolam* (Hope Sustains The Farmer) Covering the years 1225 to 1961 of the Tilghman (Tillman) and Allied Families' (4th edition, Washington, D.C., 1962). It provides details of 5677 members of the family, gleaned by the writer 'from old English records to be found in the Library of Congress, Washington, D.C.; Revolutionary War records in the library of the DAR and in the National Archives; U. S. Census Returns; and from data furnished by living members.' More recently, the indefatigable research of an English member of the family, Miss Elizabeth Tillman, has cleared up much confusion present in the American accounts and her exhaustive work must surely make them one of best documented of all families. This chapter draws heavily on her research and I am indebted to her for so willingly sharing her discoveries.

Some American families have difficulty in tracing the moment when their forebears left England, but the Tilghmans find precise details recorded in a family manuscript dating back to 1540. (I should like to know where it is now.) Richard Tilghman (1627-1676) obtained a grant from Lord Baltimore of a manor in Maryland and sailed to settle there in 1661. The old manuscript was among his possessions brought from England and it includes notice of a birth on board the ship. The gist of the Latin original is as follows:

> Near Bermuda, latitude 34.43, longitude 34.55, in the ship Elizabetha & Maria, captain Richardo Hobbs, the 21 January 1662, before 2 in the

afternoon, Richardus Tilghman was born, and he was baptized on the 28 of the same month.

From this Richard, a surgeon, many of the American Tilghmans are descended. But what of the family before they emigrated, and of those first thirty (English) members listed in *Spes Alit Agricolam*? John Philipott's *Villare Cantianum* (published after his death in 1659) includes the following (p.322):

> 'There is a second seat in Snodland called Holoway Court, and in the Book of Aid mention is made of one Henry de Holoway that held it in elder times, about the beginning of Henry the Third, but upon a serious perusal of the evidences and muniments which did relate to this Mansion, I found it, as high as they reached, that is to the reign of Edward the Third, to be the Inheritance of the Tilghmans; and several very old Panes of Glasse are coloured with that Coat of Arms which the Tilghmans are entered with in the last Visitation of Kent [1619], and in this Name was the Possession for many Descents permanent till some forty years since or more it was by sale conveyed to Clotworthy.'

Philipot's statements cannot be dismissed lightly. Clearly he visited the families in drawing up the 1619 Visitation and presumably took the opportunity to consult documents held by them. Unfortunately we do not know what these were so far as Holloway Court is concerned, but those currently known indicate a somewhat different state of affairs. Miss Tillman has found that the family originated in Norfolk before establishing bases in the West Country and in Kent. In the fourteenth century Tilghmans were living in Pluckley and it is here that we must seek the origins of the Snodland branch. She suggests that Philipott may not have looked too closely at names on the deeds in the Tilghman chest and that it is likely that the early ones derived from previous families.

Such lists of Snodland parishioners as have come down to us (particularly tax returns), and other early documents such as wills, indicate that we need search no earlier than the late fifteenth century to find when the Tilghmans came to Snodland. The key figure is a William Tilghman who died in London in 1493/4. This man held the post of Clerk to the Privy Council and thus was among the most important 'civil servants' of his day. Official documents, beautifully written by him, are preserved in the Public Record Office. Miss Tillman has traced his activities to as early as 1446, so he must have been an old man at his death. His will shows him to have been a prosperous man, a pupil of Thomas Kent, one of the founders (with John Kent) of a Chantry in Headcorn Church in 1466. He requested that he be buried in the church of St. James Garlickhithe and clearly he was, for John Stowe recorded a monument to 'William Tiligham' in his *Survay of London* of 1598. He appears to have died childless, for none are mentioned in his will, and it was his nephew William to whom he bequeathed land in Snodland, Halling, Paddlesworth and Birling:

> I will and ordeyne...that...my...feoffees at such tyme as they shall be desirid or required on the behalf of my godson William Tilghman the younger, oon of the soones also of the said Thomas my said brother, shall make or do to

TILGHMAN

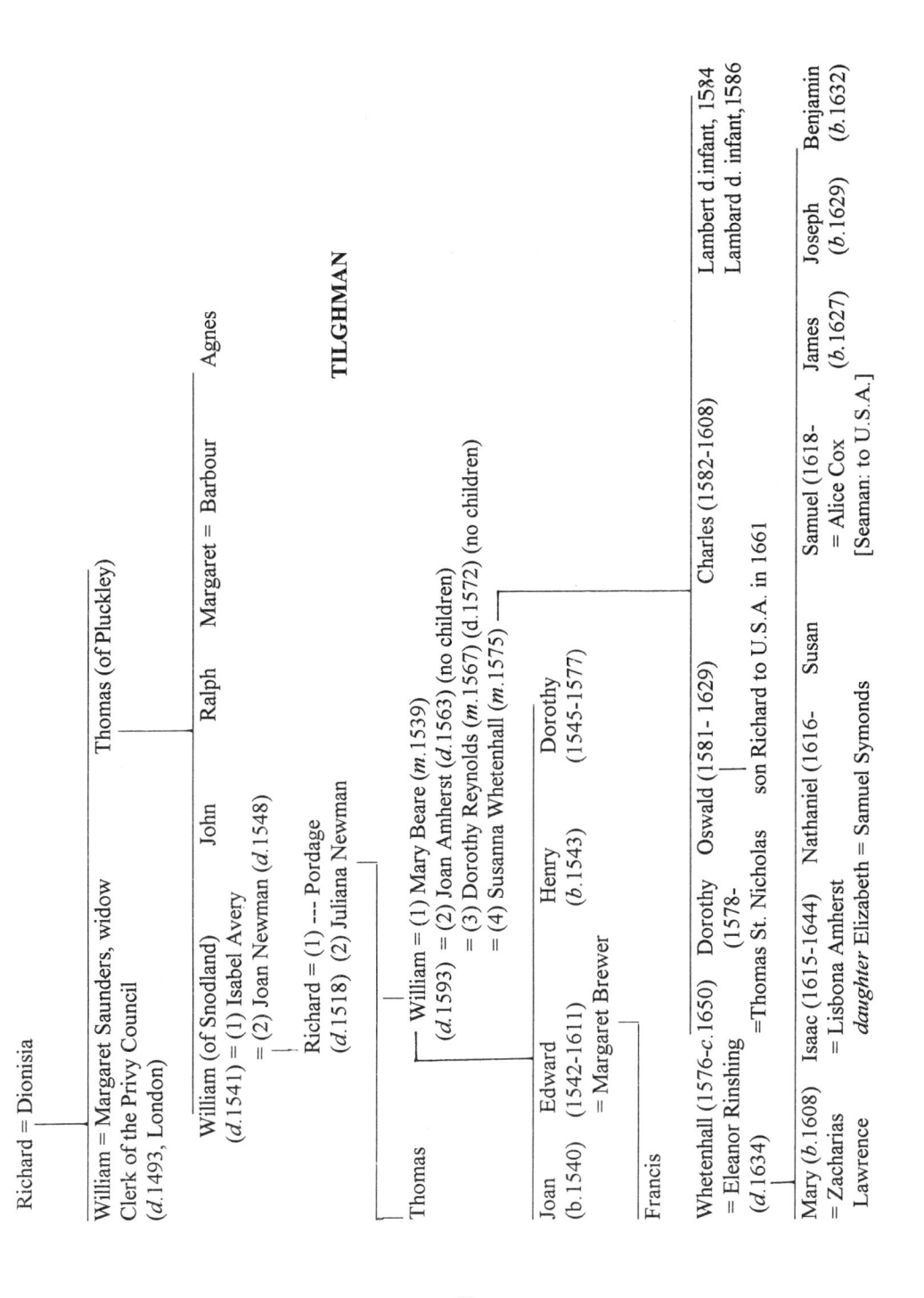

Richard = Dionisia

William = Margaret Saunders, widow   Thomas (of Pluckley)
Clerk of the Privy Council
(d.1493, London)

William (of Snodland)   John   Ralph   Margaret = Barbour   Agnes
(d.1541) = (1) Isabel Avery
        = (2) Joan Newman (d.1548)

Richard = (1) --- Pordage
(d.1518) (2) Juliana Newman

Thomas — William = (1) Mary Beare (m.1539)
        (d.1593) = (2) Joan Amherst (d.1563) (no children)
                 = (3) Dorothy Reynolds (m.1567) (d.1572) (no children)
                 = (4) Susanna Whetenhall (m.1575)

Joan   Edward   Henry   Dorothy
(b.1540) (1542-1611)   (b.1543)   (1545-1577)
          = Margaret Brewer

Francis

Whetenhall (1576-c.1650) Dorothy   Oswald (1581-1629) Susan   Charles (1582-1608)   Lambert d.infant, 1584
= Eleanor Rinshing   (1578-   son Richard to U.S.A. in 1661   Lambard d. infant,1586
(d.1634)   =Thomas St. Nicholas

Mary (b.1608)   Isaac (1615-1644)   Nathaniel (1616-   Samuel (1618-   James   Joseph   Benjamin
= Zacharias   = Lisbona Amherst   = Alice Cox   (b.1627)   (b.1629)   (b.1632)
Lawrence   daughter Elizabeth = Samuel Symonds
                                                       [Seaman: to U.S.A.]

be made unto the same William or unto such p[er]sons as he will thanne assigne a sufficiant estate in the law of and in all my landes and tenements, rentes, medowes, pasture, leses and woodes wt [with] their appurtennces sett lying and beying as well in the p[ar]ish of Snodland, Hallyng and Paddellesworth as in the p[ar]ish of byrling in the said countie of Kent, to have and to hold the same londes and ten[emen]ts, rentes, medowes and pastures, leses and woodes wt their appurtennances unto the said Willm Tilghman and to his heires and assignes forev'more condicionally as it folowyng that the same Willm Tilghman the younger his heires and assignes shall kepe or do to be kept yerely from that tyme forth during the terme of 80 yeres thence next ensuing in the said parish church of Snodland an obite solemply by note after salisbury use for my soule and the soules of margarett late my wiff and of Thomas Saundre sumtyme her husband and for all cristen soules att such tyme of the yere as it shall fortune me to departe out of this wreched worlde expendying in the said obite so yerely to be kept as above to preestes, clerkes, children, almes to poure people, bred, ale, chese, wax and Rynging of belles to the sexteyne durying the said terme of 80 yeres by the oversight of the p[ar]son there or of his deputee there for the tyme beyng 4s.

(For a musician like me, it is very exciting to see, even in a small parish like Snodland, the instruction for the priest to commemorate William Tilghman 'solemply by note after salisbury use' - that is to sing the service using the chants established at Salisbury, but which were widely used in southern England). No doubt Tilghman himself had heard them frequently at the Chapel Royal, Westminster, or St. Paul's, all of whom had adopted them. It is probably also significant that Snodland's rector at this time was the Oxford-trained John Perot, who went on to be Precentor at York Minster; a Precentor is particularly responsible for leading the singing. One's impression from the will is that William Tilghman of London considered that Pluckley rather than Snodland was his home: he bequeathed an altar cloth and book to the church there, he left money for the keeping of a yearly obit and for a priest, and virtually all his other bequests of land were in that parish. Tilghmans continued to live in and around Pluckley for some considerable time thereafter.

Nevertheless, together with his nephew, he had bought land in Birling from 'John Boteler of Snodland' on 7 October 1489 and the will shows this was just part of a larger holding in the area. The seventeenth century list previously mentioned also records that John Holway conveyed his properties to Bennet Phillip and others in 1468 (one of whom may have been William Alisander) and that these had passed to William Tilghman the younger by 1504/5. More was added as time went on.

Enough evidence survives to show that William Tilghman the nephew settled in Snodland, establishing himself as one of the principal parishioners. By the late fifteenth century he was a churchwarden and he is mentioned in several wills: John Andrew 1491; Margery Canon 1503; Andrew Berrard 1505; John Ussher 1522; John Taylor 1527; Walter Stonyng 1532; Agnes Stonyng 1540. Tax lists for 1524 and 1538 show him to have been among the most prosperous villagers. He was married twice: first to Isabel, daughter of Thomas Avery, and second to Joan Amherst. A brass memorial now in the South aisle of All Saints church, Snodland, records them (Plate x):

> Pray for the soules of William Tilghman thelder & Isabell & Joane his wyves, which William decssyd the xxvij day of August ano dni MCCCCCXLI, on whose soules Jesu have mercy.
> As you ar so was I, and as I am so shall you be.'

The memorial also incorporates the Tilghman arms. William's will shows that he leased the mill and forge at Holborough from the Bishop of Rochester and that he farmed much of the land in the village. William's son and heir, Richard (of Snodland), had died in 1518. Richard was married twice according to the Visitation. His first wife was the daughter of William Pordage, his second was Julian[a] Newman. Two sons, Thomas and William are mentioned in his will, but further references to Thomas have not been traced among the Snodland records and he may have lived elsewhere, perhaps at Pluckley. William, on the other hand, succeeded his grandfather in the Snodland estates and developed them further. He married four times and some of the first entries in the Snodland church registers refer to his growing family. The Tilghmans were undoubtedly the most prosperous and important land-owners in the parish at this time and when William made his will in 1593 he incorporated a long list of houses and lands which he had acquired, the rents of which mostly passed to his wife Susan. He was careful to attach certain of these to the tenement called Nasshenden 'where I now dwell' and others to 'Hollwayes'. He concluded:

> my minde and desire ys that the litle mesuage and garden at Holberth in the parishe of Snodland nowe devided into twoe dwellinges wherein widow Blacke and Johane Valentyne do nowe inhabit and dwell shall allwayes be ymployed as an Almeshouse to the use of the poore for ever by my said wife or such myne heir as shall from tyme to tyme inherit my mansion house wherein I nowe dwell and that she or such heir shall allwayes nominate and appoynte twoe poore persons to have theire severall dwellinges therein paying none other Rent to my sayed wife or heir but only twoe pence yerelie which cometh to a penny a peece for the Lordes rent therof.

No other reference to these almshouses has come to light. Indeed, the picture of the Tilghmans, who are well documented in wills and deeds of the sixteenth century, now becomes somewhat blurred. Susan Tilghman, assured of a steady income from the rents, continued to live in Snodland. She is last recorded in a tax assessment of 27 March 1613, but was only valued at a quarter of the amount charged to Edward (1542-1611), William's eldest son by his first wife, Mary. Edward's wife, Margaret (d. 1613), came from the Brewer family of Ditton, and was bequeathed his estate with the proviso that she paid £14 a year to their son Francis for his maintenance. In 1610 Francis had already received a substantial amount of land and property in Snodland and Birling from the estate of his godfather, John Trevett. Probably Francis soon sold up, for on 15 June 1615 he married Margery Sprackling of Ellington-in-Thanet and they set up home in Sandwich. This would explain how about half of the Tilghman property in Snodland may have come into the hands of a London lawyer, Thomas Clottery of the Inner Temple, passing at his death in 1631 to his sister Elizabeth Williams and then to her son Thomas. In the meantime the lease of the mill 'and the two little houses over against the said mill' (could these have been the almshouses?) had been taken over by William Gyles (*d.*1614).

The other half of the land descended to Susan Tilghman's eldest son, Whetenhall, named after her family from Hextall's Court at East Peckham. A 1634 map of the Bishop's manor of Halling (printed as the flyleaf of *Across the Low Meadow: A History of Halling in Kent*, by Edward Gowers and Derek Church, (Christine Swift, 1979)) shows fields occupied by 'Mr Clottery' and by 'Mr Tillman'. A deed of 1 December 1640 transfers Whetenhall's property, including the house in which he was then living, to his eldest son and heir, Isaac, and all this passed in turn to Isaac's only daughter and heir Elizabeth, wife of Rev. Samuel Symonds of Murston, Kent. Finally, in 1682, she sold the farm of Nasshenden and the other land to Sir John Marsham of Whorne's Place, Cuxton, who was gradually acquiring most of the land in the parish.

Of the other sons of William, it is probable that Henry (*b.*1543) died young, for nothing further is heard of him. Similarly both boys called Lambert/Lambard, after William Lambarde the famous Halling lawyer and historian, died in infancy. Charles was buried at Snodland, aged 26, on 25 May 1608. Oswald moved to Wood Street, London and became a grocer and member of the Grocer's Company. He made his will on 6 January 1629, desiring to be buried in the churchyard of St. Mary Abchurch. To his daughter Abigail he bequeathed

> the Cheste of Lynnen in my upper Chamber, next the streete, and the vallence for a Bed and wrought Cupbord cloth, and Cubbard cloth of Holland marked with A:T: and all the plate marked wth AT wch were given to my Daughter Abigail by her grandmother and mother and a wine cup wch her Grandfather gave her.

OSWALD TILGHMAN

= (1) Abigail Tailor, St. Michael Bassishaw, London, 13 Jan 1612
(she died 29 June 1621)
daughters Abigail, Mary; *sons* Francis, John

= (2) Elizabeth Packham/Packnam, 15 Nov 1625 or 1626.
(she died *c.*1634)
son Richard, bapt. St Mary Abchurch, London, 23 Sept 1627

Oswald buried, St. Mary Abchurch, 1628

Three other children by his first wife are not mentioned and probably died young. Nor does he mention Richard, his infant son by Elizabeth his second wife. The latter would appear to have been orphaned in 1634 and his guardianship was entrusted to his step-sister Abigail during his minority. This Richard became a surgeon and married Mary Foxley. A daughter Mary was christened at St Olave, Hart Street, on 14 December 1656 and and unnamed infant of 'Mr. Tilmans the chirugeon' was buried at St. Dionisius Backchurch in 1661. Within the year he and his family were on the ship *Elizabeth & Mary* intent on starting a new life in Maryland.

THE SIXTEENTH CENTURY

As the centuries pass our picture of the village and its inhabitants becomes increasingly vivid. New series of documents, imperfect though they are, add life to the tale. First there are the church registers, dating from 1559, which chronicle the births, marriages and deaths of the parishioners. Then a limited group of papers from the local Quarter Sessions informs us of some of the misdemeanours here. Returns of taxes provide lists of householders at various times, while wills and deeds, now usually in English, fill in details of friends and families and of the exchange of property.

William Tilghman	lands	£21. 4s.	William Canon	goods	£6.	
John Galden	wages	20s	Edmund Salmon	goods	40s.	
Roger Mores	wages	24s.	John Chapman	goods	£6.	
Walter Stonyng	goods	£23.	John Parment[er]	goods	£3. 6s. 8d.	
William Spayn	goods	£30.	John Springfield	goods	£3. 6s. 8d.	
Humfrey Mordale	goods	£6.	William Ussher	goods	£20.	
Edward Mordale	wages	20s.	John Taylor	goods	£5.	
Robert Mordale	wages	20s.	William Howlet	wages	20s.	
John Berde	wages	22s.	Stephen Wadman	goods	£5.	
William Lambe	goods	£14.	John Sherwoode	wages	20s.	
Roger Andrewe	wages	40s.	John Molle	wages	40s.	
John Stalworth	wages	40s.	John Roger	wages	40s,	
James Girlington	wages	40s.	Richard Taylor	wages	40s.	
Thomas Tannton	goods	£13.	Walter Andrewe	wages	40s.	
William Smyth, junior	goods	£6.	Roger a Downe	goods	£4.	
Thomas Thorpe	wages	40s.	Richard Winstanley	wages	40s.	
John Crosseby	wages	40s.	Thomas Mores	wages	40s.	
Roger Parment[er]	wages	40s.	Henry Chetinden	wages	40s.	
Thomas Ifilde	wages	40s.	Thomas Coker	wages	40s.	
Alice Taylor, widow	goods	£4.	Henry Southward	wages	40s.	
Walter Lulke	goods	£3.	John Chapman	wages	40s.	
Laurence Hollet	goods	£5.	John Gayton	wages	40s.	
Thomas Carter	wages	40s.	Thomas Hemewell	wages	40s.	
John Hatcher	wages	40s.	John Sannder	wages	40s.	
John Lulke	wages	40s.	Laurence Crossely	wages	26s. 8d.	
John Syble	goods	£5.	John Carter	wages	40s.	
William Watts	goods	£5.	Robert Lancastre	wages	40s.	
John Canon	goods	£6.				

Paddlesworth

William Danke, junior	goods	£37.	William Bone	wages	40s.	
Edmund Danke	wages	40s.	William Upton	wages	40s.	
Martin Sendell	wages	20s.	William Danke, senior	goods	40s.	

1524 : Assessment of Snodland Parishioners

A good starting point is the list of taxes imposed in 1524, which probably records most of the householders then in the village and their relative worth in lands, wages, or goods, on which the tax was based.

Stonyng, Spayn, Lambe, Tannton and Ussher stand out with Tilghman as the most prosperous. No other reference to Tannton has been found, but William Lambe appears in other tax lists until 1547. The families of Spayn and Ussher have already been noted in the fifteenth century and together with others like Andrewe, Stalworth, Parmenter, Lulke, Watts, Canon and Taylor, testify to their being well-established in this place. Wills give us snippets of information about these men and their fathers. John Smith (*d.*1513) had a 'bote and netts'; John Chapman (*d.*1524) was a carpenter; William Smith (*d.*1528) lived in a house called 'Coppid Hall'; Walter Andrewe (*d.*1532) had a house in Northstrete (Holborough Road); Nicholas Chitenden (*d.*1540), perhaps son of Henry, was a 'Matrismaker'; Steven Wadman lived in a house called 'Arnolde' and owned another one called 'Stocks'; Marian Spayn (*d.*1543) left a 'house in Brokegate strete [Brook Street] wich John Bregge hath in occupying' and another 'that Bartholomew Bekytt the parish Clarke of Snodland now dwellyth in'; John Springfield (*d.*1546) lived in North Street and made provision that 'Alis my daughter as often tymes as she comythe from London to Snodlande as a Geest shall have thuse and occupying of my plowre [parlour] where I nowe dwell with the bedde and other thyngs now being there.'; William Ussher (*d.*1545) owned five houses in Snodland and Halling, one 'at holbergh which I now dwell in' ...and another 'in holbergh, whereof the one is called Lamkyns, the 2d I laytlie bought ... of John Taylor of neyther Hallyng, and the Thredde ... standythe nye unto the myl at holberg wich I laytlie buylded'.

Walter Stonyng (*d.*1531) owned houses and land in Snodland, Milton and Luddesdown, but his prime interest was in ships. He bequeathed to his wife Agnes, daughter of William Nicholson of Wouldham,

> my shippe called the *new Inne* with all ye takeling and ymplements belonging to her to give or to sell at her pleasure. I will that my new Shippe called the *Mary marten* with all the takeling and Implements to her belonginge be solde by myn executors and overseer and of the money thereof coming I will that Margaret my daughter have £80 at her marriage and £10 more to an honest prest to sing for my soule in the parrysh churche of Snodland.

Mention of Margaret brings us into touch with another prominent Snodland family of the time. She married Allen Wood, son of John Wood of East Dereham, Norfolk, and they settled here. Margaret died sometime before 1540 and I wonder whether the brass of three figures now in the chancel of All Saints church is in memory of Walter and Agnes Stonyng and Margaret. Its inscription is lost, but I do not hold to the view of those who believe it belongs with the Tilghman brass: the size is wrong and the quality is poor when compared with the latter. Experts date the brass to around 1530. Allen Wood acquired land from the Crown in addition to farming fields leased from the bishop. He remarried, and after his own death in 1556, his property descended to his son William. William received a grant of

acres of land in Snodland in Wood's own occupation; (2) a house and 18 acres of land in Snodland occupied by John Bowne; (3) two houses and 8 acres in Snodland occupied by William Forster and the rector Thomas Barnard; (4) a house and garden in Snodland occupied by William Cromer. Snodland parishioners who have visited the remarkable church of Greensted in Essex have been surprised to find a memorial on the North chancel wall there:

> Here lieth Ione, sister to S^r
> Thomas Smith of Mont Knight
> Second wife of Alane Wood
> of Snodland in Kent, Gent.,
> Who living Vertuouslie 66
> yeeres, died godly the xxth
> of August 1585.
> Feare thou God, and do
> as thou wouldst be done unto.

Later another grant of arms was made to Sir John Wood of Stapleford, Essex, 'descended out of the house of Wood of Snodland, Kent', so it seems the family subsequently settled in that county.

The religious upheavals of the mid-sixteenth century created difficulties for all. Parishioners had to come to terms with the many alterations made both to the fabric of the church and to the services held in it. Images were taken down and painted over, the rood screen was dismantled and their faith was challenged. No longer could they set aside money in their wills for candles to be burned before the images of saints, nor could they pay priests to say or sing services for their souls and those of their forebears; rather all their bequests were accepted as alms in the 'poor men's box', to be distributed in charity. The rector of Snodland instituted in 1530 was Robert Truelove, who also received the living of Halstow in 1533. He was chaplain to John Fisher, Bishop of Rochester, yet was among the clergy who renounced Papal Authority in 1534. During the reigns of Edward VI and Queen Mary (1547-1558) he held a prebend in York Minster, but lost all his livings at the accession of Queen Elizabeth. William Hall was Rector here from 1540 until his death in 1571 and he had the help of curates.

As time goes on the wills begin to include more details of household property and of livestock and produce, but a precise map of Snodland and its inhabitants at this time is currently unattainable. We do know, however, that the clothier John Leeds (*d*.1585) owned the manor of Veles and bequeathed it to his son Edward. His will is a typical mix of the time. He asks to be buried 'in the churchyarde beside the Ewetree in the Sowthside of the sayd Church'. Edward is to receive 'all such corne and cattells, haye and other moveable goods and chattells belonging aswell to my husbandrie and Trade of Cloth makinge wthin the sayde p[ar]ishe of Snodlande as also wthin the Citie of London or elsewhere', 'my manner of veles and the land in Snodland, Birling, East Malling, Luddesdowne and Paddlesworthe'. His daughter Amy received '5 sylver spones .. the best horse, mare or geldinge and the best cowe and one heyffer' and her sister Elizabeth 'one

horse, mare or geldinge and the best cowe and one heyffer' and her sister Elizabeth 'one cowe and a quarter of barley.' Whatever one's trade and status, the daily sustenance of one's family came from land and livestock.

Wealth, then as now, brought temptation to others. On 10 July 1587 Robert Gyles and James Hopkyns, labourers of Snodland, stole a piece of woollen cloth valued at 30s. from Edward Leedes. On 5 June 1588 Thomas Raynard of East Peckham, labourer, burgled the house of Edward Leedes and stole 2s. 3d. belonging to Elizabeth Hurtt (presumably a servant in the house). Later that month, on 24th, he tried again and stole a frieze jerkin (18d.), a doublet (11s.), 2 pairs of stockings (6s. 8d.) and a pair of breeches (18d.). All were tried and indicted. But Leedes himself also got into trouble: on 21 April 1595 he was indicted for assaulting one Arthur Francis at Snodland, and on 20 January 1603 he was required to promise future good behaviour, having abused George Shakerley, gent., the collector of the subsidy for the hundred of Larkfield, when he came to collect the subsidy from Leedes. By their nature the Quarter Sessions records reflect local disturbances and problems, of which theft and breaches of the peace were the most common. Thomas Hollowaye of London may have been a travelling salesman staying overnight at the village, perhaps in the house of Richard and Alice Skate. On 19 November 1563, at Snodland, Richard Bartlett (also from London) stole from Holloway 'a casket with metal chains (16d.), a 'turkes' [head] mounted in a gold ring (20s.), a death's head mounted in a gold ring (30s.), a white saphire mounted in a gold ring (20s.), three gold 'hrope' rings (£3), 5 silver spoons (25s.), 6 silver pins with pearls (4s.) 3 rails (10s.), 3 headcloths (8s.), 6 handkerchiefs (12s.), 12 cottons (20s., 12 red satin purses (14s.), 4 dozen knives (40s.), 3 dozen ivory combs (15s.), 3 pounds of tape (12s.,), 1 dozen snuffers (2s. 4d.), 1 pound of counters (16d.), quarter pound of sisters thread (6s. 8d.), 3 dozen 'cullyne' knives (20s.), a child's shirt (8s.), 1 dozen wrought leather gloves (6s.), a belt (8d.), and 10d. in money. Skate and his wife were indicted as accessories, but found not guilty; Bartlett was to hang for his crime.

In the years following the Spanish Armada, it was rash of Nicholas Howlett to say publicly 'I would they [the Spanish] would come. I would strike never a blowe agaynst them'. He was found guilty of uttering seditious words, was to be pilloried in market time and remanded in gaol.

Routine matters included the granting of licences to keep alehouses. And Thomas Usher was warned that if he 'will not of his own accord deliver the indenture of Stephenson, his apprentice, then the said Stephenson when he shall be at large should go to Sir Maximilion Dallyson for his discharge.' One dramatic event occurred on 10 September 1608. John Barnes of Cranbrook, bricklayer, Andrew Whyte of Snodland, blacksmith, and William Ray of New Hythe, labourer, were talking and drinking together in the house of John Fletcher, victualler, at Snodland. A quarrel broke out between Barnes and Whyte, in the course of which Barnes stabbed Whyte with a knife and killed him. An inquisition was held at Snodland the next day by the coroner, Thomas Willoughby, before a jury of leading parishioners: Richard Argall, William Gyles, Whetnall Tillman, William Wylles, John Easdowne, George Sprinckfyeld, Alan Ussher, Thomas Mylles, Abraham Coker, Robert Rumney, Thomas Edmunds, William Benson and Robert Lane. They found Barnes guilty and he was sentenced to hang.

Beyond the changes in fashion which inevitably came and went, there would have been little to distinguish the village of Snodland in 1500 from how it appeared some two hundred and more years later. It is not likely to have changed much in size, if at all, and the farms and houses served successive generations unless, as sometimes happened, they were consumed by fire. Then it was no great matter to rebuild with wood and plaster and without foundations. Even the Plague seems to have passed by, for there is no evidence from the church registers of any sudden increase in mortality, even in the years when that scourge was dominant. The uncertainties of life in an age when communications were limited sometimes speak from surviving documents. When Joan Chauler made her will in 1523, she asked her executor 'to gif and to sell my house and garden yf that my husbonnde com not a geyn and yf he com agayn he to paye £3 to my son that he and I did borowe of hym in ouer besiness'. Richard Chauler seems to have been a man of some eminence, for there is a letter from him extant in the State Papers addressed to his 'well beloved friend, Thomas Cromwell', then a rising star at Henry VIII's court. Chauler was a merchant of the Staple in Calais, so his absence from Snodland is not surprising. More than a hundred years later, in 1638, John Cawsten, farmer at Covey Hall, bequeathed all his land, goods and chattles to his daughter Mary 'provided always that George Cawsten, my eldest sonne bee already dead. If he be livinge then I give and bequeath all my lands to him and his heires males for ever, paying to my sonne William Cawsten £300 ... .' But there was a snag:: 'provided always that if my sonne William Cawsten be already married or do ever marry or take to wife Anne Giles, sister to John Giles in the parish of Snodland, yeoman, that then hee shall have only for his porcon untill he be married to some other venter or person fortie shillings'. Furthermore if George was living and William was married to someone other than Anne Giles, then William could inherit the land. John Cawsten seems to have had another grudge too, for he bequeathed 10s. a piece to every poor widow in the parish, 'the widowe Gilbert onlie excepted'. If Ann Giles married William Cawsten, there is no record of it, at least in the Snodland registers.

The Giles family are an interesting bunch. William (*d.*1614) was the miller at Holborough and a churchwarden, as early as 1541 'servant' to William Monde, a tenant of William Tilghman the elder. The job of miller passed through his family to John (*d.*1620) and then to John Amisse, who had leased the mill for 31 years in 1617; the latter married John's widow in 1628. John (*d.*1678) achieved notoriety for his activities (with others) for

GILES

William = Joan
(*d.*1614) | (*d.*1624)

William (*d.*1616?)	John = Ann Leedes (*m.*1608)	Isabel = Thomas Short (*m.*1610)
sons: William (*b.*1608)	(*d.*1620); she remarried: John	*children:* Thomas (1611-1630)
Thomas (*b.*1610)	Amisse, 1628	Elizabeth (1614-1615)
Francis (*b.*1612)		Elizabeth (1616-
	John (*d.*1678) = Joan (*d.*1717)	John (1622-1684)

his part in the Kentish uprising against Cromwell and his forces in 1658.

It would appear that he clashed with the Roundheads who had marched from Meopham to Maidstone on 1 June 1648, where they fought a fierce battle. In 1650 Giles and others received the attention of Cromwell's administrators. The records include:

12 April 1650: Information by Col. Baseville and other against men 'as being in arms against Parliament in Kent at Whitsuntide, 1648. the list includes 'Thos. Hester' and 'John Joyles', both of Snodland.

6 May 1650: Information concerning Wm. Grigges and Wm. Yappe, both of Snodland, 'that in the late rising in Kent, Grigges rode in the King's army, and has spoken inveterately against Parliament, says that it sits for nothing but to cozen the country, and he shall live to see them all hanged, and would be the first to cut their throats if there should be another rising. Also that Yappe was a very violent actor in the late rising, forcing men and horses to serve against Parliament. Yappe was in the insurrection under Lord Goring in 1648, violently took away horses and arms from a well-affected widow [i.e. she was sympathetic to Cromwell's cause], threatening to leave her not worth a groat, and imprison her, and used gross words against Parliament.

August 1650: Giles' estate was to be seized and appraised and an inventory made. In November the prosecutor, John Abell, confessed that Giles gave him £10 as a bribe to desist from the prosecution.. Abell was ordered to pay the money to the Parliamentary committee in charge.

14 March 1651: Information renewed that Giles furnished the insurrectors with men, horses, arms, and money, and carried himself with much bitterness and malica against Parliament and the well-affected. Also that he was in the Tonbridge rising, and was a gross maligner of Parliament.

In spite of all this, on 9 April 1652 (when the War was over), Giles was granted a free discharge on the Act of Pardon because no judgement or sequestration had taken place. Joan, his wife, achieved notoriety on her own account, for the entry of her burial on 8 September 1717 reads: 'Joan Giles being as was suppos'd an hundred and three years of Age'. There is no good reason to doubt it. Their house was the former 'Benet's Place', mentioned earlier.

Apart from the insubordination of John Giles and his friends (which in any case does not appear to have occurred in Snodland itself), the village seems to have avoided any mistreatment at the hands of Cromwell's forces. Church registers throughout the land were neglected and it seems probable that the few entries in our registers between 1640 and the late 1650s, such as the following, were added later, drawing upon people's memories for the details.

> Isaac Tylghman dyed Dec: ye 21 1644 & is buried under the Great Chancell Window at the East End Snodland Church yard. Near If we can make any Guess his Father Whetonhall Tylghman of this Parrish Gent: (is deposited).

Whetenhall actually died in 1650 or later. The last known record of him comes from another of Cromwell's committees, which administered estates of Royalist sympathisers which had been seized by Parliament:

Whetenhall actually died in 1650 or later. The last known record of him comes from another of Cromwell's committees, which administered estates of Royalist sympathisers which had been seized by Parliament:

> 16 August 1650. Whetenhall Tilman of Snodland, Kent, petitions that in 1606, Edward Nevill, Lord Abergavenny, sold him for £120 an annuity of £20 on Rotherfield Manore, Sussex, which he received during the life of the said Edward and that of Henry, his son and heir; but it ran into arrears during the troubles [the Civil War], and the manor is now sequestered for delinquency of John, Lord Abergavenny, son and heir of Henry. Whetenhall 'has always been faithful' [to Parliament], is 80 years old [actually he was just 75], and has no other subsistence.

A hundred years later John Thorpe recorded the grave 'On an Altar Monument, about six or eight feet East of the S.E. corner of Chancel is the following inscription: 'Here lyeth the body of Isaak Tilghman, son of Witenhall Tilghman of Snodland, Gent. who dyed the 21st day of December 1647 aged 36 years, and Lisbona his wife, who dyed the 10th day of September 1678 aged 58 years and of their two daughters Elizabeth and Elinor.' Such discrepancies are difficult to solve. All that remains of the 'Altar Monument' is one slab, now illegible and at grass level.

A tax rated according to the number of hearths in each property was begun in the 1660s and at least three lists for Snodland have survived. Here are the names (1662-1664):

Chargeable	[Hearths]	[House, where known]:	[buried on]:
Thomas Ray [1662-4]	5 [4 in 1663]		
Richard Evens [1662]	3		
John Shorte [1662,1664]	2	[Acacia Cottage?]	2 May 1684
John Curde [1662-4]	2		31 October 1668
James Grinstead [1662]	2 [1 in 1663; not chargeable in 1664]		
John Scarlett [1662-4]	2		5 February 1670
Nicholas Staines [1662-4]	1		7 March 1670
Lawrence Dutch [1662-4]	2		4 July 1671
Stephen How [1662-4]	2 [4 in 1663]	['Moules']	16 October 1678
Richard Parker [1662-4]	4	[Mulberry Cottage]	15 October 1678
William Read [1662,1664]	2		25 October 1678
George Savage [1662-4]	4	[Grove Farm]	19 April 1670
Thomas Pound [1662-4]	1		5 January 1689
Thomas Mercer [1662-4]	2		21 January 1671
William Lambert [1662-4]	1		
John Giles [1662-4]	5	[Benet's Place]	20 September 1678
John Mercer [1662-4]	4	[Newhouse = Woodlands]	
Thomas Cox [1662-4]	2 [1 in 1664]	[Frogwell]	2 February 1694
Henry Collison [1662-4]	2		20 April 1681
Widow Roberts [1662-3]	2		23 February 1667
Widow Bance [1662]	3		
Robert Bance [1663-4]	3		
Mr [Thomas] Williams	5 [3 in 1664]	[Holloway Court]	8 June 1672
Thomas Wells [1662-4]	5		
The widow Wells [1663-4]	5		

John Lamb [1662-4]	2 [1 in 1663]	[Holborough Mill]	[1667]
James Pack [1662-4]	3		23 December 1670
John Lander [1662-4]	1	[Gilder's Farm]	
Thomas Butler [1662-4]	1 [not chargeable 1664]	[Holborough]	29 June 1680
William Gull [1662,1664]	2	[Holborough]	28 August 1664
Thomas Martaine [1662-4]	2		6 March 1671
Elizabeth Causten, widow	6 [five in 1663]	[Covey Hall]	11 December 1679
Mr Garraway [Rector]	3	[Rectory]	21 February 1667
Hamon Ray [1662-4]	3	[Paddlesworth]	18 June 1675
John Flowere 1663-4]	1 [2 in 1664]		6 January 1671
John Vowsden [1664]	2		10 February 1673
William Oldment [1664]	2		
William Pack [1664]	2		

Not chargeable

Richard Pierson [1662,1664]	1		
John Carrier [1662]	2		23 October 1675
Thomas Carrier [1664]	2		
Thomas Howlett [1662,1664]	2	[Island Cottage]	
Thomas Parsons [1662,1664]	1		11 March 1694
Henry Gilbert [1662,1664]	1		15 January 1681
Richard Johnson [1662,1664]	1		22 March 1686
Robert Wellard [1662,1664]	1		26 January 1675
Widow Smith	1		
Widow Mumford [1664]	1	[Holborough Forge]	[wife of George Mumford]
William Goteer [1664]	1		14 September 1670
Widow Palmer [1664]	1		
John Matthews [1663]	1		7 May 1693
John Cozens [1664]	2 ['empty house']		

It has to be said that this was not a popular tax and many in the country sought to evade it, at least in part, by blocking up fireplaces and chimneys.

One member of a prolific family, and son of Thomas Godden, the farmer at Paddlesworth, remembered the village where he had been born. Edward Godden, baptised at Snodland on 13 January 1600, had prospered as a 'Citizen and Haberdasher of London'. He established a charity by his will dated 8 February 1662, in which he devised

> 20 acres in Ivychurch to Brett Netter and his heirs to the intent that they should pay yearly to the church wardens and overseers of Snodland £10 on trust with £5 thereof to put forth one poor child male or female apprentice to some honest trade or calling.

This is still administered by trustees today and the income has increased.

Meanwhile Holloway Court was transferred from Thomas Williams to Sir Richard Manley. He appears little in the village records, although he was a churchwarden here and a Justice of the Peace. But when his wife Martha died in 1682, he commissioned a memorial in the church which recent expert opinion suggests was made by Arnold Quellin (1653-86), a partner of the famous woodcarver Grinling Gibbons, so clearly he was a man of some refinement, in touch with the most fashionable sculptor's workshop in London.

His own simple memorial, required two years later, has disappeared. Holloway Court was sold by their son Charles to a Rochester man, Robert Conway.

A census of the number of communicants, catholics ['papists'] and non-conformists in the county was taken in 1676, the 'Compton Census'. It revealed

Snodland: Conformists: 100; Papists: - ; Non-conformists: 40
Paddlesworth: Conformists: 5; Papists: - ; Non-conformists: -.

The position of Grove farm, on the Snodland-Birling boundary, caused difficulties since it was never clear to which parish it belonged. The text of an agreement was inserted in the Snodland church register:

> Memorandum that, whereas there has formerly been a Difference between the Parishioners of Snodland & those of Berling concerning Grove's House; it was unanimously agreed upon by both Parties (haveing put the Businesse to Arbitration) that the said House should hereafter be ever accompted & acknowledged to stand entirely in, & to be part of the Parish of Snodland, in consideration of four pounds & ten shillings, to be given by the Minister & Parishioners thereof to the Inhabitants of Berling aforesaid, & that the said sum was actually given and received accordingly upon ye 21st day of Novembr: 1693: In Testimony whereof they have hereto set their Hands:-

Theo Beck, Vicar de Birling; [the marks of] John Carnall, William Flood Churchwardens; William Pain [and others]; John Walwyn, Rector of Snodland

Edward Hasted tells of a plan to pipe water from Holborough to the Medway Towns:

> Sir John Marsham, bart., and Sir Charles Bickerstaff, had a design of supplying the towns of Stroud, Rochester, and Chatham with fresh water by bringing it from the spring rising at the foot of Holborough hill, and others thereabouts, by a cut or channel through Halling and Cuxton thither, four miles of which was through Sir John Marsham's own lands, but after they had proceeded two miles, finding some obstructions, which could not be removed, but by an act, this was procured for the purpose in the 1st year of James II [1685-6], but nothing further was afterwards done for it, for what reason does not appear.

THE EIGHTEENTH CENTURY

Two new sets of documents add their own perspective to the history of the village at this time. The first is a series of inventories of the goods and chattels of deceased persons, made between 1688 and 1766, not a large collection, but of great interest, especially when we can identify the houses which are described. Here are three examples. The first is for 'Mulberry Cottage' in the High Street, the second for the Courtlodge formerly beside All Saints church, and the third for Covey Hall farm in Holborough Road.

William Manley, Maltster

Made by George Wray of Paddlesworth and John Taylor of Snodland, yeomen
8 January 1711

Imprimis his wearing cloths and ready money　　　　　　　£26. 0s. 0d.

In the Hall

Item. a porridge pott and hooks, two spitts, one own lidd fir pan and tonges, a paire of andirons, one dripping pan, two box irons, Shilliards and some small things. Nine pewter dishes, two dozen pewter plates, A Clock and case, a warming pan, six earthen plates, two tables, two stoole, five chairs, two Cowper and small things and some Bookes:
£7. 13s. 0d.

In the Parlor

Item. for a small Table, six caine chairs, a pair of cole Racks　　£1. 12s. 6d.

In the Buttery

Item. one powdoring Tubb, one small table and a Frying pan　　12s. 6d.

In the Drink Roome

Item. two powdoring Tubbs, Six drink vesells, two Funnells and some small things　　　　　　　　　　　　　　　　　　　　　　　　　　　£1. 7s. 0d.

In the Backhouse

Item. three dozen of bottles, three sives, one wheele, one reele(?), one melle Tubb, two trayes　　　　　　　　　　　　　　　　　　　　　　　£1. 1s. 0d.

In the Milkehouse

Item. three iron potts, three kettles, three skilletts, Seven Milke bowles, two trayes, two platters　　　　　　　　　　　　　　　　　　　£1. 13s. 0d.

In the Brew House

Item. One Copper and old kettle, a Brewing Tubb, a Tun Tubb, a Bucking Tubb, eight Kellers, two staldors and Funnell, some wood, two hogg Tubbs　£4. 16s. 6d.

In the Best Chamber

Item. One feather bedd and Stradle Curtaines and Vallence and all belonging to it, Six small chairs, One Chest of drawers, a lookeing glass and small things upon it, a pair of andirons, fire pan and tonges, some small things, sixtene pair of sheets, eight pair of pillow Coates and twelve Table Cloathes, Three dozens of Napkins, Twelve Towells and a peece of Damaske　　　　　　　　　　　　　　　　　　　　　　　　£20. 6s. 0d.

In the Chamber over the Hall

Item. one flock bed and Stradle Curtaines and vallence and all belonging to it. One chest of drawers. One chest, two stooles, two chairs　　　　　£2. 13s. 6d.

In the Chamber over the Buttery

Item. one Fether bedd and Stradle Curtaines and Vallence. One chest, one box, one Trunck	£3. 3s. 6d.

In the Chamber over the Drincke Roome

Item. one Truckbedd, one Chest, one box, one Cradle, a parcell of Hopps, a spinning wheele and three Beehives	£1. 14s. 0d.

In the Malt House

Item. for forty quarters of Malt	£4. 10s. 0d.
Item. One Oasthaire, two shovell, eight sacks and the measurers	£1. 6s. 6d.
Item. In the Barne for fother [fodder]	£2. 0s. 0d.
Item. a Cart and Ladder, a hearne, three pammells, a pillion	£3. 12s. 0d.
A Horse, one Cow and calfe, one heiffer, four ...[?]	£9. 17s. 0d.
Item. Hoppoles upon the ground	16s. 0d.
Dung in the yard and a Malt Bin	15s. 0d.
old iron and Lumber	12s. 0d.
Debts due and oweing to the said deceased	£32. 0s. 0d.
Total:	£79. 1s. 0d.

John Crow the elder, Ropemaker

Made by John Weekley the younger and John Taylor
22 March 1714

Imprimis in Ready money	£4. 7s. 1d.
Item his wearing Appàrrell	£6. 15s. 0d.
Item his Debts good & bad	£31. 17s. 0d.

In the Kitchen

Item one payer of Coale rack wth all things thereunto belonging; one payer of Potthangers; one payer of large broad headded Andirans; one Gridiron; fower Spitts; & a little Spratt Spitt; two payer of bellowes; one fire Shovell; three payer of Tongs; a payer of Tobacco tongs; five Iron Candlesticks; one tin Candlebox; one wooden tinder box; one Tosting Iron, one pott Iron; three husseys; two frying pans; one Kettle; Two Dressers; one Cubbord; one Jack line & weights; two tables; three Joine-stooles; five brasse Candlesticks; one brasse Morter & pestle; Two brasse savalls; one brasse skimmer; one brasse flower box & two pepper boxes; one Tin flower box; two parcels of pewter; 18 peeces of Earthen ware; fower Rush bottom Chayers; fower Cushens; one Clock & case; line & weights; a pcell of books; two small lookeing glasses; two blew stone Muggs; one little stoole; one Iron Chafing dish; one brasse warming pan   £9. 10s. 0d.

In the Brewhouse

Item: one Copper furnace; one brasse furnace; one breweing tubb; one buckeing Tub; Thirteene other tubbs; two water tubbs; one Charne; two Rowling pins; fower wooden platters; forwer Iron potts; three brasse Kettells; one brasse sawse pan; one Iron oven lidd; one Iron slice; one Tin Cullender; three latten pans & a Tin sawse pan; one white Earthe bason; three pailes; one Table; one wooden pye peete; one pott brasse skillett; one wort sive; two Earthen platters; & trenchers; one Cleaver; one bill & one stalder

£5. 12s. 0d.

In the Celler

Item: five drinke vessells, two stalders, one Tiller, 16 Glasse bottells   18s. 0d.

In the Parlour

Item: 12 pictures, three ovell Tables; six turkey worked Chayres; five rush bottom Chayres, one Court Cubbard; one Glasse case; two wooden cupps ... one large stone bottell & a wooden platter; fower drinke glasses; one Greene glasse punch bowle & wooden stan; one lookeing glasse; 3 large Earthen Dishes; Five Earthen basons; one Glasse Cup & one water glasse   £2. 15s. 0d.

In the drinke buttery

Item; one great Powdring Tub & the Porke in it; three drinke vessells; one little Powdring tub; a flower tub; two sives; one wooden can; five ...[?] & 5 pans; three wooden Platters; two bowles & a Shall; one Funnell; one Stalder; one little Table & one Meale Bag

£2. 15s. 6d.

In the Chamber over the Kitchen

Item: one feather bed; one feather boldster; two feather pillows; three blanketts; one Coverlett, Bedstedle, Matt & cord curtaines & vallence; the window Curtaines; one Chest of Drawers; two pre of brasse Andirons; one pre of Tongs; one fire shovell; one warming pan; one Table & table cloathes; a ... chair & four other chairs; one Chest; one Trunk, 18 pictures little & great; a parcell of Earthen ware; one Presse; one pre of bellows; one lookeing glasse wth a pcell of odd things in a Closett in the same roome £7. 10s. 0d.

Item: one silver Tankard; one silver spoone; a silver laster & silver Thimble

£5. 0s. 0d.

The Linnen

Item: five shifts, two dia..ly wascoates; 6 pillow Coates; fower Aprons; 3 whit hoods & one handkercheife; 14 Capps and suite of quivers; two payer of fleeces; 13 Coarse Cloathes; 4 Course Napkins; one bagg; a little Table cloath; a little fine Towell; 4 little window curtaines, 9 coarse Aprons; 14 payer of sheets; one damaske Table cloath; one fine Table cloath; 6 fine Napkins; 6 flaxen Napkins; 6 damaske napkins; three Table cloathes & two towells; 6 shirts; 6 ells of New dowlas & Course Table Cloathes; 6 Course Towells; two little baggs   £9. 17s. 6d.

In the Chamber over ye Buttery

Item. one feather bed, two feather boldsters; one flock boldster; two Ruggs, Bedstedle, Matt & cord curtaines & vallence, 2 Chests   £1. 15s. 0d.

In the Chamber over ye Parlour

Item: one feather bed, two feather boldsters, 4 pillows; two blanketts & one Rug, Bedstedle, Matt & cord curtaines & vallence; three Chests; one Chest of Drawers, one Table & three Chayers, three bus: of wheat £4. 12s. 0d.

In the Chamber at ye Top of ye Stayers

Item: one Conney Flax bed; two feather pillows; one feather boldster; two blanketts; one Covrlett Bedstedle Matt & cord curtaines & vallence; one Trunk £2. 7s. 6d.

In the shopp

Item: fower Cheeses & a halfe; three pre of scales; one dozen of Candles; three ... of Drawers, one Co... a pcell of soape, a Jare of salt, a pcell of pipes; a pcell of Crocks wth tape binding Tobaccoe & other shopp goods £3. 2s. 6d.

In the worke house

Item: his workeing stuffe and workeing tooles	£12. 10s. 0d.
Item: the Dray in the Barne & fire wood	£1. 5s. 0d.
Item: his boat & oars	£3. 10s. 0d.
Item: his horse Bridle & Saddle, Pommell & Pillyon	£7. 0s. 0d.
Item: one Cow & one calfe, one Bullock, one budd	£6. 10s. 0d.
Item: things unseene & forgotten	5s. 0d.

Total: £124. 14s. 1d.

John Wingate, Farmer

Made by William Wingate and Thomas Larking
11 May 1752

Imprimis for all the Hop poles on the Ground	£160. 0s. 0d.
Item four cows, three Calves, fifty five sheep and forty four lambs	£61. 0s. 0d.
Four ploughs, four Harrows, one Roll Compleat	£4. 5s. 0d.

In the Oast House

Two Oast Hairs, a parcell of Coal, four Binns, four Sieves, one Rake, six Pooks, four Binn Cloths and other small things £5. 11s. 0d.
Seven Hoggs & a pr of Scoops £5. 17s. 6d.

In the Barn

Item a parcell of Wheat and Barley, one ery, One Bushell and some Oats. Some forks and Rakes £3. 13s. 0d.

In the Yards

Two Waggons, two Dung Carts, one Carriage, Six Horses and all the Harness and other Utensils in the stable £53. 0s. 0d.

Twenty Acres of Wheat on the Ground, work and seed	£33. 0s. 0d.
Seed and Sanfoine in the Ground	£1. 10s. 0d.
Two Acres of Peas, work and seed	£2. 2s. 0d.
Twenty Acres of Oats, work and seed	£17. 0s. 0d.
Fifteen Acres of Barley, work and seed	£25. 0s. 0d.
the seeds on Twenty four Acres of Land	£3. 12s. 0d.

In the Kitchen

One pair of Brand Irons, One pair of fire Doggs, One fire pan & Tongs, One fender, one pot Iron, One Grid Iron, One pan Iron, two Box Irons and Heaters, One Roasting Jack compleat, six candlesticks, One Lamp, One Coffeepot, two Drudgers, One pair of Steelyards, One Curtain and Rod, two forks, a Hook and Skewers, One Warming Pan, One Glass, One Cupboard, Nine Pewter dishes, twenty four pewter plates, One Clock & Case, three Small Tables, One Iron Rack, One Candle Box, One Gunn, Six Chairs, two forms, One Brass Sconce, One spit, One Basson   £8. 0s. 0d.

In the Parlour

Item One Cloaths Horse, One Sive, Glasses & Delft Ware, One Sadle, One pillion
£1. 17s. 0d.

In the Brewhous

Item One Copper, three Tubbs, five Keelers, One Brass Kettle, two potts, one pair of Potthangers, One slice, One pair of Bellows, three Saucepans, one Cover, One skillett, One pair of Scales & Weights, One Cullendar, Six Trenchers, Four Pailes, two Butts, One platter and small things   £5. 12s. 0d.

In the Pantry

Item One safe Cupboard, three Brine Tubbs, One frying pan   £2. 1s. 6d.

In the Dairy

Item Two Milk Leads, one Churn, one Bowl   £1. 3s. 0d.

In the Cellars

Item A Barrel, 1 Brasse Cock, 1 stalder, 1 Trundle, 6 Glass Bottles   £1. 17s. 0d.

In the First Chamber

Item One Feather Bed compleat, One Chest wth Drawers, Ten pair of Sheets, One Table Cloth, Ten Towells, Six Napkins   £13. 0s. 0d.

In the 2d Chamber

Item One Feather Bed compleat, Two Chests, One Table, One pair of Brandirons, Fire pan and Tongs, One small Bed, Six Chairs, One pair of bellows   £6. 4s. 0d.

In the 3d Chamber

Item One Feather Bed compleat, Two Chairs   £2. 0s. 0d.

In the 3d Chamber

Item One Feather Bed compleat, Two Chairs	£2. 0s. 0d.

In the 4th Chamber

Item a Flock Bed compleat, a pair of Coal Grates	£1. 10s. 0d.
Item The Wearing Apparell of the deceased	£5. 0s. 0d.

Total: £424. 5s. 0d.

These inventories were taken by friends or neighbours of the deceased, who made an estimate of what he (or she) was 'worth'. The estimates differ enormously from one another and cannot truly reflect relative values. Some provide very detailed lists while others are content with 'In the Kitchen: £5. 0s. 0d.' and the like. The three examples given are of prosperous Snodland people and large houses. John Crow in particular seems to have lived in some luxury with his large collection of pictures, oval tables, turkey-worked chairs and so on. While he describes himself as a ropemaker, his shop seems to be more of a general store, and maybe the boat and oars were put to use as a ferry. Compare these lists with one for Thomas Hodges, who presumably was someone's lodger, since there is no mention of any furniture:

Thomas Hodges

Made by George Courthop and John Martin
13 September 1731

Item. His Wearing aparell and Money in purse	£6. 0s. 0d.
Item. Two horses	£5. 0s. 0d.
Item. Eight sheep	£3. 0s. 0d.
Item. For other small things	1s. 6d.

It is greatly to be regretted that the earliest manorial records of Snodland, which belonged to the Bishop of Rochester and were kept with the cathedral archives, seem to have been thrown out (with much other material) about 100 years ago. What survives of our series begins in 1702. The books summarize the meetings of the Court Leet and Court Baron, which controlled the affairs of the parishioners as tenants of the Lord of the Manor (the Bishop of Rochester). Twice a year, in the Spring and Autumn a representative of the Bishop came to the Five Bells at Halling (for the Manor covered not only Snodland but also Halling and Cuxton) and all men aged 16 or over were obliged to attend. A 'Homage' of around a dozen householders attending from the three parishes acted as a jury. Some might make excuses for non-attendance; failure to do this resulted in a fine for the defaulters. The business of the Court Baron would concern surrenders and transfers of land, and 'escheats' - the disposal of land of those who died without heirs, together with discussion of the general management of the agricultural affairs of the manor. The Court Leet dealt with minor offences against the community - blocked ditches or roads, lack of maintenance of hedges, and so on; it also regulated the quality of ale and bread and considered public disturbances. Each meeting elected a 'Borsholder' or constable to oversee the nuisance problems and an 'aletaster' to check the bread and ale. One notices that the 'borsholder' tended to be elected from those *absent* from the meeting, while the reverse was true of the aletaster!

Such meetings had been held for centuries and by the time these records come into play the routines and serving of penalties had grown somewhat lax. There are few notices of persons being called to account for misdemeanours and no evidence that the fines were insisted upon. Lists of those excusing themselves from the meetings are ominously large as are those of the defaulters. Rich landowners like Lord Romney, John Coney and Thomas Dalison never bothered to attend. The value of these documents for us lies more in the regular lists of names supplied and in the brief notes recording transfer of property and land than in the occasional reprimands:

> 12 October 1738
> The Road leading from John Costen to Wm Best's leading to Holborough containing 40 Rods to be greatly out of Repair.
> Also the s[ai]d Jurors further present the Ditch from Cacons Pond to the Lower side of Mr Austin's Hop-Ground containing 100 Rods lying against the Lands of John Fletcher, John Cawstin, Stephen Manley and Mark Aston and order each of them to cleanse the same against his land in Two Months and do amerce every of them who shall neglect so to do in the sum of Ten shillings.

From 1747 there are records of the Court of Petty Sessions which took place at West Malling. And here we come face to face for the first time with the another strand of life at that time, the struggle of those without permanent homes, who offered themselves as labourers on farms or in households, to be hired on an annual basis. The problem was that if they fell on hard times, they then became a potential burden on the parish and all parishes naturally were anxious to avoid calls on their limited funds. Strangers were allowed to settle in a new parish if they could produce a certificate from their home parish which guaranteed to take them back if they needed to claim poor relief. It fell to the Court to pass judgement on disputed cases:

> 4 January 1766. Gates Kempton, now residing at Snodland; about 8 years ago hired himself for one year to Edward Ashdown of Cuxton, farmer, and about 6 years ago for one year to Ed. Gilder of Snodland. Married in the said year between Haying and Harvest time. (Adjudged to remove to Cuxton with his wife Annie and daughters Elizabeth and Ann). [Gates Compton and Ann Figg, both of Snodland, were married at All Saints on 19 July 1760.]

> 3 February 1759. William Knight, now residing at Snodland, on Oath saith that about 12 years ago he was bound an Apprentice by Indenture to John Elvey of Rainham in the said County, Butcher, for 7 years. That he served the said John Elvey about 3 years when he and his Master parted by consent. That soon after he set up his Trade in the said parish of Snodland. Saith that he hired a House, Barn and Slaughter House in Snodland of Mr

George Courthop at the Yearly Rent of £7. 10s. 0d., a peice of marshland in Snodland of Mr Fletcher at the Yearly Rent of 10s., A Slaughter House in Snodland of Robert Austen at the Yearly Rent of £1., and a Peice of Ground in East Malling of Thomas Wray at the Yearly Rent of £1. (Adjudged settled in Rainham with Anne his wife, the hiring being looked upon as fraudulent; order made to remove them from Snodland to Rainham.)

Some fared better. Richard Austen, for instance, became a stalwart of the community:

2 February 1760. Richard Austen, now residing in Trottescliffe, on Oath saith that he was born in the parish of Birling. And that his Father after his birth removed from Birling to Snodland. And that the Parish Officers of Westerham in this County, where this Examinant's Father belonged, gave a certificate to the Parish of Snodland acknowlegeing this examinant's Father to be their Parishioner. Saith that his Father hired a tenement in Snodland of Three Pounds a Year of one [Mr] Field; And also a House and Land in Snodland of Mr Thomas Whittaker, of Nine Pounds a Year, all which he used and occupied for severall Years. And this Examinant lived with this said Father whilst he used and occupied the said Tenements. And saith that he this Examinant never gained any Settlement for himself other than by liveing with his said Father as aforesaid. (Adjudged settled at Snodland with wife Elizabeth; to remove from Trottescliffe to Snodland.)

A few of the entries are extremely informative, enabling us to recapture elusive images of life at that time:

7 December 1765. James Aldridge, now residing at Snodland; born at Saxmundham, Suffolk, mariner. About 17 years ago was apprenticed to William Reynolds. Saith that the vessel belonging to his said master was burnt by accident at Shadwell Dock and that his Indentures were burnt on Board the said vessel; and saith that after the said vessel was burnt this Examinant within three or four days came to reside with his brother Francis Aldridge at Snodland, his master giving him leave to quit his service; and continued in his brother's service on board his vessel about four or five months, when he was pressed into his Majesty's service and went to sea. Saith that after he was discharged from his Majesty's service he agreed to serve his said brother Francis Aldridge on board his vessel for a year at 20s. a month. And saith that during the said year he was ill upwards of six weeks and then was ashore at his brother's house in Snodland. And saith that he lived a whole year with his said brother'.

James remained in Snodland, but in later years became one of the village paupers, forced to rely on poor relief. Petty disturbances sometimes came before the Court:

5 April 1783. Thomas Alchin of the Parish of Birling, on Oath saith that this Day he was attacked by Thomas Jeffery of Snodland, butcher, as he was riding on horseback in the said parish of Birling. That he the said

Thomas Jeffery struck at the said Thomas Alchin several times and pushed him and his horse into a ditch.

What the Court ordered concerning this tiff is not recorded. Incidentally, it seems that Thomas Jeffery took over the premises of William Knight (noted above), but in July 1783 these were described as 'very ruinous and decayed'. Then there were problems with orphaned or illegitimate children:

> 14 October 1775. Jane Butler, wife of John Butler of Snodland. Upwards of 5 years ago he left her in Snodland and went to sea. She did not see him for upwards of 3½ years; was informed that he was dead. During his absence she was delivered of a female child, baptized 'Sal' in Ash next Ridley; the said child was maintained in Meopham by Margaret Ashenden, Jane Butler's mother. John refuses to maintain the child, delivered about 6 months before he returned.

> 1 December 1788. Sarah Broad of Snodland, singlewoman, says that she is with child and that Edward Ort, now or late of Gravesend, smuggler, is the father of the said child.

And so to the village itself, and to the half-dozen honest, hard-working, thrifty, un-paid men who had the responsibility of maintaining order and of collecting and distributing the money which kept the poor alive. They were Parish Council, Parochial Church Council, Police and Social Services in one. Two Overseers, Two Churchwardens, Parish Constable and Parish Clerk were generally in charge at Snodland, drawn, as always, from the householders of the place. They were elected at the annual Vestry meeting. Two sets of accounts were drawn up, one for the church fabric and one for the poor, and a rate was set for each to be paid by all who owned property in the parish, whether or not they lived here. Snodland's accounts, which commence in 1769, were meticulously kept and beautifully written by William Lewis, schoolmaster and parish clerk between 1763 and 1797. The poor rate was

> (1) 'for setting to work the children of all such whose parents shall not be thought able to maintain them';

> (2) 'for setting to work all such persons, married or unmarried, having no means to maintain them, and who use no ordinary or daily trade of life to get their living by';

> (3) 'for providing a convenient stock of flax, hemp, wood, thread, iron and other ware and stuff to set the poor on work';

> (4) 'for the necessary relief of the lame, impotent, old, blind, and such other among them being poor and not able to work'.

John Butler, home from the sea, made peace with his wife. Their son William was baptised at All Saints on 28 July 1776, but the family struggled to make ends meet. During May 1773 and April 1774 they received 5s. a week poor relief from the parish and in August 1776 10s. 6d. was paid 'To Jno Butler to get his son into the Hospital'. Apparently he recovered and the churchwardens found John a little casual employment, paying him 6s.

for three days' work in the churchyard (January 1777) and 2s. for one day 'Cleaning a Dyke' in December 1778. Ten years later, in the summer of 1788, it seems John fell ill and was unable to work, for he received 3s. 6d. in August 'going to Dr Milner' (perhaps at Malling). In October £1. 1s. was spent 'to Lodging' for the family and another 14s. the next month. 'John Butler, aged 40 years', was buried at All Saints on 1 December 'by the Parish' - that is the parish had to pay the £1. 1s. costs of his funeral as the accounts show. It is to be hoped that he was aware in the last week or so of his life that the Overseers had paid out £2. 2s. 'To Mr Mackpharson taking Wm Butler Apprentice' and another 10s. for his indentures.

And what of Sarah Broad. She must have been the bane of the Overseers. Perhaps an orphan, there are regular payments to provide her with clothing during the 1770s, until John Heaver took her as his apprentice in October 1778 (which cost the parish £2. 7s.). The affair brought to light at the Petty Sessions meant more expense:

December 1788: To Oath for Sarah Broad: 1s.
                 To a Warrant to take Edwd Ort: 1s.
                 To Expenses at the Sitting: 3s. 6d.
December 1788 to March 1789: monthly payments of 2s. a week
April 1789:   To Sarah Broad's Lying in: £2.
April 1790:   To Sarah Broad's Child 35 weeks pay: £3. 10s.
April 1791:   To Sarah Broad 55 weeks: £5. 10s. [and so on]

Baptisms at Snodland:

12 April 1789: Henry, son of Sarah Broad, Base Born.
10 June 1792: Wm, son of Sarah Broad, Base Born.
8 June 1794: James, son of Sarah Broad, Base Born.

Maybe she had tried to settle in Northfleet, perhaps with Edward Ort; if so the Overseers there were alert to the fact that they would soon have another illegitimate child claiming some of their precious resources. On 2 February 1792 the Quarter Sessions issued an Order to remove Sarah Broad from Northfleet to Snodland. It was a wise move. Sadly, we note the burials of 'Wm Broad, son of Sarah Broad, 5 months, by the Parish' on 28 October 1792', and of 'James, son of Sarah Broad' 3 months, by the Parish' on 31 August 1794. The parish continued to pick up the bill: 'Burial fees for Sarah Broad's child: 3s. 6d.' (Oct 1792); 'To a midwife for Sarah Broad, 5s.' (May 1794) and 'Expenses Sarah Broad's Lieing in: £1. 15s.', and 'Nursing ditto', 6s.' (June 1794); 'To the Burial of Sarah Broad's Child, 5s. 6d.' (August 1794). And later, in March 1796, 'To Cloaths for Sarah Broad's Child, 15s.'. Henry Broad (1752-1843), not confirmed as a relation, also depleted parish funds in October and November 1792 when his family received 5s. a week relief. The reason is apparent from other entries: 'To Hy Broad to pay his Lodging in Gaol, £1. 1s.'; 'To the Collector of Excise for Broad's Discharge, 4s. 4d.'; 'To Gaol Fees &c., 16s. 6d.'.

So often these accounts make sad reading, for of course they are concerned with the poor and needy. The mentally unstable and mentally retarded would sometimes be shared among the parishioners, lodging with different families in turn. They were given casual work whenever possible. Let us follow the stories of just two parishioners who fell upon hard times. When the accounts begin in 1769, we meet Jane Couche, paid 'for washing &c.

Bethlehem Hospital' and 1s. 6d. 'For Signing her Certificate'. 3s. more went to Mrs 'Keable going after Jane Couche', with 12s. 6d. to 'Mr Brown's Expenses going after ditto'. It seems from this that Jane had run away from Snodland, but the next month finds 'Dame Keable washing and looking after Couch and Cole' and in May 'Mr French' (at the 'Red Lion') took his turn. 'Expences keeping Jane Couche 27 weeks' amounted to £5. 8s. in March 1771. Then a whole series of entries shows that she was finally admitted to the Bethlehem Hospital:

May 1771: Expences Carrying Jane Couche to Bedlam: £2. 8s.
Paid for Signing Jane Couche's Certificate: 2s.
To Mr Manley Carrying Jane Couche to London: 12s.
June 1771: To Keeping Jane Couche 8 Weeks at 6s. per week: £2. 8s.
July 1771: Paid Messrs May what they paid for Jane Couche's Admittance into Bethlem &c.: £4. 10s.
December 1771: To Bethlem for Jane Couche: £2. 4s. 6d.
To Expences Going to London after Jane Couche and Removing her from Bethlem to Hexton: £2. 16s. 9d.
February 1772: To Ticket, Bond &c for Jane Couches Admittance into Bedlam again: 3s.
May 1772: To Isaac Wenman 4 Weeks Lodging Couche: 4s.
Paid Richard Seaton for Jane Couche's Board &c.: 7s.
October 1772: To Jane Couche at Bedlam: 2s.
August 1773: To removing Jane Couche from Bedlam: £.3. 3s.
July 1773 to July 1776: regular payments for board for Jane.
August 1776: To the burial of Jane Couche: £2. 1s. 8d (but it is not entered in the church registers).

Among the cases heard at Malling Petty Sessions on 7 December 1765 was that of George Nebbs

> now residing at Snodland, on Oath saith that about 7-8 years ago he hired himself to Robert Austen of Birling, farmer, for one year, and served one year. Since he left Mr Austen's service he was bound by indenture to Francis Aldridge of Snodland, hoyman, for three years, for which the said Francis Aldridge was to pay this examinant twenty pounds at three different payments. Saith that he served the said Francis Aldridge three years, sometimes on shore at Snodland, but chiefly on the water. Saith that he believes he was never ashore at Snodland forty days at any one time during his apprenticeship. Saith that his father Thomas Nebbs was a Certificate man from Yalding to Snodland and saith that after he quitted Mr Aldridge's service he hired himself to John Brown [farmer] of Snodland. (Adjudged to be settled at Snodland).

He did his bit to rid the parish of unwanted animals, for which the churchwardens offered money: 23 July 1769: 'Paid George Nebbs a Hedgehog, 4d.'; 16 October 1770: 'To George Nebbs a Badger, 1s.'. But his first appearance in the Overseers' accounts is a poignant one: 12 March 1771: 'Gave George Nebbs to bury his Wife, £1. 1s.'. She was buried the next day. The church registers are silent concerning the names of his children - maybe they were baptised elsewhere - but the parish 'Paid Mr Hubble for Shoes for

George Nebb's Children, 7s. 3d., and 'Mr Austin for Cloaths and making for ditto, £1. 5s. 7d.' and 'Nichs Hadlow for George Nebbs Children, 5s.'. Also they 'Paid Ann Heaver for Nursing George Nebb's wife, 8s.'

In June he ran away and Nicholas Hadlow was sent after him, without success. The Overseers arranged for the children to be put with William Adams at Bearsted, although they continued to pay their maintenance. In October 'To Advertising George Nebbs twice, 7s.' failed to bring results, but a year later £1. 1s. was 'Paid for taking George Nebbs', and £1. 5s. 6d. 'Expences carrying him to Bridewel [prison] &c.'. On 6 December another 8s. 10d. went as 'Expences taking George Nebbs out of Bridewel' and 8s. 9½d 'To Mr Austin for Bed Ticking for George Nebbs'. The children returned to Snodland, with Thomas Larking, Robert Austin, Mrs Crispe, Mrs Hadlow, Thomas Hubble and Mr Craft all helping with their upkeep and clothing, for which they were remunerated by the Overseers. George Nebbs had another brief spell in Bridwell in April 1774, but later seems to have pulled himself round. On 27 September 1785 he married again - to Mary Langridge - and raised a new family (his older children having grown up). 'George Nebbs, labourer' was buried at All Saints on 20 March 1803.

THE MAY FAMILY

On the south wall of the nave in Birling church is a memorial:

> Sacred to the Memory of John and William May sons of John and Jane May of this Parish. William May ob. [died] 25th August 1777. aet. [aged] 41.
> John May ob. 2nd September 1805. aet. 71.

('1805' has previously been misread as '1803' - it is not easy to spot the difference). In her book *Birling - A Backward Glance* (1982), Margaret Collins suggests that John May senior lived in Sandy Lane. During the 1730s, through bequests, he inherited cash, securities, leases and stock. We shall see that at that time he bought the Snodland Court Lodge estate and built (or possibly rebuilt) the paper mill. On 18 October 1738 he acquired further property, including the 'Red Lion', Shernall and hopground in Birling, Hope's marsh and a tenement in Halling. He added other property in Borden, Bredgar, Halling, Luddesdown, Meopham and Tunstall. He died in 1760 and was buried at Birling on 24 November. In his will he shared his property between his two sons William and John (his wife having pre-deceased him). In Snodland William received the Courtlodge estate (including the paper mill and 'Red Lion') and John the Holborough Court estate which his father had bought from Thomas Pearce. When William died in 1777 John inherited his share.

John May junior was baptised at Birling on 12 May 1734. (A previous son John, baptised on 31 May 1732, had died a year later). By 1777 he had become an extremely wealthy man. But as we shall see, he established two endowments for the village in 1800 which have earned him much praise and thanks in succeeding years. *The Gentleman's Magazine* reported his death:

September 1, 1805. 'At his house at Snodland, in Kent, aged upwards of 70, lamented by all who had been honoured with his acquaintance, or had shared his bounty. John May, esq.. He went to bed seemingly in good health the preceding night, and was found dead in the morning.'

He was buried at Birling on 6 May. His will is lengthy and complex, since he had no family, and was entrusted to four executors. It begins by wiping out debts of £4000 owed to him and then lists his property as follows:

Godings farm in Wrotham with 28 acres; Wyarton House in Boughton Monchelsea with 215 acres; three cottages with 5 acres in Boughton Monchelsea; 8 more acres; Holloway Court in Snodland and Halling; Lad's farm in Snodland and Halling; Halfhead's in St. Margaret's parish, Rochester; Gassons in Snodland; Rumsey's; Rectory of Halling; house and 89 acres in Luddesdown and Meopham; Birling Hole and land in Birling; Whitehorse woods in Birling and Luddesdown: 126 acres; house and Boghurst Down (6 acres) in Luddesdown; several houses and planted woodlands in Birling, Leybourne and East Malling; 'Butlers' and 'Peat Pale' in Birling; house called 'Contaers' there; house and 1 acre planted with ash in Birling; three acres in East Malling called 'Hynes' and 'Barrams'; 6 new hopkilns and land called 'Boarfield' and 'Lodge Brooks' in Wrotham (8 acres); Snodland Court Lodge in Snodland and Birling (50 acres); Manor of Veles in Snodland; Snodland Mill and Wharf.

The will concludes with a few monetary bequests. His own debts and responsibilities satisfied, the four executors could each receive the rents of various parts of the property and could jointly administer or dispose of it, which they gradually did.

THE NINETEENTH CENTURY: A GENERAL VIEW

Before separate discussion of some particular developments in the life of the village, it would be valuable to set out the broad perspective. The first big change occurred early in the century. The deaths of John May in 1805 and of Robert Lord Romney in 1794 meant that ownership of virtually the whole of Snodland parish changed hands within a decade. John May's trustees took charge of his estates, Holloway Court, Lad's Farm and 'Gassons' passing to Edward Wickham, and the Manor of Veles with Courtlodge to Thomas Beech, and the mill to Thomas Spong. Lord Romney's lands were put up for sale in July 1808 and were purchased as follows:

Punish Farm	William Tidd	£3600
Middle Farm (with Buckland Tithe) [= Covey Hall Farm, Grove Farm and Mark Farm]	Thomas Whittaker	£4500
Cox's Farm	William Gorham	£4000
Austin's Farm	Thomas Beech	£2300
Holborough Farm	Edward Wickham	£2000
Gilder's Farm [Holborough]	John Goodhugh	£2120

Year	Males	Females	Total	Houses
1801			312	
1811	174	176	350	53
1815	198	186	384	
1821	240	198	438	59
1831	271	247	518	73
1841	271	229	500	102
1851	299	318	617	118
1861	552	525	1077	205
1871	954	890	1844	372
1881	1478	1348	2826	521
1891	1642	1545	3187	575
1901			3091	

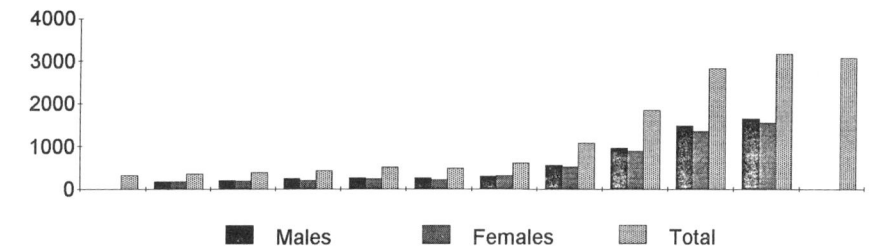

Place	Males	Females	Total	Dwellings
Burham	129	107	236	45
Leybourne	143	157	300	53
Ryarsh	182	177	359	60
Snodland	240	198	438	59
Birling	239	220	459	82
Aylesford	565	571	1136	192
W. Malling	557	648	1205	219
E. Malling	700	703	1403	219

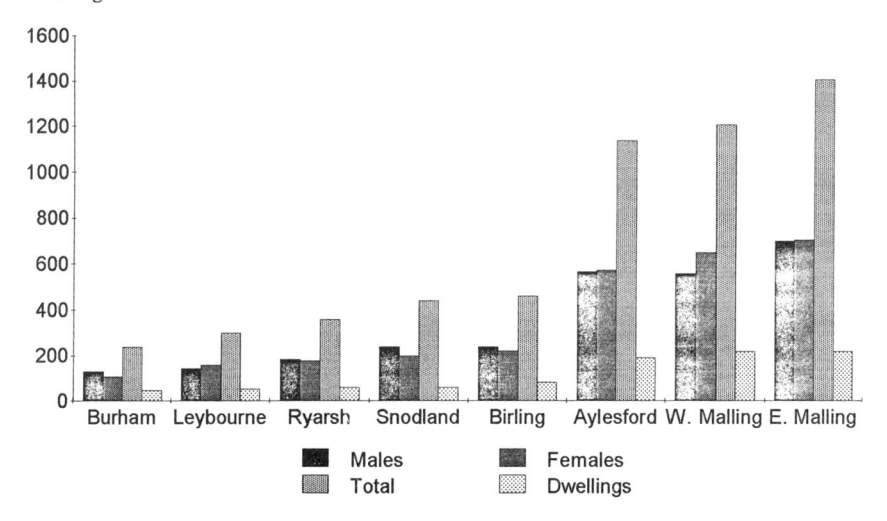

49

Every ten years from 1801 a census was taken. We are left only with the barest statistics for the first three of these, but from 1841 onwards full lists of names of parishioners are given, and the censuses from 1851 add more precise details concerning their ages and places of birth. The 1815 census in the list seems to have been made by the Rector on his own initiative.

Comparions of the relative sizes of local parishes early in the nineteenth century are startling. The second set of figures and chart are for 1821, which shows that Snodland then was actually smaller than Birling and Ryarsh, and little larger than Leybourne. It can be seen that there was a slow population growth during the first half of the century, becoming static around 1840. But the enlarging of the paper mill and the growth of the lime and cement industries, drawing people from the land and attracting workers from other parts of the country, and above all the building of the railway, caused a tremendous leap in the size of the village after 1860. Close study of the family names and their places of birth shows that many of the 'immigrants' were related. Overcrowding in the houses was a fact of life - divide the total population by the number of houses in the table above and the result averages from five to seven people per house, a very high overall rate. Even small houses might have their share of lodgers living with work-mates or relatives.

The censuses enable us to trace not only the families who lived here, but also the development of the village itself as new houses and new roads were built. The opening of the Strood-Malling Turnpike road around 1826 created the present Malling Road, while the sale of land to finance the National School resulted in May Street and East Street. The first occupants of May Street seem to have been moved there from the very bottom of the High Street, where it turned right along 'Mill Street' and 'The Wharf' and where there were many houses leading up to the mill. As the mill grew these were progressively demolished and only one or two now remain. Charles Townsend Hook and William Lee, owners of the Paper Mill and Cement Works respectively, recognised that new houses were needed for their growing numbers of workers and many of the rows of terraced houses in Birling Road and Holborough Road were built for this purpose. On the other hand, some land and property was lost to the South Eastern Railway in the early 1850s.

One of the most valuable documents is the map drawn up in 1844 to show the ownership of the houses and land in Snodland. By the Tithe Commutation Act of 1836 the former tithes (theoretically a tenth part of one's income which went towards the maintenance of the Rector) were turned into rent-charges. The map, on which every plot is numbered, together with its schedule of owners and occupiers, was drawn up for the Commissioners appointed to negotiate the values. The detailed Ordnance Survey maps from 1868 onwards show how the village grew.

The South Eastern Railway branch line from Maidstone to Strood was opened in 1856 and undoubtedly contributed enormously to the prosperity of the village, allowing easy movement of people and goods - and especially the products of the factories. Timetables were published each month in the local newspapers. In December 1873, for instance, there were eight trains daily each way between London and Maidstone which called at Snodland (five on Sundays):

To London: 7-30; 8-42; 10-38; 10-53; 3-53; 5-53; 8-03; 10-03.

To Maidstone: 8-17; 10-59; 2-17; 4-26; 5-32; 7-38; 9-19; 11-10.

There were no stations yet at New Hythe or Halling. To reach London took an hour and a half, including the shunt from London Bridge to Cannon Street and on to Charing Cross, which all trains were then obliged to do. A journey to Maidstone took eighteen minutes. Newspaper reports also show that the railway frequently laid on special trains, for instance for the factory outings which were such a keenly-anticipated event in the village each year. On a sadder note, it also provided the train for the funeral party of Mrs Hook in November 1881.

The river, of course, retained its value as a transporter of bulk items, but lack of a bridge was a handicap, particularly to those from Burham and Wouldham who worked here and also to the factories on that side which needed to load their goods on to the railway. Much of the cement from Peters' works, for instance, was brought across the river on barges and then transferred to railway trucks using a small intermediate railway track running between the river and the station alongside the churchyard. During the 1870s plans were formulated for a bridge or subway from Snodland to Burham, to be subsidised by the Rochester Bridge Trust, but after nearly thirty years of wrangling these came to nothing.

Much of the routine life of the village (and its more eventful happenings) can be traced in local newspapers such as the *Maidstone Journal and Kentish Advertiser* and later the *Kent Messenger and Maidstone Telegraph*. We have a splendid scrap-book of the years 1865-1882 compiled by two Snodland rectors; directories, church magazines and pamphlets also contribute to the story. They tell of improvements to the houses, water and drainage, to the roads and footpaths, and to the lighting - by gas. There were plenty of societies, sports and entertainments of all kinds, and a good round of fetes and festivities. In 1867 Snodland boasted its first resident doctor, so it was no longer necessary to dash to West Malling for help; others soon followed. A fire in the barn opposite All Saints church on 11 July 1881 was just prevented from spreading to the church itself. The Non-conformists were busy building new churches: the Primitive Methodists in Malling Road in 1872 and the new Congregational Church in the High Street in 1888 (replacing their earlier building in Holborough Road). On 10 October 1893 Christ Church was consecrated as a Chapel-of Ease in Birling parish to serve that end of the village and also Ham Hill. A cemetery was consecrated in 1894 and in that same year the Parish Council began its work. Some of these items will be treated more fully later in this book; others can be found in the two collections I have previously published: *Snodland: 1865-1882: A Selection of Newspaper Cuttings* (Snodland, 1991); and *Notes from Snodland Rectory: 1865-1882: Compiled by Rev. Carey and Rev. Bingley* (Snodland, 1992)

THE PAPER MILL: EARLY HISTORY

There has been a mill on the site of the present paper mill since earliest times; no doubt one of the three mills mentioned in the Domesday survey was here. But when it became a *paper* mill is much more problematical. Henry Scryvener called himself a miller in his will of 1477, but may, of course, have worked at Holborough. John Poulter (*d.*1590) refers to 'Goodman Leedes' as his landlord, which suggests he lived here in the manor of Veles, but the picture is confused by a sad entry in the church registers: 2 June 1588: 'Deborah the daughter of John Powlter, miller, wch was drowned in the mill pond at Holborough, was buried.' Possibly Powlter was there assisting a fellow miller; there are no further clues. John May senior acquired the Snodland Courtlodge estate in 1732, when the deeds described it as containing 'Houses, Oasthouses, Dovehouses, Barns, Stables, Edifices, Buildings, Mills, Malthouse and Maltmill and Cistern therein' - no mention of paper. The next document in the sequence is dated 24 January 1743 [1744], when John Hicks was in 'actual possession' of the property for a year. It refers not only to the Courtlodge, but also to 'the Paper Mill, Drying Houses and other Erections and Buildings lately Erected and Sett up by the said John May on the said premises', and then goes on to make the same list as before. We know that earlier owners like Edward Leedes, John Crow, John Weebly and others were not themselves papermakers, although that would not rule out their leasing the mill to others (as must have happened). The burial of James Smith, papermaker, in 1705 has been noted by previous writers, but he seems unrelated to other villagers of the time. Nevertheless, we cannot insist that he did not work in Snodland, but unless new evidence comes to light, any history of paper-making here prior to the 1730s must remain conjectural.

The eighteenth-century mill would have been a small affair, perhaps worked by just two or three men. On 2 July 1748 at the Petty Sessions, 'Robert Cummings, now of Snodland, on Oath saith that he was bound an Apprentice and Served 7 years to one Luke Bale of Duffeild in the County of Derby, Papermaker, and that he has not gained a settlement since'. The judgement was that he belonged to Duffield, so on 2 May 1752 he tried again, having married in the meantime. Again the Court made an order to remove him. A third attempt on 3 February 1759 to gain a settlement here met with the same response. This time he noted that 'he served ... Luke Bale ... about three years when he the said Robert Cummings ran away from his said master'. In spite of his failure to gain a settlement in Snodland, Cummings remained here with his wife Anne and children Anne and Robert. Records for 1754 and 1757 note that Richard and John Eason, Francis Aldridge and Elizabeth his wife, and Robert Cummins and Ann his wife freely held two tenements, two barns and three pieces of land (*c.*5 acres), occupied by Richard Eason, John Craft and Richard Hales, and that these were alienated (= transferred) to Hales in the latter year. It is probable that this property was the 'Old Bull' with adjacent houses and land on the east side of Holborough Road at the corner with the High Street. (Older parishioners will remember them as the 'World Stores' and 'Baldock's' electrical shop). At any rate, after living in the village for at least 33 years, 'Robert Cummins, Paper-maker', was buried on 4 September 1781. His son became a butcher, moving to Teston in 1780.

The Petty Sessions also tell of another papermaker, Charles Lock - perhaps the same man that married Elizabeth Clampard on 30 January 1749:

> 3 November 1764: Charles Lock, now residing at Snodland, born at Ansham, county of Oxford; was bound apprentice to William Fachion of Woolvernett, Oxford, Papermaker, for 7 years (and served 5 years and 4 months); then was a journeyman in Worcestershire of 11 weeks; then about 3 weeks in Shropshire and three years with Thomas Overton, a Papermaker.

He married (a second time?) in 1761 and a son Thomas was baptised on 9 November 1764, perhaps the reason he applied for settlement. Further evidence that a paper mill was here comes from the lists of alehouse-keepers which shows that Jane Munt was victualler at 'The Paper Mill' at least between 1746 and 1759 (the records are intermittent only). The site of this alehouse is currently unknown.

John May the elder died in 1761 and his Snodland property was divided between his two sons William and John. William it was who received the Courtlodge and paper-mill estate; at his death in 1771 it passed to John May the younger. But at least as early as 1748 the paper mill manager was Jasper Crothall, from Benenden. Unfortunately the Benenden registers are defective so we cannot trace his birth and family there. Crothall leased the mill from the Mays paying the parish rates on it. By 1758, although he owned another house in Snodland, he himself was living in 'Prospect Cottage' in Holborough Road, the old house next to the Willowside estate. Almost certainly it was he who had the brick part added to the property, because it dates from around 1780. He was a prosperous man, owning three houses and land, and able to make bequests of around £1000 in his will. After his death in 1781 the mill was run by his nephew Isaac Wenman, also born at Benenden. Isaac was working in Snodland no later than 1765. Among the apprenticeship records of Birling is one of 1781 for George Edmeads to Isaac Wenman of Snodland, papermaker. Edmeads fell ill in October 1791 and the parish paid him poor relief, followed by £1. 5s. 'To Nursing & Burying G. Edmeads' (but not at All Saints). When Wenman died in 1785, aged 46, the mill passed in turn to his son Isaac. On 2 September 1805 he went to the Petty Sessions with a complaint:

> Isaac Wenman of Snodland, Paper Maker, on his Oath saith that his apprentice William Hadlow hath in his Service been guilty of several Acts of Misbehaviour. And particularly on the 26: of August last he quitted his Service & went to Strood Fair without his knowledge or Consent. (Hadlow was committed to hard labour for 14 days.)

Disaster struck on 17 December 1807, reported on the 22nd in the *Maidstone Journal and Kentish Advertiser*:

> Thursday night a very alarming fire broke out at Snodland paper Mill, which in a short time entirely consumed the same and all its contents, the whole to a very considerable amount. The great Double Barrelled Engine of the Kent Fire Office arrived at the spot with great expedition, but two [*sic*] late to effect any good purpose, as the destruction was complete.

A note in the Overseers accounts acknowledges that Wenman's rates would need modified: 1 May 1808: '2 sets allowd as agreed at the Vestry for Mill being destroy'd by fire'. The manorial records make it clear that the estate had previously been divided into two parts, separating the mill from the farm. By his will John May had left the estate to Mary Simpson, widow of Thomas of Rochester, but with her as one of the four executors was John Spong of Southwark, hop-factor. He already owned some property in Snodland. It is not until the manorial meeting of 25 October 1810 that the minutes record the alienation of Snodland Court Lodge from John May (who had died in 1805) to Isaac Wenman and William Spong. The church registers show baptisms of five children of William Spong between 1812 and 1820, describing him as 'papermaker', so he seems to have been in partnership with Wenman. And when Wenman died in 1815, 'from 'unskilful treatment of an abscess' according to the rector, his widow Ann alienated Snodland Court Lodge (being a house and 22 acres) to James Martin. On 28 October 1818 the manorial meeting minuted:

> Be it Remembered that at this Court the Homage [Jury] present that James Martin some time since purchased of the Representatives of the late Isaac Wainman a Messuage, Barn and about twenty two acres of Land, being part of Snodland Court Lodge Farm and that the remainder of the said Farm, consisting of a Paper Mill, Six Cottages and about eight acres of Land, is now the property of Willm Spong and which he purchased of the late John May. The whole of the said premises are held at the annual rent of 18s. 8d. And the Homage apportion the Rent as follows: vizt. the said James Martin to pay the annual sum of 6s. and the said Willm Spong to pay the annual sum of 12s. 8d.

A List of Papermakers at Snodland: 1748-1833
Dates of known employment

Name	Dates	Name	Dates
Edward Brown	1831	Joseph Mayatt	1817-1831
Thomas Cooke/Edmeads	1797-1816	William Mayatt	1829
Jasper Crothall	1748-1781	Thomas Mullard	1823
Robert Cummings	1748-1781	Thomas Oliver	1831
Daniel Dean	1832-1833	Stephen Outridge	1801-1814
James Dickson	1813	James Proctor	1826-1833
Thomas Fielder	1816-1818	William Randall	1816-1818
William Fryer	1825-1827	**William Spong**	1811-1823
William Hadlow	1805	William Streeton/Stratton	1824-1825
Daniel Hurd	1822	Samuel Tovey	1828-1830
William Jordan	1820-1826	**William Trindall**	1821-1823
William Joynson	1823-1833	Robert Waghorn	1813-1825
James Line	1826-1829	Constantine Weedon	1823
Charles Lock	1749-1764	**Isaac Wenman [I]**	1765-1785
James Loosely	1810-1813	**Isaac Wenman [II]**	1785-1815
John Lynn	1830	Thomas Wright	1825

Thomas Fielder took over between 1816 and 1818 and in 1823 William Joynson came from High Wycombe (one of the English centres for papermaking) to run the mill; several Snodland papermakers and other parishioners seem to have made the journey with him. Some of them moved on with him in 1833 when he went to St Mary Cray. The Land Tax Assessments (and later the censuses) show that the house formerly in the High Street, eventually occupied and enlarged by the Hook family and named 'Veles' by them, was also the home of most of the previous mill managers, beginning with Isaac Wenman the younger (1796-1806). Others who lived there were Thomas Cleaves (1807-10) - not known to have been a papermaker, William Spong (1811-23), William Joynson (1823-33) and John Clark (1834-41). When Joynson left Snodland, Spong leased the mill to Reuben Hunt of Wooburn (near High Wycombe), but he immediately re-assigned the lease to John Clark, who probably came from the same area (the 1841 census does not specify exact places like the later ones do). Clark evidently felt the need to modernise the mill and borrowed money to do so. In 1838 the rates were increased because the mill had been 'improved'. A detailed description survives of the machinery at this time:

2 October 1838

One Rag Engine with Shafts and Drivers in the Mill worked in Gear by Water Wheel or condensing Engine. One set of Glazing Rolls attached to paper machine - one Knot Strainer attached to Paper Machine. A Small Steam Engine of two Horse power - Two Board Tables in the Soll - One pair of small Rollers with swing Shafts and Wheels and Timbers erected in the Soll for rolling Boards - Tube Steam Boiler fourteen horse power high pressure - A large cylinder steam Boiler of Twenty horse power with cocks, pipes and valves erected in the Yard - A sixteen horse power steam engine high pressure and condenser with pipes and cocks; balance wheel, Spur Wheel and large Shaft erected in the new building in the Yard - a Rag Duster with Drivers - Two washing Engines with Rolls, plates and pinions; Water pumps to supply the same erected in the new building in the Yard - A new Bleaching Chest with Racks for braining stuff erected in the bleaching house - A Rag Cutter with Shafts and Drivers - Four shaving Boilers with Pipes and Cocks in the lower Drying House. A Pair of large Mill Board Rollers for Glazing with Shafts and Wheels erected in the Soll. A Grind Stone with Shafts and Wheels erected in the Soll. A Grind Stone with Shafts and Pinions - sixty pairs of new Trebles marked J. C.

Clark planned more and drew up an agreement on 1 June 1840 for

A New Steam Boiler of 20 Horse Power - A New High and low pressure Steam engine of 20 Horse power, with Shafts and Blocks and pinions and the apparatus therewith as going gear connected - Four new Cast Iron Rag Engines with pumps and Apparatus complete - A New Paper Machine with Drying Cylinders, Machinery, Utensils and Apparatus

and a splendid diagram and code survives which shows the position of the machinery new and old. Unfortunately Clark went bankrupt and the plans for this second phase fell through. For a time the mill was leased to Henry Holden, a papermaker of Fulham, who perhaps ran the business from London; certainly the house in the High Street was not regularly occupied until the next manager, Henry Atkinson Wildes, took up residence in 1847. In 1854 the business passed into the hands of Charles Townsend Hook, whose name it still bears.

THE LIME AND CEMENT INDUSTRY

The Medway valley has been marked for generations by the scars of chalk quarries. Chalk was excavated in a small way from Roman times for the making of quick-lime. We have already noted William Lambarde in 1596 recording William Tilghman 'throwing downe a part' of the tumulus at Holborough 'for the use of the chalke', and the small pit above Paddlesworth (actually in Birling parish) was created in the eighteenth century. Nearby was 'Lime-Kiln field', for the chalk was put on an iron grid inside kilns and slowly heated by a charcoal fire to 900 degrees C, when it changed to quick-lime.

During the nineteenth and early twentieth centuries a whole series of cement works grew up along the banks of the Medway from Frindsbury to Burham, each with its pits, industrial railways, works, wharfs and barges. The earliest of the group, at North Halling, began in 1799. A map of 1823 shows the beginnings of the chalk workings on the Halling-Snodland boundary (which eventually extended to Upper Halling). At the manorial meeting held on 27 October 1819, it was recorded that John May's executor Edward Wickham, who took over the Holborough Court estate after May's death, was transferring it to Thomas Poynder and William Hobson. A deed dated 31 December 1819 confirms this, stating Poynder was 'of Clapham Common' and Hobson was 'of Stanford Hill, Middlesex'. Further additions to their holdings were made in 1821 and 1826, when they were described as 'Limeburners'. The 1823 map refers to Holloway Court as 'Mr Poynder's house', so presumably he lived there at that time. In 1845 the partnership changed to 'Poynder and Medlicott' in the Overseers accounts, and the following year another transfer took place. By deed dated 31 December 1846, Thomas Poynder of Wimpole Street (son of the one mentioned above) and Edward Medlicott, Lime Manufacturers and Lime Merchants of Earl Street, Blackfriars, made over Holloway Court, Holborough farm and Gassons to William Lee 'of Rochester'. (Thomas Poynder and William Medlicott also owned works and kilns in Halling.) William Lee, born in 1801, the youngest son of a Lewisham building contractor, had already worked as manager of lime works at Burham since 1826. Another deed of 30 May 1850 gives his address as Satis House, Rochester, but the 1851 census, taken of 30 March, finds him settled at Holborough with his wife Christiana, his son and partner Samuel, and six servants. The Poynder family seem to have retained some land in Snodland as William H. Poynder (the next generation) continued to pay rents into the 1850s and indeed he is described 'Lord of the Manor' in the 1882 Kelly's Directory.

One name which dominates cement-making in the area is that of Peters. It is interesting to note that William Peters, the earliest of the family to become established here, is described as 'Conductor of the Lime Works' and 'Agent to Mr. Poynder' in the Snodland church registers. He lived in the house now isolated from the main road some 200 yards north of Holborough mill, and had certainly settled there by 1823. The 1841

Plate 1

Holborough Knob, 1930.

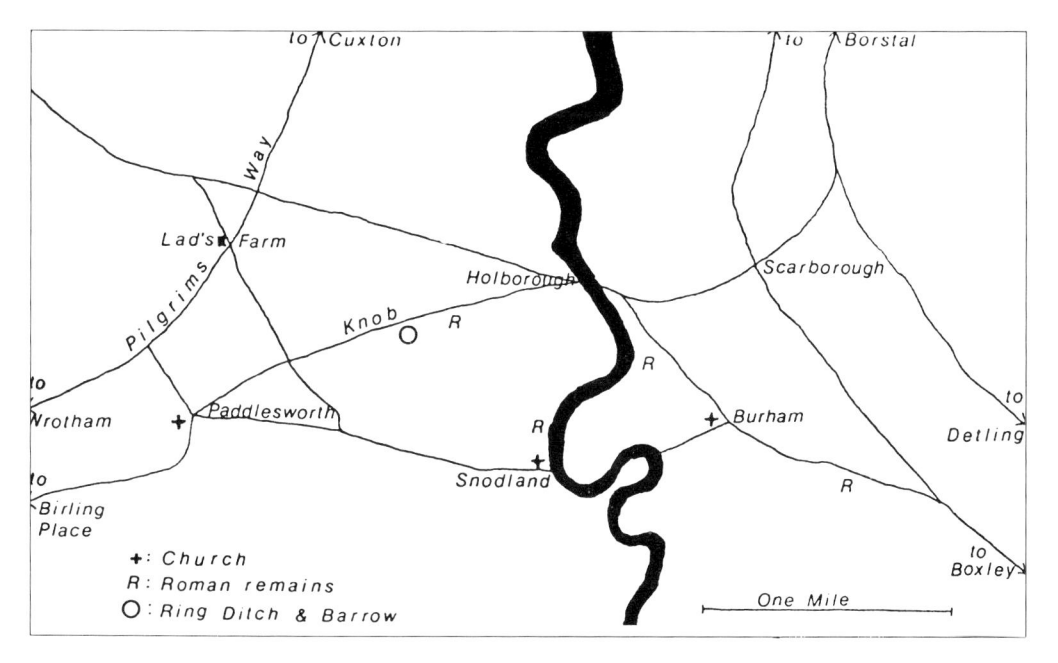

Early tracks around Snodland.

Plate 2

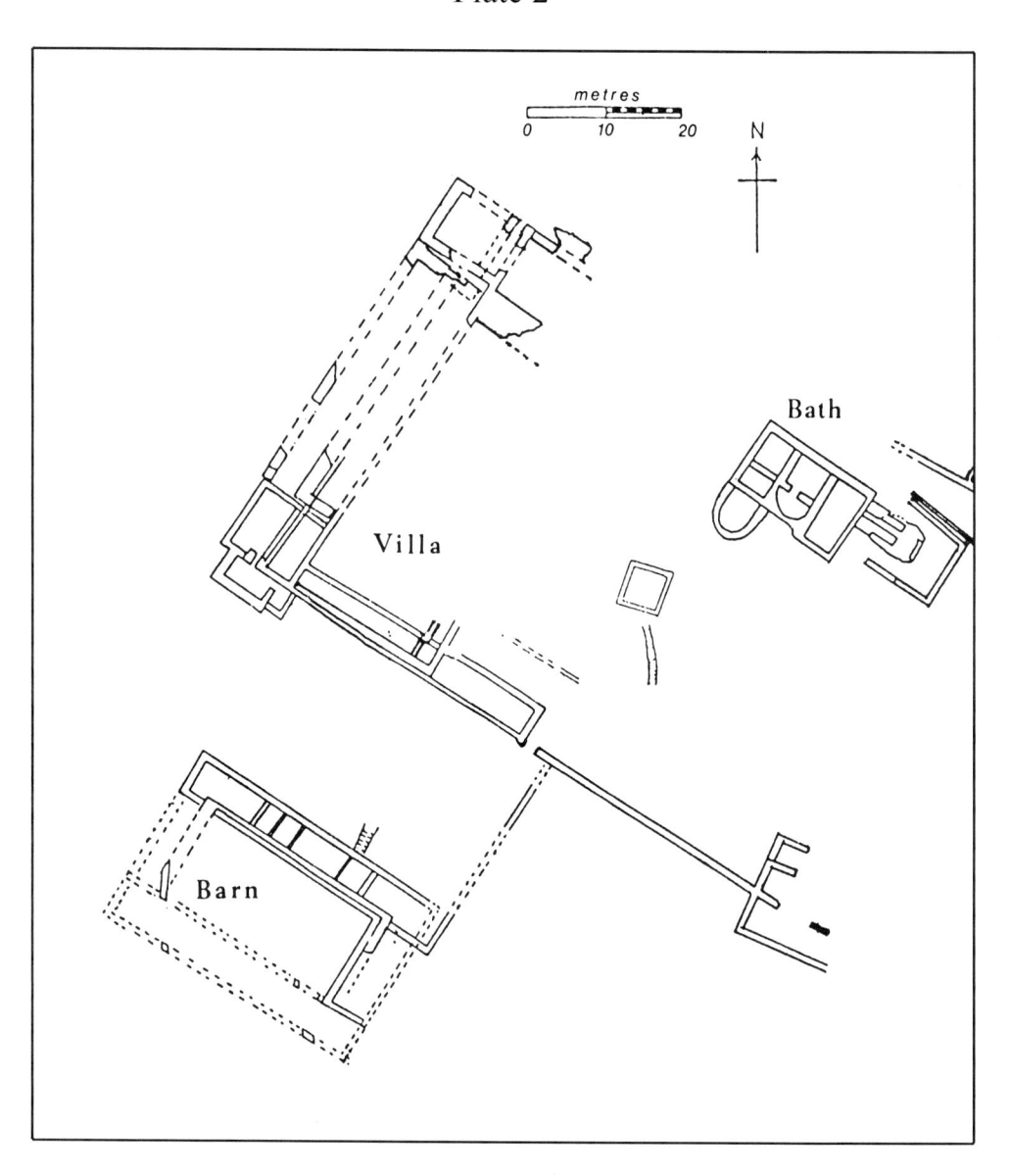

Snodland Roman Villa

Plate 3

The charter of 838 A.D.   (courtesy of British Library)

Snodland ferry 1924

Plate 4

Courtlodge, Drawn by William Twopenny 1821-28 (Courtesy of British Museum)

All Saints church and the foundations of Snodland Courtlodge. 1881?

Plate 5

Edward and Margaret Bischoptre. Brass, 1487

William Tilghman and his wives: Isabell and Joane. Brass, 1541

Plate 6

All Saints church interior, about 1900

Snodland Brook with 'Blackbrook Bridge', about 1900

Plate 7

Charles Townsend Hook (1831-1877)

The first Independent Chapel in Mill Row

Plate 8

At the Paper Mill fire, 12th August 1906

Salvaged belongings in the station yard after the Paper Mill fire

Plate 9

'The Veles', home of the Hook family

High Street, 1864; site of New Jerusalem church on left; Gorham; cottages on right

Plate 10

'Mulberry Cottage' before restoration 1933

Woodlands Farm before rebuilding and enlarging 1880

Plate 11

John May (1732-1805)

William Lee; his daughter Ann Robert; her son William Henry Roberts; His son William Lee Henry Roberts. 1878

Plate 12

Covey Hall farm, probably painted by Agnes Hook in the 1860s.

Holborough Road in 1926, before it was widened; 'Prospect Cottage' on right

census shows only that he was born outside Kent, but we might guess that he came here in the company of Richard (1791-1880), perhaps a brother, who was born in Brentwood. Although Richard became a grocer, he spent some time as a lime labourer and so did five of his sons. He had lived for a time in Dorking, where his son Thomas William was born. A James Peters, limeburner, was also born in Dorking around 1808, but evidently was not a close relation because his daughter Emily married Thomas William at Snodland in 1851. Brothers William and Henry Peters developed their own works at Wouldham during the 1850s.

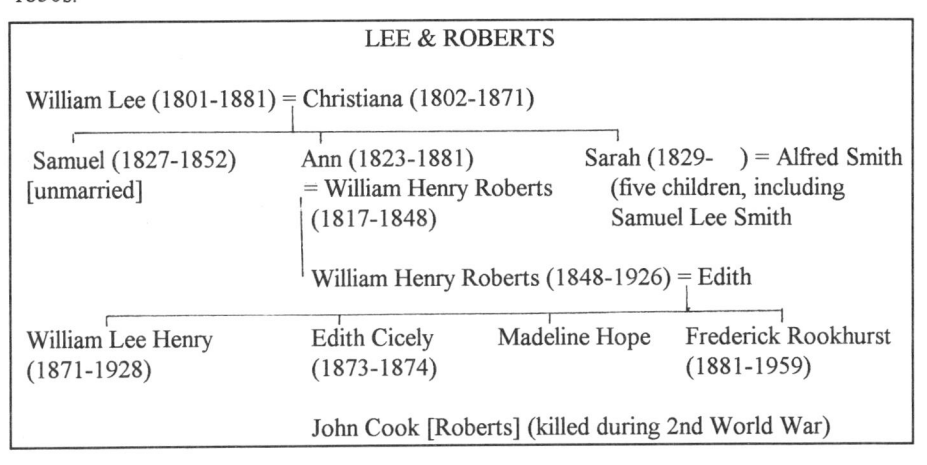

```
                              LEE & ROBERTS

    William Lee (1801-1881) = Christiana (1802-1871)
    ┌──────────────────────┬──────────────────────────┬──────────────────────────┐
    Samuel (1827-1852)     Ann (1823-1881)            Sarah (1829-  ) = Alfred Smith
    [unmarried]            = William Henry Roberts    (five children, including
                             (1817-1848)               Samuel Lee Smith

                           William Henry Roberts (1848-1926) = Edith
    ┌──────────────────────┬──────────────────┬──────────────────────────┐
    William Lee Henry      Edith Cicely       Madeline Hope              Frederick Rookhurst
    (1871-1928)            (1873-1874)                                   (1881-1959)

                           John Cook [Roberts] (killed during 2nd World War)
```

Samuel Lee died in 1852. Soon after, William Lee added Portland Cement to his firm's products. Two kilns were all that existed when he took over the Halling works, but the business quickly expanded. The title changed to Lee, Son & Smith when a new partner was appointed - Alfred Smith of Rochester, who had married William's youngest daughter, Sarah. Around 1876 his grandson Samuel Lee Smith joined the business and following William's death in 1881 another of his grandsons became a partner. William Henry Roberts (1848-1926) was a cavalry officer and a friend of the Prince of Wales (later Edward VII). The company was renamed again, William Lee, Son & Co. Ltd., but the Halling works went into liquidation in 1912, when they were acquired by B.P.C.M (British Portland Manufacturers Ltd.). William Lee Henry Roberts (1871-1928), son of W.H.R., was the last managing director of the company, but around 1923 he established a new cement works at Holborough, known as the Holborough Cement Co. Ltd. This was sold to A.P.C.M. Ltd in 1931.

Holloway Court, rebuilt in the late eighteenth century by John May, (and of which one picture seems to have survived somewhere in America) was pulled down in 1884. In its place Holborough Court was built nearby. This was designed by Hubert Bensted and incorporated 'a considerable amount of the materials' from the old house; it was ready for habitation in 1886. William Lee Henry Roberts (1871-1928) succeeded to the property and when he died it passed to his nephew John Cook of Royden Hall, on condition that he took the name Roberts. He did, but subsequently sold the estate to A.P.C.M. and the house was promptly demolished. Some of the ancient fittings were saved and now form part of the furnishings of Paddlesworth church.

THE NATIONAL SCHOOLS

Returns made by Snodland's churchwardens in the first half of the eighteenth century occasionally state categorically that there was no school in the village. On 25 May 1716, for instance, John Goffe wrote 'Our Minister does not reside [in Snodland] but Mr White his Curat does and p[er]forms his Duty. Concerning Schools, Schoolmasters, Physitians, Surgeons and Midwifes: None in the parish.' That situation changed with the arrival of William Lewis following his marriage on 1 June 1762: 'William Lewis of Cuxton, singleman, and Sarah Wingate of Snodland, singlewoman'. William was the son of William and Mary Lewis of Cuxton, and was baptised there on 26 February 1739. Whoever taught him did a fine job, for Lewis acted as parish clerk in Snodland and his books are the most beautifully written and organised of all the parish records. He lived in Brook Street, using his house as a school, so there cannot have been many pupils. When Jasper Crothall made his will in 1780 he made provision for his young nephew George:

> I will and desire that ... George Crothall be put to School to William Lewis, Schoolmaster, of the Parish of Snodland aforeasaid, to Board with him, at Sixteen Pounds per Year until he be put Apprentice or otherwise provided for.

Jasper actually owned the house occupied by Lewis and after his death ownership passed to George! The Land Tax assessments hint at a change in 1793 when the former valuation of £7 is divided into two parts: £3 for the house, with one for £4 assigned to the 'free school'. It seems likely that some kind of benefaction had been agreed to supply free schooling for at least some pupils. Lewis died in April 1797 and his place was taken by Samuel Maurice Hitchcock (1755-1811). In 1799 the ownership heading in the tax list, which is 'Free School' between 1793 and 1798, changes to 'John May'. May evidently intended to set the school up on a proper footing and took steps to make provision for its future. On 10 October 1800, he drew up a scheme for two charities, one of which concerned the school. He sold to those who were to be trustees for the scheme the house then used as a school and four acres of land belonging to it, with twenty acres of salt marsh. From the rents of the marshland the schoolmaster was to receive £20 a year, on condition that he taught reading, writing and arithmetic to twenty poor children from Snodland and ten each from Birling and Halling. (This did not restrict him from taking other scholars whose parents paid for them.). The schoolmaster also had free use of the house and four acres. Future appointments were to be made by the clergy of Snodland, Halling and Birling, or by Magistrates in case of their neglect or disagreement.

Following Hitchcock's death in 1811, the new schoolmaster was William Higgins. He had married Mary Butler at All Saints on 13 May 1809. Eleven children were born to them (although three died in infancy), no doubt helping to sustain the school numbers at this time. In the 1831 will of John Goodhugh, grandfather of Thomas Fletcher Waghorn, Higgins was described as his nephew and was bequeathed £25. When Mr Woolmer compiled his *Historical Jottings of the Parish of Snodland* in 1894, he seems to have drawn upon memories of elderly parishioners for some reminiscences of village life earlier in the century. He writes that the school was originally

> a long and narrow red brick building with tiled roof, being well lighted with three or four large square windows on either side. It contained two large rooms, porch, and a house for the master, and stood nearer the street than the present fabric - on the site now devoted to the boy's playground. In the front were well-kept palings, painted white, and at the back was an extensive playground for both boys and girls. In the very large wash-house, at the back of the master's house, could be seen some fine old beams of timber, and from one of these Mr. Higgins, a former master, hung himself, and strange to say, his nephew who came to the funeral, shot himself in Church Fields, near the railway arch.

Higgins was buried at All Saints on 5 March 1836, aged 48. A report by the Charity Commissioners in 1839 notes:

> The property devised for the support of the School consists of a good dwelling-house, with two schoolrooms, a barn, oast-house, and four acres of land, and a right of common for two cows, which premises have been occupied rent free, by the schoolmaster for the time being.

> The late schoolmaster died in February, 1836, and it has been thought advisable to take this opportunity of putting the school-house in complete repair, the expense of which is estimated at £54, by pulling down some of the out-buildings, which seem to be of little or no use, and selling the materials... .

> A schoolmaster has been appointed by the Rector of Snodland and the Vicar of Halling, on an understanding that he is to receive no emoluments other than the occupation of the school premises and what he may obtain by admitting pay scholars, in addition to those who are to be taught free on the foundation, until the expenses of the repairs were defrayed.

John Cogger was the replacement for Higgins and held the post until 1842. The 1841 census gives his age as about 60, with his daughter Eliza, aged about 30, as the schoolmistress. Edward Jupp, son of William and Eliza of Birling, took over, his wife Susanna (born in Rochester) becoming schoolmistress. Next was William Thomas Wood and his wife Emma (1854-56), then Walter Rumble (1856-66). Both Wood and Rumble had a second job as the village postmaster. Rumble and his wife both came from Wiltshire and in later years he received great acclaim as a story teller at some of the village entertainments. In February 1873, for instance, at one of the series of 'Penny Readings', the newspaper reported that '"Jonas Grubb's Courtship," a Wiltshire tale, in the hands of Mr. Rumble left nothing to be desired; the lingo he introduced being given with great humour. In this style of piece Mr. Rumble is unrivalled, nor does he ever fail to raise a hearty laugh from all'. Unfortunately within a few years he had blotted his copybook. He had become assistant Overseer in 1862, responsible for collecting land tax, income tax and rates. Early in 1880, having played his part in the Easter entertainments as usual, he absconded with the money, leaving a deficit in the parish accounts of £270. 15s. 11d. Yet his wife and son continued to run the Post Office for many years after.

Woolmer gives another story of the early school - clearly a policy of carrots as well as sticks was the order of the day:

> Some years ago, even as late as 1865, there used to be a curious custom in vogue at the National Schools. The then schoolmaster, in order to promote the good behaviour of his scholars - some of whom, at that time, might almost have been called young men - took note of his scholars' conduct during the whole of the week, and those who stood highest on the merit sheet for that period were alowed to indulge in a little recreation on the Friday afternoon. Tickets to the number of the competitors were shook up in a hat, and each lad drew his ticket, which was numbered. The schoolmaster then produced from his desk a small parcel, containing half-a-crown, also with a number on it, and the lad who drew the number corresponding to that on the parcel, won the much-coveted prize. With a change in the management of the school, this custom disappeared; but no doubt this plan had proved to be a great boon in keeping up the tone and good conduct of the school in those days.

Tom Hilder, aged 21 and born at Tonbridge, was appointed at Easter 1866. The next month he married Ellen Seers of Mid Comp at All Saints church. There are several photographs of the school staff and children taken during Mr. Hilder's headmastership. This he resigned in 1882, having replaced Walter Rumble as Assistant Overseer. In view of his precessor's actions, Mr Hilder was required to put up £300 security, later reduced to £200. He continued to serve the parish in various capacities, as organist at All Saints (until 1897), as postmaster and as clerk to the Parish Council. He died in June 1927. His successors at the school were Arthur Verriour (1882-87), followed by Charles Godfrey (1887-1925). Godfrey also took over as organist.

In 1853 the school was enlarged; repairs in 1859 were funded from Godden's charity. But further expansion was needed and in 1867 the School Trustees sold the land which had hitherto provided the rents to pay the schoolmaster. The rector gives the details:

> One portion, viz. that in front of the Queen's Head Hotels, hitherto let for £13. 10s. per ann., was divided into 25 lots, and sold for £2402. The extent was 2¾ (about). The other portion, hitherto let for grazing purposes, situate next the river, and fetching £20 per annum, was sold for £500. Its extent was 16 acres (about). Thus the whole realised £2902. Of this sum the Charity Commissioners permitted £800 to be set apart for the erection of the new buildings - the same to be repaid (without interest) by yearly instalments of £27 each in 30 years. The remainder, after legal and other expenses had been paid, was invested in the 3 p. cent consols, and ordered to be paid half-yearly to the local trustees of the school. In addition to this sum of £800, the Committee of Council gave £277. 8s. 9d., and the remainder necessary, amounting to £516. 8s. 6d., was raised by private subscription. Total cost £1593. 17s. 3d. The new school, designed by

Edward Stephens Esq. of Maidstone, and built by Mr. T. Clements of Rochester, were begun August 14, 1867, when a solemn service was performed and the stone under the great West window in the Infants schoolroom laid in the presence of many people; and they were finished Tuesday February 11, 1868, one which day they were formally opened after service in Church, by the right Rev. Thomas Legh, Lord Bishop of Rochester. ... The schools consosts of two large rooms - one for boys and girls, the other for infants. Adjoining the first is a classroom capable of holding 30 children. The house contains on the ground floor two sitting rooms and a kitchen, and on the first floor three bedrooms. A new well was dug at the time of the building, but the old well was left untouched, in the boys' playground.

Further extensions were made in 1871, 1877 and 1895, by which time they had come under the Free Education Act of 1892 and could accommodate 420 children. Rev. Wall notes that the School's income in 1909 was 18s. 7d. a quarter, out of which the building had to be kept in repair! (By this time teachers were appointed and paid by the Local Education Authority.) Investments by the Charity Commissioners eventually put matters to rights and assured an income of £70 a year. Following the opening of the Central (now Holmsdale) School in 1931, further improvements were made to the Brook Street buildings. On 9 July 1948 the former National Schools became 'Snodland Church of England (Controlled) Primary School', with the Kent Education Committee having responsibility for maintenance, the School House excepted. The latter was transferred to them in 1967, when it provided additional space for staff rooms and storage. Plans for an entirely new building at Roberts Road were made and temporary huts had to be employed for a time due to the expansion of population. With the impending construction of the Snodland-Halling bypass the new school was built and the Brook Street school closed on 26 November 1979. It was demolished shortly afterwards, although the Foundation Stone, laid by Mrs. Anne Roberts on 14 August 1867, has been preserved.

THE BRITISH SCHOOLS

A strong streak of non-conformity runs through the history of the village: for instance 40 of this persuasion were noted earlier in the 1676 Compton census. In the nineteenth century the papermaker managers in particular were leading Non-conformists and supported their cause through many generous contributions to improve village life. A family called Bateman appear to have come to Snodland with William Joynson from Wooburn, Bucks. John, perhaps the father, Thomas, Joseph and Jabez are all listed in the 1841 census, of whom Thomas and Jabez were papermakers and Joseph a grocer. Thomas at least went briefly to St Mary Cray (which is where William Joynson was) around 1842, for his son William was born there, but he was back in Snodland soon after, becoming a grocer at what had previously been 'The Old Bull' on the High Street/Holborough Road corner. In the words of Woolmer:

> A few members of the Congregational Chapel wished for a school of
> their own to which their children might go, and thus be free from that class

of religious instruction usually taught in Church Schools. Their desire was soon carried into effect, for in the vestry of the Congregation Chapel the Nonconformists started a small school, under the charge of Miss George. Afterwards it was fortunate when there was a great increase in the child population of Snodland, and a corresponding necessity for another school beside the National, that the late Mr. Thomas Bateman was able to prevail upon his friend, the late Mr. Joynson, of St. Mary Cray, to build these schools (in 1857). At a meeting, the latter gentleman presented them to the people of Snodland, but unfortunately did not place them in the hands of a legal trust, or form a committee of management. The inhabitants, as a recognition of the gift, presented Mr. Joynson with a Bible, as a token of their thankfulness for his benevolence.

For a lengthened period the working of the Schools appears to have been unsatisfactory, and ultimately a disagreement arose with some of the persons concerned, which led Mr. Joynson to have the school materials put up for sale in one lot, to be cleared away in a short time; and the house and ground in another lot. The school materials were bought by the late Mr. Charles Townsend Hook, who asked several of the leading Nonconformists what was best to be done about the school-house and ground, which had been bought by Mr. Collier of Greenhithe. In the end, the two gentlemen arranged matters, Mr. Hook purchasing the house and ground from Mr. Collier, who gave a donation for the benefit of the Schools.

No doubt the fact that William Joynson lived some distance away hindered his appreciation of the difficulties the school had faced. But certainly under the direction of the Hook family it soon prospered and received high praise from visiting Inspectors. Following the death of C. T. Hook, his sisters took over the school and promptly gave it the tower by which Snodland is so well-known today. It incorporates a stone on the south side, inscribed:

> This Clock Tower is erected in Loving Memory of
> CHARLES TOWNSEND HOOK,
> Of "Veles", and the Paper Works, Snodland,
> by his sorrowing mother and sisters.
> Died 11th February 1877.
> Deeply loved and mourned.

Numbers increased to such an extent that it outstripped the National School and expansion was called for. The Misses Hook offered 1000 guineas for the adjacent Providence Chapel, which the congregation accepted, and which subsequently became the infant department of the British Schools. Accommodation was thus increased from the former 430 places to 320 boys and girls and 190 infants. It remained busy until the opening of the Central School on 19 May 1930, to which the children were then transferred.

The Hooks were not only very much alive to the needs of the village, but had vision (and money) to keep abreast of new developments. As an offshoot of the British Schools they built and funded a technical workshop. Woolmer describes it:

The British Schools Manual Training Class Room, situate in [the] High Street, is one of the first of its kind in Kent - there being but one other in the county - and was erected by the Misses Hook in the year 1893, as a means of supplying the need of technical education for the advanced scholars of the British Schools. The building is constructed of stock bricks, being well lighted, and thoroughly fitted with benches and tools for the training of boys in woodwork. An able instructor is provided by these benevolent ladies to teach the scholars. Although no charge whatsoever is made for instruction, skill in drawing, the passing of the fourth standard, and regularity of attendance in the Schools, are the only qualifications for entering this Manual Training Instruction.

HENRY DAMPIER PHELPS

The Rev. Henry Dampier Phelps (1777-1865) was Rector of Snodland for sixty-one years between 1804 and his death in 1865. Born at Sherborne in Dorset, he was himself the son of a clergyman, Rev. Thomas Phelps (1740-1811), vicar of Haddenham, and of his wife Elizabeth Dampier (1739-1825). Henry went up to Hertford College in the University of Oxford on 18 May 1795, graduating four years later and achieving his M.A. in 1801. In 1799, the year of his graduation, he took Holy Orders and went to Haddenham as curate to his father. His uncle, Thomas Dampier, was already Dean of Rochester, but was elevated to Bishop of the See in 1802. As Dean he had been able to put his brother-in-law into the vicarage at Haddenham; now, as Bishop, he appointed Henry to be Rector of Snodland, where the living was worth £300 a year. He was inducted on 3 July 1804. And here Henry stayed for the rest of his long life, unmarried, but with two nephews nearby playing their part in the cure of souls: Henry Dampier Phelps (1811-1864), Vicar of Birling, and Thomas Prankerd Phelps (1814-1903). The latter clergyman (and the family background) are the subject of a fine book by Gerald van Loo, *A Victorian Parson: The Life and Times of Thomas Prankerd Phelps, Ridley, Kent. Rector, 1840-1893* (Upton-upon Severn, 1989).

Phelps spent a great deal of money in maintaining and beautifying the fabric of All Saints Church: a little book of expenses totals £1644. 5s. The east wall of the church was completely rebuilt at his expense and he also commissioned stained glass windows, some of which survive. The east window of 1846, portraying four christian martyrs, was destroyed in 1941. The old village market cross stood on steps outside the Red Lion, but by Phelps's time a tree was growing where the cross had formerly been. In 1846 he caused the steps to be moved to the churchyard and had a large new cross erected on them there. It is said that he is buried close by but the 'small square stone' marking the place cannot now be traced.

Between 1812 and 1825 Phelps decided to add in the burial register some notes of the causes of death: 'In order to ascertain what disorders are the most prevolent in the Village, I mark the disease of which each of the Parishioners die'. Thus we learn that Isaac Wenman died after 'unskilful treatment of an abscess'. 'Thyphus Fever', 'Dropsy',

'Consumption' and other diseases are recorded. Jane Hadlow, aged 96, and other elderly parishioners quite reasonably succumbed to 'Decay of Nature', but the Rector can hardly have endeared himself to the relatives of the couple buried after 'the effects of debauchery throughout life'! One guesses that he was not on the best of terms with some of his flock and there was an attempt on his life, recounted by the curate who helped him during his last few years:

> I must here relate one very odd story which he himself told me. He was a great foe to Smugglers, of whom in the old times there were many, and he had taken a somewhat leading part against them. Now Mr. Phelps was in the habit of walking one day in the week across the Medway via Wouldham to Rochester and back again - a walk of many miles. Very likely he may have been known to go to his Bankers on such a day, but at any rate he was a marked man, as the sequel will show. Fortunately for Mr. Phelps - unfortunately for another individual, a certain Tailor in Rochester, also a diminutive man of small physique - the latter took it into his head to walk towards Snodland through some woods where the path lay; and coming along unwittingly was pounced upon by one or more of the "Smuggler" party and cruelly murdered then and there - by mistake of course, but a very convenient one for Mr. Phelps, who had that day left Rochester somewhat later on his return walk to Snodland. Suspicion appears to have fallen upon the right party, and at the Coroner's inquest on the Tailor which was held at Cuxton, Mr. Phelps was chosen foreman - his would-be murderer being also present under arrest, and the two facing one another. I recollect how the old gentleman related to me his own feelings at the time under such extraordinary circumstances, knowing well he was himself the "*corpus*" intended, over which the inquest was being held. It was satisfactory, however, that the murderer was so promptly brought to justice and in due course duly hanged.

I wonder if this was the Thomas Mills, aged 51, 'Drowned in the Medway' and buried on 21 March 1813. More than once Phelps notes 'smuggler' as the occupation given in the church registers, again hardly a friendly act! The curate, the Honorable and Reverend Edward Vesey Bligh, wished to marry the daughter of the Earl of Abergavenny - but his father-in-law insisted that she should marry a clergyman, so forcing Bligh to leave the Diplomatic Service for the Church. He spent a brief time at Snodland after his marriage in 1854, leaving us with a picture of old Phelps and an astonishing complaint that 'The Lodge' built by Thomas Waghorn was far too small to accommodate his own little family:

> We, Father, Mother and Baby, took up our permanent quarters in a very tiny habitation near the Bull Inn and Old Turnpike at Snodland. A more undesirable locality could not well be: even worse now with 4000 people, but it was then in its babyhood, and I think the population - nearly all cement and lime burners - was little over 700. Quite flat, smoky, without a single real gentleman - much less a lady - the one redeeming point was the close neighbourhood of Birling Manor where at any rate was refuge for the Curate's aristocratic wife. The old Rector of Snodland was a positive

curiosity - quite an old fossil, an antique Bachelor, who lived in two small rooms of his Rectory tended by a beaming Housekeeper called 'Kitty'. W. Phelps - that was his name - was nearly 80 years of age, a very short man, dressed always in a long tailcoat down nearly to the ankles, with an old-fashioned white choker round and round his neck and a 'Mother Gamp' large umbrella. On Sundays he wore his University gown, which he had had at Oxford or Cambridge 50 years ago, and which from black to brown had lapsed into a dingy floor colour: he always marched down the Village on his way to Church and back again in this manner. ... On quarter days, when my stipend of £25 was due, the old gentleman would triumphantly march up the village to our house and put the money down in hard cash or otherwise, and good-naturely dispose of his debt for my humble services as if I was the biggest '*dun*' or 'Old Clother' London Jew craving for a prompt settlement! He also solemnly confused me when I first took up duty (no reflection of course on the services which I preached subsequently) as to the proper length for such discourses, using the phrase (as I well remember and also to my astonishment) "Twelve minutes is long enough for any *Monkey* to be talking to a lot of others". Peculiar indeed and hardly encouraging exhortation to a newly ordained Deacon. Old Phelps was a character, and the oldest clergyman in the diocese. [Esme Wingfield-Stratford: *This was a Man* (1949)].

THE TOLL ROAD

To journey from Snodland to Malling in the old days, one took the road up the High Street, then left on the Birling Road, before branching off down 'Hollow Lane' to Ham Hill, then into Lunsford Lane and so on to Malling. There was no 'Malling Road' running south from the 'Bull'. A Turnpike Road from Strood to Malling was authorized and opened in 1825/6 with toll-gates at Strood, Snodland and Leybourne. New sections of road were built from the Bull direct to Ham Hill and from the end of Lunsford Lane to Leybourne. Annual bids were made by those wishing to collect the tolls and these were allocated to the highest bidders. Successful bids for the Snodland Gate generally averaged around £250 and were usually made by persons from far afield who then put in collectors to live in the toll-house and receive the money on their behalf. Administration of the road seems to have run smoothly and the trustees rarely needed to comment. At the meeting on 25 March 1850, an improvement was proposed at Holborough 'by making the Road thro' the Blacksmith's Forge and across the Field in front of Mr Lee's residence'. This was agreed if William Lee would pay for it; the trustees had insufficient funds to make the alteration, but would maintain it thereafter. So the old road past the mill and - more to the point - past William Lee's front door was abandoned. He built the road on the line it still holds, adding an extended driveway, wall and gatehouse to his property. Other alterations had been made by William Poynder in the early 1850s and which were noted in the last manorial minutes of 1 January 1858:

William Poynder Esq. hath encroached upon the Manor of Snodland by holding a Court about 3 years ago at The Bull Inn, Snodland, and claiming and having enclosed a portion of the mill pond. And that certain other encroachments have been made by turning the road leading to the Bishop's land. And that the said Wm. Poynder Esq. hath sold certain portions of the Manor of Snodland to the North Kent Railway for the sum of £200. And the Homage present lastly that the beforementioned encroachments have very much improved the locality generally, that is to say as far as the Pond and Roads are concerned.

On 23 March 1868 'Mr Lee having suggested an improvement in the Road at Holborough; Ordered that it be carried out at an expense not exceeding £15 if Mr Shaw and Mr Drage upon viewing the spot approve it'. What this change was is not known.

15 March 1869: 'Ordered that Mr Shaw and Mr Lee be empowered to ascertain what alteration can be made at the Snodland Gate to give a better view of things passing there and that a sum not exceeding £15 be expended for that purpose'.

19 March 1877: 'The desirability of making a footpath along the side of the Road from the Bull at Snodland to Holborough for the convenience of the public having been considered: Ordered that if the Parish do carry out the same one third of the expense of contracting thereof be paid by the trust'. The Parish Vestry minutes show that this was done by public subscription at a cost of £290.

A year later the toll system ceased and the 'little weather-boarded house' for the toll-keeper was pulled down:

'At a Special Meeting of the Trustees of the said Road held at the Institute at Snodland on Tuesday the 8th of October 1878. Present: W. Lee, Chairman; The Rev. J. G. Bingley; W. H. Roberts Esq.

The Trustees took into consideration the disposal of the Toll Houses & Gates and the Malling Highway Board having given notice of their intention to take off a small portion of the site of the Snodland Toll House to improve the rounding of the corner of the Highway: there Ordered that the Toll House be pulled down and the Materials be sold.

Ordered that the remaining site thereof be offered to the owners of the adjoining Land for the sum of £12. 10s. - and if they decline to take it that the offer of Mr Bingley to purchase it at that price be accepted.

Mr Bulmer having agreed to purchase the Temple Toll House for £45: Ordered that his offer be accepted. Ordered that Messrs Burgess & Langridge's offer to give 5 guineas for the materials of the Snodland Toll House, thirty shillings for the two Turnpike gates & posts at Snodland & Strood and Twenty shillings for the small House and Side Bars at Ham Hill be accepted.

Ordered that a special Meeting be held at this place on Tuesday the 17th of December next at Eleven a.m. to finally wind up the affairs of the Trust. [Signed] William Lee.

THOMAS FLETCHER WAGHORN

Snodland's most famous parishioner actually spent most of his life away from the village. But many members of his family were here and his ties with the place were close. His father was a Rochester butcher (whose shop later seems to have been taken over by Thomas's brother, Edward), who married Ann Goodhugh of Snodland at All Saints on 28 July 1794. (The family tree shown gives only the bare genealogical bones). Thomas Fletcher Waghorn was baptised at St Mary's, Chatham, on 16 July 1800. He entered the Royal Navy as a Midshipman at Chatham in 1812, serving in H.M.S. *Bahama*. In 1817 he passed the examination for commissioned rank, but reductions in the size of the navy at that time prevented his promotion and he was paid off. He immediately joined an Indiaman and sailed to Calcutta as third mate. In 1819 he was appointed to the Bengal Marine Pilot Service and spent the next five years on the Hoogly River.

The First Burmese War erupted in 1824 and Waghorn was given command of the Hon East India Company's Cutter *Matchless*. He fought with distinction, and was wounded in the thigh. During the war he had been impressed by the performance of a steam ship owned by the company, and after a brief return to his pilot duties in 1827, persuaded the Calcutta merchants that a steam ship service from England to India via the Cape would improve upon that then in force. He met with opposition both from the East India Company and from the Post Office, but was given an unexpected opportunity when Lord Ellenborough, President of the Indian Control Board, commissioned him to take dispatches to India - but via Egypt and the Red Sea. This Waghorn did, leaving London on 28 October 1829 and reaching Bombay on 21 March 1830. In spite of the hazards and delays he encountered on that initial journey, the experience convinced him that the route

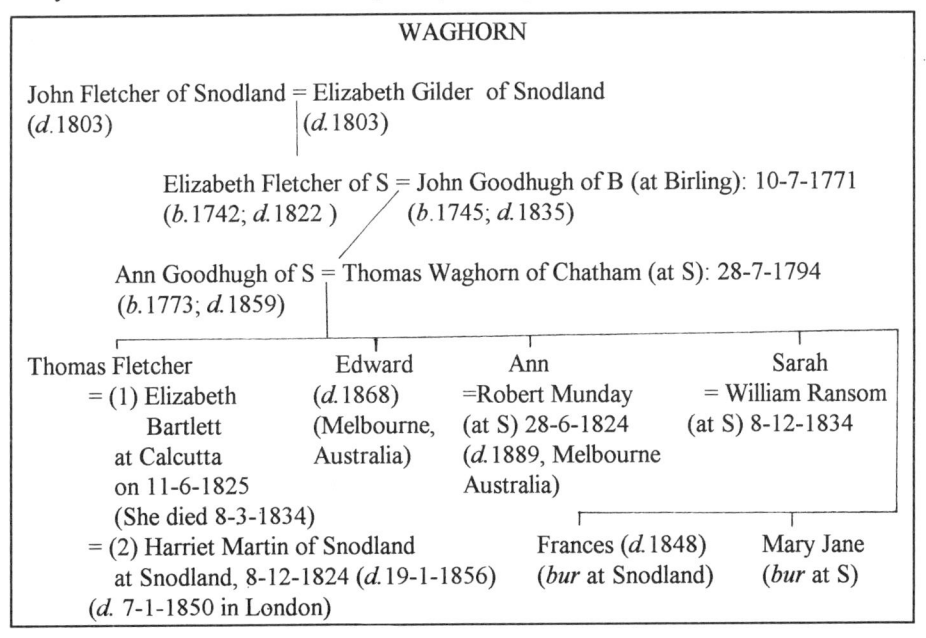

WAGHORN

John Fletcher of Snodland = Elizabeth Gilder of Snodland
(*d.*1803)   (*d.*1803)

Elizabeth Fletcher of S = John Goodhugh of B (at Birling): 10-7-1771
(*b.*1742; *d.*1822)   (*b.*1745; *d.*1835)

Ann Goodhugh of S = Thomas Waghorn of Chatham (at S): 28-7-1794
(*b.*1773; *d.*1859)

Thomas Fletcher | Edward | Ann | Sarah
= (1) Elizabeth | (*d.*1868) | =Robert Munday | = William Ransom
Bartlett | (Melbourne, | (at S) 28-6-1824 | (at S) 8-12-1834
at Calcutta | Australia) | (*d.*1889, Melbourne
on 11-6-1825 | | Australia)
(She died 8-3-1834) | |
= (2) Harriet Martin of Snodland | | Frances (*d.*1848) | Mary Jane
at Snodland, 8-12-1824 (*d.*19-1-1856) | (*bur* at Snodland) | (*bur* at S)
(*d.* 7-1-1850 in London)

would be the best one for communicating between England and India, so his earlier scheme was abandoned in favour of this Overland Route.

Waghorn received no official support, so resigned from the East India Company to promote his schemes independently. He spent three years in Egypt, living as an Arab, and developing that part of the route. He gained the friendship and respect of the Pasha Mehemet Ali, which ensured that the route would be safe for those using it. In 1839 Waghorn was invited to escort the Earl of Munster and others from Bombay to London. It took them 35 days, cutting 55 days off the time taken via the Cape. A company 'Waghorn & Co.' was formed, with offices at 34 Cornhill, to transport goods and mail along the route, but still the government and French government proved hostile to his efforts, and they set up their own couriers in direct competition with him. One ray of light came on 23 March 1842 when the Admiralty at last promoted him to lieutenant. But he had used up all his resources in funding the venture and when the Government and East India Company each granted him pensions of £200, these were swallowed up by his debts. By now a sick man, he lived for a time in Malta, returning to Islington on Christmas Day 1849, where he died on 6 January following. He was buried near others of his family in Snodland churchyard on the 14th of that month.

There are many papers and letters concerning Waghorn's schemes among the collections of the British Library. Most are letters to or from him in pursuit of support for the Overland Route. Just what was involved can be deduced from manuscript drafts of the European route (avoiding the hostile French) and of the Egyptian leg of the journey (which of course was well before the Suez Canal was built):

A quicker Route to Egypt without going through any part of France

London to Antwerp by steam: 20 hours
Antwerp tp Liege by Railway: 5 hours
Liege to Aix la Chapelle by Land: 4 hours
Aix la Chapelle to Cologne by Railway: 2 hours
Cologne to Mannheim: 19 hours
Mannheim to Insbruck by Kempten: 45 hours
Insbruck to Venice: 35 hours
[Total] 135 hours
As above: London to Venice: 5 days 10 hours
A first rate steamer at 10 miles an hour, can go from Venice to Alexandria and vice versa, distance 1204 miles in 5 days 10 hours.
[Time between London and Egypt: 10 hours 10 days]

Government Despatches from London to Alexandria can thus be conveyed within Eleven Days.

The Austrian Government will grant our Courier all the privileges enjoyed by their own Diplomatic ones - The most perfect secrecy would be secured, together with a shorter conveyance than at present, free altogether of France by a Treaty with Germany &c for that purpose.

The Plan

It is proposed during the summer months of the year, viz. from April to December, that a small Iron Steam Boat 80 feet long by 20 feet broad [Note 1], to draw within 30 inches water, should be built and always in waiting at Alexandria for the arrival of the Mail from England, that she should receive it and the passengers on board and proceed as speedily as possible via the Rosetta branch of the Nile to Cairo. This can be done with certainty during these months within 28 hours.

[Note 1: During the winter months from 1st December to 1st April, the Iron Steamer will ply from the end of the Canal at Atfeh to Cairo, (for certain local seasons, occasioning no loss of time) having a Track boat on the canal for the conveyance of mails and passengers to Atfeh to join the steamer there.]

It is further proposed that Mails and passengers should remain in Cairo 20 hours for rest and refreshment and for the purpose of preparing carriages to convey them to Suez. Five carriages of roomy dimensions should be built to convery the Mails and 8 passengers each besides servants and light baggage on the roof to be drawn by Mules to go at the rate of 5 or 6 miles p. hour (of which only four (of these carriages) will be required at one time). These mules to be changed every 16 miles where halting places or stables will be erected at the expense of His Highness the Viceroy [Note 2]. This can easily be done on an excellent road of 82 miles.

[Note 2: 1st Halting place at A two miles from Cairo at the Caliphs Tombs
    2nd ditto   at B,   18 miles from ditto
    3rd ditto   at C,   34 miles from ditto
    4th ditto   at D,   50 miles from ditto
    5th ditto   at E,   66 miles from ditto
    6th ditto   at F,   82 miles from ditto

By this arrangement it will require 30 Mules for each carriage or 120 Mules for the four carriages in use, which leaves 30 available for loss by death or for being disabled and also for drawing heavy baggage across in 3 or 4 carts.]

At 34 miles from Cairo it is proposed to erect the principal halting place C on a large scale for refreshments and repose if necessary for 6 hours each way. The whole of this part of the journey, including the above stoppage of 6 hours, may be accomplished with the greatest ease within 24 hours.

The 'Total first outlay' estimated by Waghorn was £13,342.

Waghorn's grandfather, John Goodhugh (1745-1835), was a carpenter from Birling, who moved to Holborough after his marriage. He inherited property there which descended to him from the Gilder and Fletcher families on his wife's side and he both built and bought more. These included Island Cottage, Mill Stream Cottage (with the attached farm of 23 acres), the blacksmith's forge and two adjacent houses (one of which became

'The Rising Sun'), and three houses at that end of Holborough Road which he had built himself. He had also bought the village poor houses at the bottom of the High Street. T. F. Waghorn was an executor to Goodhugh's will (dated 22 November 1831) and was bequeathed 'my silver pint tankard', a portion of the household goods, and the 'Old Poor House' after the decease of Goodhugh's son John (which was in 1842). Waghorn seems to have paid the rates on Island cottage (where his mother lived) from 1827 until his death. His own house, the Lodge, in the upper High Street, was built in about 1841, perhaps the time when he was most optimistic about establishing himself as manager of the Overland Route.

Waghorn married twice. His first wife was Elizabeth Bartlett, daughter of William and Ann, born in Calcutta on 28 March 1805. They were married by license at St. John's Cathedral, Calcutta on 11 June 1825. She died aged 28 years 11 months and 7 days and was buried at Calcutta on 8 March 1834. Later that year a double wedding took place at All Saints, Snodland, when Thomas Waghorn, widower, married Harriet Martin, spinster, and William Ransom of St. Mary Rotherhithe married Sarah Waghorn, Thomas's sister. Harriet Martin was the daughter of the miller at Holborough. It appears that Robert Munday, Thomas's brother-in-law, assisted him in his endeavours, for the address of both of them is given as 'Cairo' in the 1847 poll-book.

There is a fine portrait of Waghorn painted by Sir George Hayter (kept at the National Portrait Gallery), but our only glimpse of him at Snodland comes from an account given by the celebrated local antiquarian Charles Roach Smith in his *Retrospections, Social and Archaeological* (1883):

> Not unfrequently, I accompanied him on Saturday afternoons to his residence at Snodland, staying with him and Mrs Waghorn until the Monday mornings when we returned together to London. In everything he was scrupulously methodical, but not fussily so. The chaise was always ready waiting for him at The Bull's Head at the corner of Cuxton Road at Strood. He drove rapidly; quite as fast as the horse, which was a swift one, could canter or gallop, calling for five minutes at the White Hart at Cuxton, and for one minute, on his mother, who lived in a neat cottage, on the right, near the brook at the entrance to Snodland. [At this time the road forded the mill-stream at Holborough.] He would often say "These are my only times of real enjoyment - which they unquestionably were.
>
> In his own house, a neat comfortable habitation, he was reflective; cheerful he always was, his conversation ever taking a somewhat serious turn; but never touching on his own eventful life. He was deeply benevolent without the slightest ostentation. I had many opportunities of knowing his warmth of heart and his deep attachment to his mother, wife and sister. Usually I met at his house a few of his neighbouring friends, specially invited. The evenings were always agreeable, as the conversation ever took an intellectual turn, and instead of being trite and commonplace, usually ranged to character and men and manners. He adored Shakespeare.

In later years Charles Roach Smith was a frequent visitor to the village to give dramatic readings, at which he excelled, and perhaps these visits were the more appreciated because of his former friendship with Waghorn.

THE FERRY

While the ferry at Halling is mentioned in early times, that at Snodland is not. Nevertheless we can be sure that inhabitants of the area were able to cross the river here. Certainly there were boats available for them to be able to do so, but how 'official' the service was is unknown. In the story of the attempted murder of Rev. Phelps, printed above, it seems significant that he crossed by the [Halling]-Wouldham ferry. Surely he would have taken the Snodland ferry if there was one?

However the Snodland ferry is marked on the 1844 Tithe commutation map. It would appear that for some time at least, it was part of the emoluments of the rector. The ferry house is built on what was glebe land, perhaps at the initiative of Rev. Phelps, who would have charged the ferryman rent. In a memorandum dated 20 August 1874 the then rector, Rev. Bingley, set down the outcome of a meeting which he held with the ferryman, Edward Baker, concerning the rent of the ferry. After much argument, it was agreed that Baker would pay the Rector £30 instead of £20 as formerly. Baker, of course, charged those who used the ferry to pay this rent and earn his living. In 1880 it was said that around 600 persons a day crossed every day to and from the factories lining the river. The service operated from 6.a.m. to 10.p.m. A wire was anchored at the bottom of the river and when the tide was going out, the ferrymen found it sufficient to man-handle the boat across using the wire, allowing the river to exert any pull that was necessary.

Edward, son of John and Frances Baker, was born on 24 October 1810. John appears in the registers as carter, labourer and smuggler! Edward too is called labourer, lighterman and barge owner; he is first described as ferryman in 1853, but may well have operated the service as much as twenty years earlier. He made a good living from it and in the 1860s was able to build a large house called 'Nephalite Villa' (where the library now is). By the 1870s he employed three men to operate the boat, the senior of whom was John Gorham. All the while there were factories active on both banks of the river, there was a demand for the service. For a time the proposition of a bridge or subway threatened its existence, but that passed. Nevertheless, there were those who felt sympathy with the view expressed by one anonymous individual when the discussions about the bridge were at their height: 'The country on the other side of the river is a boggy marsh, and it can be of no advantage to anyone from this side to have easier access to it; in fact, the further off it is kept from us the better.' One by one the cement works closed: the Wouldham Cement Co. in 1902, Peters' Wouldham Hall works in about 1930 and the A.P.C.M. at Burham in 1941. This sounded the death-knell of the ferry and it closed in 1948, having been operated in its later years by the Stevens family.

THE HOOK FAMILY

Samuel Hook, his wife Anna Maria and their five children moved from Chalford, Gloucestershire to Tovil, Maidstone, in 1852, when Samuel took a partnership in the paper mill there. Two years later his son Charles Townsend, aged twenty-two, acquired the Snodland mill and they all moved to the house in the High Street called 'Acacia cottage' in the 1851 census, which had been the home for previous papermaker masters. It was on the south side, just where the by-pass is today, and the Hooks lost no time in rebuilding the property to make it a large and imposing building, filling the space between Brook Street and May Street [PLATE   ]

```
                              HOOK

Samuel                  =  Maria Anna, daughter of Charles Townsend
(b. 7 Jan 1797, Devizes)   (b. 10 Jun 1803, Bures, Essex)
(d. 16 Jun 1866, Snodland) (d. 20 Nov 1881, Snodland)

Charles Townsend        Edith Anna              Maude Midsummer
(b. 30 Apr 1832, Norwich) (b. 1835, Norwich)    (b. 1841, Chalford, Gloucs.)
(d. 11 Feb 1877, Snodland) (d. 1 Mar 1892, Snodland) (d. 29 Sep 1930)

Agnes Darlington        Eustace = Evelina Augusta Bull (b. 1847, Chatham)
(b. 1846, Chalford, Gloucs.) (b. 1843, Stroud, Gloucs.)
(d. 12 Sep 1903, Snodland)   (d. 1890, Hove)
```

Charles Townsend Hook breathed new life into the paper mill. When he took over, production was about 5 tons a week 'from 20 to 30 hands'. In 1859 *Kelly's Directory* described it as 'a manufactory of writing paper from straw which employs about 70 persons. By the 1871 census there were 129 men, 35 women and 12 boys and in the 1882 *Directory* the mill was 'employing about 350 persons and manufacturing weekly more than 90 tons of paper. But for a detailed account of the mill the reader is referred to Kenneth Funnell's *Snodland Paper Mill* (Snodland, 1979 and 1986).

Following C. T. Hook's death, the family soon appointed a retired army officer, Lieutenant-Colonel Trevenen James Holland (1836-1910), as manager of the mill. He built Ivymeath (now the offices of the Mid-Kent Water Company) during the 1880s, but lived there for only a few years before moving to Tunbridge Wells. Nevertheless, he remained formally in charge until his death in 1910, although William Dedrick, the General Manager, effectively and efficiently ran the business, which contined to prosper, even in difficult times. There was one blip, however, which the company preferred not to disclose:

> £100 reward. Wanted on warrant for Fraudulently Embezzling certain sums of money to the amount of £2000 and upward, the monies of his employers, Messrs. HOOK & Co., Paper Manufacturers, Snodland, Kent, between the 6th October 1885, and the 10th September 1887.
>
> ALEXANDER EDWARD ROLLASON late Cashier in the above firm, and who absconded on the 9th September last.

> He is about 45 years of age, height 5 feet 9 inches, spare gaunt man, light thin and straight hair, quick and abrupt in his manner, good regular white teeth, a little inclined to stoop, short-sighted in one eye, uses glasses, one a magnifier the other plain, sober man, not in very good health, fond of physicking himself with Homeopathic medicines, speaks French, well read and well informed. Has a wife but no children. Has resided abroad, and been employed as commission agent and manager of stores in London, Paris, New York, Montreal, &c.. May seek similar situations.
>
> The above reward will be paid by "Colonel Holland, C.B.," Ivymeath, Snodland, Kent, for information that will lead to the Apprehension and Trial of the accused (Police included). Information to be given to Superintendent Richard Hulse, Kent County Constabulary, West Malling, who will forward Photographs of the accused on application. West Malling. Jan. 2nd. 1888.

All members of the Hook family went out of their way to support and help the community and many memorials of their generosity remain for the benefit of succeeding generations. The list below makes no mention of the smaller but continual charitable acts which one finds in written accounts of the time. We might note two. Following one particularly harsh winter, Charles Townsend Hook called a meeting of the parents of pupils at the British Schools. He expressed his concern that they had had an especially hard struggle 'to pay the school pence at that time', and refunded them their money. Woolmer goes on to note:

> During the year 1887 (the Jubilee of Her Majesty the Queen's Accession), the Misses Hook not only contributed liberally to the fund raised for the festivities, which took the form of a feast to the aged poor as well as the children; but they had struck, by a Maidstone firm, at their own expense, and from their own design, a number of very pretty little silver brooches, one of which they presented to each mother who had children attending the Schools, as a commemoration of the event.

c.1870? Acquisition of the British Schools by Charles Townsend Hook. The Hook family paid all expenses apart from a £90 government grant.

1870: Stained glass windows in All Saints Church given by Mrs Eustace Hook. She later contributed to the cost of the tiles in the chancel floor.

1877: Clock Tower built in memory of Charles Townsend Hook.

1878: Gas lamps for the parish, gas supplied from the mill gasometers.

1881: Temperance Coffee Tavern in May Street opened.

1882: New Jerusalem Church consecrated on 27 June.

1887: Providence Chapel sold to the Misses Hook to enlarge the British Schools

1893: Three almshouses erected in memory of Eustace Hook opened on 27 December. One house was for a member of the New Jerusalem Church; one for a member of the Church of England nominated by the Rector; one for a person elected by the

Nonconformists. A second building divided into four tenements was erected later by Agnes Hook in memory of Amelia Drummond, governess to the Hook family.

1893: The Technical School on the corner of Waghorn Road and the High Street erected; it supplemented the work of the British Schools.

1895: Devonshire Rooms erected.

1923: Sale of land for Fire Station (now the garden at the end of Waghorn road, next to the Devonshire Rooms).

Of course, to some extent all this charitable activity was geared to the family's involvement with the Swedenborgian movement (discussed later) and to welcoming and encouraging the villagers into that Church. Among the collections of the Kent Archaeological Society is a privately printed pamphlet, written by the sisters supposedly as an account of their summer holidays in Devonshire (hence the 'Devonshire Rooms'), but taken up mostly with religious and moral preaching. Nevertheless, their contribution to the life and well-being of the village was outstanding and we still reap its fruits today.

Agnes was an artist, but if her pictures have survived, the whereabouts of most them is unknown. We have two which may be by her and two very rough sketches from the 1930s which may have been based on two more. The latter are mid-nineteenth century views of the paper mill - just what one would expect from the daughter of the owner.

THE PAPER MILL FIRE OF 1906

On Sunday, 12 August 1906 the paper mill was destroyed by fire, unquestionably the most dramatic event in the history of the village. The following account was printed in the *Kent Messenger* of 18 August. The reporting puts all modern efforts into the shade: finely written and extremely comprehensive, it vividly covers not only the disaster, but also the first relief efforts, not forgetting enterprising actions from some ready to feed the curiosity of those drawn to view to scene. Together with the many surviving photographs of the event (some of which were advertised), the horror is fully realised, as is the splendid and immediate response of the Parish in mitigating the distress of those affected:

A fire occurred at Snodland on Sunday which is without parallel in the annals of the village, and which is one of the most serious known in Kent for at least 20 years past. It entirely burned out the papermaking mills of Messrs Townsend Hook and Co., leaving only the carpenters and fitters' shops standing at one end of five or six acres of ruins.

It created in a few hours damage estimated at from £150,000 to £200,000; Deprived nearly 400 people of their ordinary employment; Caused 31 families to leave their cottages; Imperiled the Parish Church; Filled the air with fragments of burnt paper - resembling a snowstorm - which the wind blew about for a distance of seven or eight miles; and Engaged the services of six fire brigades. We are in a position to announce, however, that The mill will be rebuilt without delay; That, by arrangement with the Insurance Companies, as many of the mill-men as circumstances permit will be employed on the work which is immediately possible; That a relief fund has been started with subscriptions of £20 from Colonel Warde, M.P., and £15. by Mr. W. H. L. Roberts, J.P.;

That the Parish Council have undertaken the administration of the money, in conjunction with other prominent inhabitants; and That the Council have accepted the offer of the 'Kent Messenger' to acknowledge the sums received through its columns.

Origin of the Fire

The fire owed its origin to some repairing work which was in progress on Sunday morning. A paper mill, especially one supplying the wherewithal for the printing of the London dailies, knows neither night nor day from Monday morning till Saturday night, and it is only on Sundays, when it is still, that the machinery can be overhauled. On Sunday last the opportunity was being taken to splice one of the driving ropes in the machine room, the work being in the hands of a Lancashire firm. The men were early at work, and to assist them had in use a paraffin lamp, and it was in some way through the presence of this lamp no doubt that the fire occurred.

Unfortunately the rope caught, and as a fire-carrying agent there was nothing in the mill to equal this, for, highly inflammatory as it was through the oil it had absorbed in the course of countless revolutions of the great wheels, it carried the flames from floor to floor, and brought about the doom of the whole establishment.

The tide was out at the time, so that in the creek, which split up the mill into two portions, a couple of barges, both heavily laden with pulp, lay high and dry, and fell a prey to the fire. There was also at this time very little pressure on the water main, and thus hampered neither the mill staff, who were on the scene in next to no time, nor the Snodland Fire Brigade, were able to make any impression on the fire; and by the time the Maidstone and Rochester, and the Malling and Halling brigades arrived, it was seen that the mill was past saving. Efforts were therefore made - and not without success - to confine the conflagration to that property. All the dwelling houses around, however, were in peril, and no fewer than 31 families, comprising upwards of 100 individuals, found it advisable to turn out, although a dozen of the families were able to move back again when the flames were subdued.

The scene can be imagined, with about six acres of buildings and their highly inflammable contents on fire, with the flames fanned by the wind, the smoke blown in great volumes over the river, the air charged with the calcined remains of pulp and paper, and around the vast cauldron of the mill a scene of chaos and havoc caused by the hurried emptying of rows of cottages. One lot of cottages, called Mill-row, ran right down to the mill gates; others, called Church-cottages, ran right and left of these and the top of the row, facing the church and the station. Mill-row was quite untenable, and the four end houses were burned beyond repair; the others were more or less damaged. In Church-row, as the backs of the houses became unbearable, the people broke the front windows and willing hands - too many and too willing - rushed out the furniture, higgledy-piggledy heedless of its nature or its value. Thence it was taken to a place of safety behind the church, or laid out in the goods yard of the station until other accommodation was found for it.

Church-row screened the Parish Church from the fire, but on top of the tower the heat was very great, and in time became unbearable to those who made the ascent in order to get a bird's-eye view of the fire. From this vantage point they say the sight was awful. First came the insidious curling of the smoke through the roofs, then little tongues of fire, then the all-devouring flames, followed by the collapse of roofs, amid still larger bursts of flames as fresh fuel was thus added to the fire below, fed as it already was by tons upon tons of paper and pulp.

One fortunate circumstance was that the wind was blowing away from the town, otherwise in all probability the fire would have travelled up the High-street, with results too horrible to contemplate. Even more fortunate is it that amid all the ruin no lives were lost nor serious personal injury caused.

With the wind as it was, it was possible to work the railway service without great inconvenience - for the mill walls abutted right on the railway line, and the mill owners had their own siding not far from the railway platform. In fact the mill, the railway station, and the church, with numerous cottages in between, amde up in a close group on the banks of the Medway a not unimportant part of the village.

An Eye Witness's Description

An eye-witness of the fire, who also knows something of the mill, helped us to some valuable information. He explained that the rope which caught fire was of cotton, of innumerable strands, twisted cable-fashion until it formed a rope of about two inches in diameter. It was the driving rope of the great double crank engine, which with its enormous wheels, 140 or 150 feet in circumference, worked the whole machinery of the mill. From the engine room, the flames "ran along them like fireworks." First they led to the beating room, the floors of which were laid in pitch in order to make them drip-proof. Therefore the fire at once obtained a substantial hold, and the further it spread the more perishable were the materials it found to feed upon. There were at least 100 tons of rosin; a thousand tons of printing paper in reels ready for delivery; a large number of parcels of paper; many sacks of waste paper from the Government departments; quite 400 tons of dry wood pulp, and one stack of not less than 900 tons of wet pulp, which, in spite of its wetness, was burnt to ashes. There were also the two barge-loads of pulp, each containing about 100 tons.

The barges, which lay fast on the mud-banks, belonged to Messrs. Goldsmith, of Grays. One was practically burnt to the water's edge, and the other, though an iron one, is probably past repair. Both were inhabited when the fire caught them, and the wife of one of the captains had to leave in dishabille.

We gathered, further, that there were five modern paper-making machines in the mill; that seven new patent "tower-beaters," which were an excellent invention, had been installed hardly 12 months; and that the output of the mill was 200 tons a week or more.

Curiously, the only machine saved is the very first one installed in the mill by the late Mr. Townsend Hook and originally worked by water power; while another remarkable fact is that the great engine, from which the fire spread, is believed to be capable of repair. Other survivals are the carpenters' and fitters' shops, which stand on the Maidstone side of the creek amid the buildings that formed the old mill and are now utilised for storage.

Yet another interesting fact pointed out was that the iron frame of one of the large sheds had been in two fires. It was part of the Crystal Palace, and after the fire there was purchased by Colonel Holland and put up here. The girders and standards are still intact, though somewhat bent by the heat.

A word of praise is due to the fire brigades. They, it appears, had no chance with the mill from the first, but great as was the conflagration, it would have been greater still had they not been present. The Snodland Brigade naturally were the first on the scene, and with some of the mill men, had just got the hose attached to the gas engine for pumping, when, to avoid risk of explosion, the gas was turned off at the gas works, and they were helpless. Halling, Malling, Rochester and Chatham, and Maidstone Brigades afterwards arrived, and the Maidstone engine probably pumped as much water on the buildings as all the rest put together. Among much efficient and well-directed service - rendered with almost miraculous immunity from serious accident - our informant singled out that of Captain Stevens, of Snodland, and Captain Gates, of Maidstone, for special praise, and his tribute was, from all we hear, well deserved. But, as he says, from the first everything was in favour of the fire: the inflammable material, the high wind, the low tide, and (at first) the low pressure on the wate main. The direction of the wind was fortunate, however, for it blew away from the town and from the manager's house, which is within the mill enclosure. Had this caught it would have brought the fire within reach of a densely populated locality.

The loss to the cottagers: Monday

Every train today, up and down, brought crowds of people curious to see the havoc wrought by the fire, and it was not until the shades of evening fell that the animation in the vicinity of the church and the ruins at all subsided.

As I write this evening, the flames still keep spurting out from among the debris, the Halling and Snodland firemen, from the half-dozen Fire Brigades summoned, are still active and are likely to be throughout the night.

It is truly a scene of ruin from which the two tall chimney stacks of the mill - the old and the new - seem to rise Phoenix-like. The oldest of these, which has for some time been decapitated for safety, stands well away from the buildings which have now been gutted by the fire. The other was at the very centre of the conflagration. As people look at [it] - it may be their imagination - they declare they see it sway in the breeze; and it is probable that it will have to be demolished. However, for the time being, there it stands sentinel over the ruins - the skeletons of iron and brickwork and tons of useless debris.

It is the mill that represents loss and ruin, but the pathos of it all is most vividly realised when one returns to the cottages and the churchyard. Some of the upper rooms are absolutely denuded of their windows, and the rooms themselves are empty. Downstairs one sees furniture of all kinds crowded promiscuously into one confused heap. In teh churchyard are fragments of crockery, broken ornaments, dresses, mattresses, chairs, washing stands and all sorts of domestic utensils, unusable, abandoned, showing the panic with which they were tumbled out - anywhere away from the fire.

The dispossessed cottagers come and sadly survey these remnants of their goods, and search for that which they cannot fins, and prompt as were the steps taken for their assistance by a provisional Committee, many must suffer the loss of goods rashly precipitated from the tenements by thoughtless but well-meaning persons.

I learn from Mr. Hilder that as early as 12 o'clock on Sunday morning a number of prominent inhabitants formed themselves into a Committee to cope with the emergency arising among these cottagers. The Rector (the Rev. Finch-Smith), who is away on holiday, was represented by his father, and there were also present the Revs. Hetherington (curate), Galpin (Congregational), and Ronald (Christ Church), Mr. W.L.H. Roberts, Mr. Streatfield, Mr. F. Roberts, Drs. Freeland, Gash and Palmer, Mr. Trechman, Mr. J.H. Burke, Mr. Gooding, Mr. T. Hilder, and subsequently Mr. Hodgkinson. Mr. Roberts was appointed chairman, and Mr. Hilder secretary. They at once proceeded to deal with the accommodation of the dispossessed tenants, and during the day the whole 31 families had been temporarily provided for. By the close of the day, 12 families had been able to return to their homes. Other moved their furniture back into the rooms, and were taken in by friends. Others went into the empty cottages which were found here and there in the village, and several families found accommodation at the old Post Office, placed at their disposal by Mr. Roberts, while a quantity of furniture was stored in the sheds behind the building. The Committee made themselves responsible for the rent where necessary, and Mr. Roberts opened a relief fund with a promise of £15. Today he has lent seven or eight vans, which have further assisted in the removal of the furniture to the new abodes of the owners. I find today all who are in a position of any responsibility impressed with the seriousness of the outlook.

The service at the Parish Church yesterday morning was abandoned, the curate simply reading the Litany to the Rector's father, while in the evening only a shortened form of service was read, owing to the want of gas.

The station-master (Mr. Horton), whose first duty was to have three trucks removed from the mill siding, had for some time an anxious task in looking after the safety of passengers, who even on Sunday evening poured intot he village in immense numbers to see the fire. Three down trains had to be run past to Maidstone on the up line, which entailed special signalling on the line; and, in fact, the precautions had to be maintained on Monday and Tuesday, when the wall overlooking the line was pulled down as a precaution at the instigation of the Railway Company. The station premises were also made good use of on Sunday, for it was here the books of the mill-owners were first removed, while the station yard as well as the church yard became the receptacle of the furniture which was summarily removed from the houses.

The urgent need for help: Tuesday

There has been a perceptable diminution of visitors today, but the deprivation caused by the loss of work and of household belongings is beginning to be keenly felt. A practical step, however, has been taken to deal with the worst phases of the distress (as reported below).

One of the most piteable cases is that of a widow and her family who lived in Mill Row. She was left with eight children, two of whom worked in the mill and are now deprived of employment. She said to a "Kent Messenger" representative:-

"I was just getting the younger children off to the Sunday school, when one of them ran back saying 'Oh, mother, there's smoke coming from the mill'. Well, smoke is a usual thing here, and I took no alarm, but soon there was no doubt that the mill was on fire. Even then I did not think the houses would be touched, and those of whom I enquired assured me that we were safe, but as the flames spead and it was seen the houses were doomed, everybody was eager to turn the furniture out. No doubt they thought they were helping, but there were so many of them that I don't know what they did do, except that in the result I lost nearly all my furniture. In the upset I even left my money upstairs - my daughter's savings and the money I had ready to pay the tradesmen - and here I am now without a penny and with very little furniture."

The family had moved into an empty house in another part of the village where, by dint of much cleaning, they had made two of the rooms presentable, and in incongruous collections on the newly scrubbed floor lay a miscellaneous assortment assortment of furniture quite inadequate for any definite purpose.

"This," said the poor woman, "I went and picked out of the heaps in the Churchyard. But what is it? Here's the top and end of a bedstead, but not a single piece to connect them; here are a couple of cot mattresses; here's a broken washstand from the back bedroom. I suppose all my best furniture perished. I have just found a couple of spoons, but I haven't a knife and only one cup and a few plates; here's part of one thing and part of another, and I feel as if I had lost all my home - and I an a widow. Both my children, you see, are thrown out of work by the fire, and so are my near relatives; and as to my little children, I lost all their clothes except what they had on - didn't even save a pinafore."

The prospect of this wrecked home was truly enough to dismay the stoutest heart. At the time we saw the mother, little was known about the relief fund, and she knew not whence her daily sustenance was coming, let alone the restoration of a home.

Other families, always used to earning an honest living and come in to a comfortable if humble abode, are in a plight only a degree less pitiable, and one can hardly imagine circumstances which should appeal more keenly to the heart of charity.

No doubt among the honestly inclined there were some nefarious robbers on Sunday, but with such a crowd as the oldest inhabitant cannot remember in Snodland, and the excitement and alarm created by such a tremendous conflagration, it is not surprising that confusion, damage and loss should have resulted.

The Parish Council as Relief Committee

Mr. W.L.H. Roberts attended the meeting of the Parish Council on Tuesday evening, and introduced the question of a Relief Committee. Directly this disaster was avident, he said, a few of us who were on the spot formed ourselves into a Provisional Committee, as we could see at once how necessary it was that house-room should be found for the dispossessed people. Now it is incumbent on us to see what we can do for them. I had a talk with Dr. Palmer this morning, and he was of opinion that it would be best if the constituted authority in the village - the Parish Council - took the matter in hand. They, it was suggested, could form themselves into a special Committee, with power to add to their number, and I for one, if they cared to elect me, would be willing to act with them;

so would others who take an interest in the matter. I have not yet been able to consult Mr. Woodburn. I went down today, but it was rather too much to expect anyone connected with the mill, fully engaged as they were with the insurance assessors, to do anything then, so I came away; but I hope before long to be able to go into the matter with him and see exactly what the Company propose to do and what they would like us to do in the face of this possible distress among their workpeople. I had a visit from Colonel Warde, M.P., who came over to know what he could do. He said he was prepared to set to work and make a collection among his friends, while he generously gave me £20 himself. Further, a friend of mine, Mr. Thynne, gave me a £5 note today, so that we have quite a nice beginning to our fund. Tomorrow, I propose to say a few words to one of the Committee of the County Council, when a good many of the gentlemen of the county will be gathered together, and to distribute bankers' slips for them to fill in. Having got the money, we shall have to consider the best form of distributing it. So far as I can gather, those likely to suffer most from the disaster will be the women who have been the support of their homes. Many of the men will be employed, I understand, in various kinds of labouring work pending and during the re-erection of the mill, and they, though inconvenienced, will not perhaps be actually distressed; but the Committee will be bound to do something for the women who were the bread-winners of their families and who have been thrown out of work. I have no doubt, from what I gather from Colonel Warde, that the county gentlemen will show their sympathy with us in this district, and help us to overcome the untoward circumstances; while, in consultation with the managers and directors of the mill, we shall no doubt be guided as to the best way to distribute the money when we have got it, and meet the cases of distress as they arise; for, under the conditions that have occurred, we cannot expect otherwise that that distress will ensue unless means are taken to alleviate it.

Mr. Hodgkinson moved that the Council express their deep sympathy with the sufferers by the fire, and their great thanks to Colonel Warde, as well as to Mr. Roberts; and further that, as Mr. Roberts suggested, the Council form themselves into a Relief Committee, with power to add to their number.

Mr. Woodburn remarked that he had already been entrusted with some money for the fund, and numbers of people had written expressing their willingness to start subscription lists; while he was sure the mill authorities would be only too pleased to help.

Replying to a question, Mr. Woodburn said that by the courtesy of the Insurance Companies the mill-owners had been given a free hand in the employment of labour where it was possible to employ it under present conditions, and they would give as much work as they could to their own hands; but they had the winter to face, and with many people out of employment and suffering the loss of their goods, he was sure there would be no difficulty in well spending all the money they received. He agreed with Mr. Roberts as to the widows and other women who earned their own living, and mentioned a sad case in which a wife with an invalid husband was the mainstay of the home through her work at the mill. He was quite sure, however, from the expressions of sympathy he had received, that once the fund was started it would be generously supported.

By the courtesy of the Chairman (Mr. Burke), a representative of the "Kent Messenger" who was present was permitted to make a few remarks, offering the services of this newspaper, both in the way of advocating the fund and of acknowledging the amounts that were received. Such acknowledgement, he thought, would be an incentive to others to subscribe.

Mr. Hodgkinson's motion was unanimously adopted, and on the proposition of Mr. Stevens, who made a courteous reference to this paper, the offer made on behalf of the "Kent Messenger" was also accepted with thanks.

First meeting of the Committee

The Relief Committee met on Wednesday evening, and adopted as a general principle that money should not be distributed if it could be avoided, but that relief should be given by way of orders on grocers, bakers and other tradesmen, and by the payment of rent. Particular care is also to be taken that there is no overlapping.

A subcommittee of seven was appointed to go into the immediate applications, and it was decided to ask Mrs. Freeland to form a committee of ladies to investigate the requirements in the nature of clothing, some of the people having been dispossessed of almost everything.

Sixpence admission

So many applications have been received, that arrangements have been made to show visitors over the ruins, on Saturday and Sunday, at a charge of 6d. each, the proceeds to go to the relief fund. The taking of photographs will be allowed only by special arrangement.

Adult schools and the Relief Fund

At the Kent Adult School quarterly Council meeting held at Tunbridge Wells on Wednesday, it was unanimously decided to ask all the schools in Kent to immediately make collections for those suffering from distress through the disaster of last Sunday at Snodland, so that the principles the Adult School movement preaches may be practised.

Incidentals

Such a crowd as gathered in Snodland on Sunday evening has never been seen in the village before. There was quite an army of snapshotters among them, but many of their products were indifferent.

The late Mr. Townsend Hook, founder of the mill, had previously carried on business at Maidstone. He commenced the mill with one machine.

The West Kent Hospital will suffer by the fire, for the present works manager, Mr. Taylor, had instituted a fortnightly collection of 1d. from each employee.

The National School children's fete was postponed from Thursday, and it is said that the money collected for their prizes will be diverted to the Relief Fund.

None of the buildings of the old mill were burned.

Between 50 and 100 firemen were engaged trying to battle with the flames. All but a few of these have been withdrawn in order to give work to the mill men.

The Company's books were saved, the office being fireproof.

The presence of thousands of old postal orders at the mill was due to a contract with the Government. They are brought to Snodland to be destroyed and be reconverted by an ingenious process into paper. An official of the post office sees to the destruction.

The Company were full up with orders, and appeared to be in for a prosperous time. Latterly their shares have risen on the market. It is providential that this disaster did not come during the depression in the cement industry, in which many of the villagers are employed.

About two dozen of the mill hands belong to the Amalgamated Society of Papermakers. Their out-of-work pay is 14s. a week.

The loss to the Company is said to be all covered by insurance. The policies were shared among several offices.

The Mill Company have made arrangements for placing their orders, and so keeping their business connection.

The capacity of the Maidstone steam fire engine is 350 gallons per minute. Thanks to the Fire Brigades, coal in the yard was saved.

SNODLAND MILL FIRE - Four photographic post-cards, 1s. post free - BROWN, Winton House, West Malling - Advt.
POSTCARDS OF THE FIRE - Five pictures for 6d., postage 1d. Shops supplied at special prices.- R. Mason and Sons, Snodland.- Advt.
Go or send to Hambrook's Bazaar, High street, Snodland, for the best photographs and postcards of the Mill Fire.-Advt.

A CHRONOLOGY OF MORE RECENT EVENTS

It is not my intention here to do more than chart some of the noteworthy events, particularly for those who have made Snodland their home in more recent years. Older parishioners have long memories - many much longer than mine -- of what life was like here in days gone by. We also have a fine series of photographs, particularly a core collection from those made first at the beginning of the century by William Bateman, who then ran the Post Office, and later a large and invaluable series by A. N. Hambrook, brother of the stationer in the High Street. During the rectorship of Rev. Charles de Rocfort Wall (1909-1930), all the parish magazines were collected and bound. A further resource is the splendid scrap-book compiled by the Women's Institute in 1955; they have continued to chronicle life here in the years since then. The list notes some of the later nineteenth-century events, extracted from the list compiled by Rev. Wall in his *Snodland and its History* (Snodland, 1928). In particular I have included notice of some of the societies which have flourished in the village.

1868. First Show of Flowers, Fruit and Vegetables. There have been Gardeners' Societies in the village since that time.

1869. Footpath added on the south side of the High Street; made by rate at a cost of £90. Hearts of Oak Benefit Society formed. A 'court' of the Ancient Order of Foresters also existed in Snodland at this time.

1870. Major restoration of All Saints church.

1871. Snodland Fair abolished.

1872. Primitive Methodist Chapel built in Malling Road (opposite Rocfort Road).

1873. 24 August: murder of P.C. May (at what is now the junction of Rocfort Road and Malling Road).

1874. Snodland Working Men's Club formed; met at the Institute, Holborough Road, from 1878 until they moved to the current premises (opposite).

1875. William Lee built the Institute in Holborough Road; demolished in 1970s.

1877. Serious flooding in February; death of Charles Townsend Hook. 9 January: opening of Snodland Working Men's Club.

1878. Footpath added to Holborough Road, paid for by public subscription at a cost of £290. Gas lighting for the parish - at the expense of the Misses Hook. Turnpike toll-house pulled down. A choral society formed - discontinued in 1881. Bicycle club founded.

1881. 10 February: Bull inn pulled down; present building erected to allow wider roadway. 11 July: major fire at the barn near the church. 29 September: death of William Lee. 14 October: violent gale. 17 December: Temperance rooms opened in May Street. Proposal to build a railway branch through the chalk hills on the Snodland-Halling boundary to rejoin the line at Northfleet.

1882. New Jerusalem church consecrated and opened. 12 June: 'Great bicycle meeting'. 11 October: Girls' Friendly Society' first meeting.; 17 November: new Mission Room opened at Holborough.

1883. The 'New Road' [now called 'Lad's lane'] at Holborough replaced the old road which went between the mill (on the south) and Holloway Court (on the north) to join the present road further up (at the bend).

1886. Holborough Court completed and Holloway Court demolished.

1887. 2 July: extent of present cricket field (part of the rector's former glebe land) agreed between the rector and Colonel Holland (who lived at Ivymeath).

1888. 1 August. Congregational Chapel in the High Street opened.

1893. Hook's Football Club founded as part of the Maidstone League. Cemetery decided upon.

1894. Inauguration of the Parish Council. Members: George Corney (Chairman), William Lee Henry Roberts (Vice-Chairman); Edwin Brazier; Joseph Deacon; T. R. Archer; H. T. Beadle; J. H. Burke; Henry Hawks; W. R. Hodgkinson; Thomas Hollands; Jabez Fowle; John Kemsley; Thomas Gash. Clerk and Registrar: Tom Hilder. Caretaker: William Fletcher.

1895. Fire service instituted on 15 October. Volunteers listed on 2 June, 1896.

1896. Cemetery open. Lodge and Chapel constructed by Hubert Bensted of Maidstone.

1898. Water laid on by Mid Kent Water Company; pumping station at Halling.

12 August 1906. Paper Mill burnt down. Lead Wool Company Ltd. built in Church Fields.

1909. Present Post Office opened.

1912. Consecration of new extension to the cemetery. Snodland Tennis Club founded (on ground next to the Wardona Cinema).

1914-1918 War. XVth Middlesex Regiment billeted in Snodland from December 20, 1914 until the following Easter Monday. Second Battery of the East Surreys billeted in Snodland for three weeks. Church bell rung daily at noon from August 4, 1914 until the Armistice on 11 November, 1918.

1919. Cenotaph erected in cemetery.

15 March, 1920. Inauguration of bus service between Maidstone and Gillingham via West Malling and Snodland.

1921. Mary Gorham Charity

1922. Ham Hill and Snodland Women's Institute founded. Snodland Bowls Club founded (Their green was at the top end of the cricket meadow. Disbanded in the 1940s.)

1923. Fire Station built on corner of Waghorn Road and High Street (next to Mulberry Cottage). Roman urns found near 'Prospect Place' in Holborough Road. New Cement Works begun at Holborough.

1924. Recreation Ground purchased by Parish Council.

1926. All Saints Dramatic Society founded. (Dissolved 1939)

1929. Electricity comes to the village. Snodland and District Choral Society founded; conductor Mr. C.F. Butcher.

1930. 19 May: County Modern School [now 'Holmesdale'] opened.

1932. Formation of first registered Scout Troop, although earlier troops were active in Snodland from around 1914. Girl Guides companies have also been active in Snodland since around 1914. Opening of Welfare Clinic in Malling Road. (Earlier welfare work had been held at the Devonshire Rooms from 1919, then the British Schools and Institute). 8 March: William Lee Roberts Memorial Fund instituted (see Charities). Demolition of Holborough Court following purchase of the estate by A.P.C.M.

1938. Introduction of electric trains on the Medway Valley line through Snodland. 21 March: opening of the Wardona Cinema. Coronation of George VI: celebrations and activities.

1939. Snodland & District Dramatic Society founded. (The Snodland Stagers are the current Dramatic Society).

1941. 21 February: Land mine fell on Gas Works, also severely damaging the church windows.

1944. Flying bomb hits Malling Road; severe damage, casualties and loss of life.

1945. Presentation of ambulance by Snodland parishioners to Royal West Kent regiment. End of war. 'Prefabs' and other houses erected in Lee Road and Covey Hall Road.

1948. Snodland Minors Football Club founded.

1949. Snodland Cage Birds Society founded.

1952. Excavation of Saxon cemetery and Bronze Age circle on Holborough 'Knob'. Coronation of Queen Elizabeth II: celebrations and activities from 30 May to 2 June.

1953. Excavation of Roman tumulus on Holborough 'Knob'.

1954. Electric street lighting introduced. New housing between Christ Church and Ham Hill.

Early 1960s. Rookery Farm estate built.

1977. Completion of housing estates to the east of Malling Road.

1978. Queen's Jubilee. Commemorative gates to Recreation Ground installed; celebrations and activities: 5-11 June.

1979-1980. Demolition of properties in Brook Street and High Street in preparation for the building of the by-pass; also of Mr. Hind's house in Malling Road and the piping of the stream in preparation for the building of Rocfort Road. New Cement Works offices in Holborough Road. Closure of Brook Street school and all activity transferred to Roberts Road school.

1982. Demolition of properties in Holborough Road in preparation for the by-pass.

1983. By-pass (Snodland end) opened on 4 August.

1984. Demolition of 'Rising Sun'; second stage of by-pass (Halling end) commenced.

1986. Twinning with Moyeuvre-Grande, France, on 22 November.

1987. Opening of Snodland Community Centre, on 4 July.

Recent. Closure of cement works; opening of new Welfare Centre and new pavilion; re-building of 'Prospect Place'; closure of Holboro' Garage and Willowside built on the site; continued building on Woodlands estate; Jehovah's Witnesses Citadel and housing in station yard; excavation of Roman villa in Church Fields; demolition of Lead Wool works buildings. Extension of the civil parish by the addition of the Ham Hill/Lower Birling area.

History is always in the making. Take note and record the changes.

Part II

AROUND THE VILLAGE

PLACES AND PEOPLE

ALL SAINTS CHURCH[1]

Exactly when the first church was built in Snodland we cannot say. St. Augustine landed in Kent in 597 A.D. and the church at Rochester was built in 604. Before long it is likely that other churches sprang up in the valley near-by, perhaps including one at Snodland. Any such building would have been flimsy and just as likely as the rest of the village to have been razed to the ground more than once as early invaders sailed up the Medway. Surviving Anglo-Saxon churches show that the tradition of entering the building from the south side, as at All Saints, dates from before the Norman Conquest. Certainly there is documentary evidence of a church here by 1000 A.D.

When All Saints was first built in stone, the workmen had some useful materials close at hand from the abandoned Roman Villa a few yards to the north. Some Roman tiles and 'tufa' can still be seen in the older walls of the present building. We can suppose that around 1100 All Saints looked very like the other two early Norman churches of the parish, Paddlesworth and Dode, although with thatch on the roof rather than the present tiles. Perhaps it was the murder of Thomas a Becket at Canterbury which prompted the substantial enlarging of the church during the 13th, 14th and 15th centuries. However, this may have been part of the great flowering of church building then in progress throughout the country; we have already seen that parishioners were only too willing to bequeath money and materials to maintain and beautify their church.

It seems likely that the original church building would have been sited where is the present nave. The central part of the west wall is perhaps the only part of that earliest stone building to survive, but maybe the chancel also dates from this time. Significantly these are the only parts of the walls which include the Roman material. Above the west window, itself dating from around 1300 or soon after, an earlier Norman-style arch can still be seen. Perhaps the chancel also had Norman windows once, but again these were replaced early on by 'Decorated' windows of c. 1300. Two only survive - on the north side nearest the east end - and one can see where a third one has been bricked in to allow room for the much larger 14th century one to be inserted. Although the window pattern on the south side of the chancel is similar, these are nineteenth-century copies added in 1870.

Expert opinion gives the arcades and pillars of the nave as 14th century work, which suggests that the north and south aisles were added then. The walls of the nave would have been pierced and the arches formed once the aisles had been added alongside. Charles Winston noted that the north aisle 'has windows of a rather later character than those in the south side'. Outside from the east and west we can see where the roof has been splayed wider to cover the aisles. The tower would have been added at about the same time. It incorporates a priest's room on the first floor (the clergy were not allowed to marry before 1561) which served as the rectory. There is a fire-place and probably the ceiling was lower than it is today. The remains of a substantial lock on the door suggest

---

1. A much more detailed account is available in my book *A History of the Parish Church of All Saints Snodland* (Snodland, 1980, reprinted as necessary), so here I have only given a brief summary of the development of the building. Similarly, for the sake of completeness, I will just note the principal memorials and other features, which again are more fully documented in the other book.

that the room may have been used as the village lock-up from the seventeenth century onwards (once a rectory had been built). Also here is an ancient door with a 'sanctuary knob' - offering the church's sanctuary to any miscreant who could seize it before capture. Two ancient benches, apparently made from another old door, once formed part of the furniture of the room.

Some other features of the mediaeval church remain. In the chancel is a fine sedilia of the 13th century - a seat for the priests and deacons to use - and a piscina beside the altar, where the priest would wash his hands before handling the bread and wine for communion. There is another piscina beside the vestry door, showing that once there was also an altar here. The font too is of great antiquity. Dividing the nave from the chancel and dominating the interior of the church was a Perpendicular rood screen, erected before the mid-15th century. This spanned the chancel arch and standing on it were, in the centre, a crucifix, with figures of St. Anne on the north side and St. John on the south. The marks where the screen was fixed are clearly visible on the side pillars. On the south wall is a small doorway which once had a staircase behind and which led up to the opening above and on to the rood screen. At the Reformation the screen was dismantled and part of it now fills the entrance to the church from the tower. Another victim of the Reformation was a remarkable etched drawing of the Crucifixion incised upon the central pillar of the south group. This was re-discovered under plaster during the major restorations of 1869-70 and was then (re)painted. The west porch is mentioned in Thomas Benet's will of 1461, when he gave money 'to ye makyng of ye same porch'. A carved head with the hand over the mouth, denoting 'silence on entering church', appears above the inner doorway.

In the sixteenth century it was decreed that a box should be kept in church in which the parishioners could place donations for the poor of the parish. Snodland's old chest dates from this time. High boxed pews probably filled the church in later years - there were none in the mediaeval period - including a special one for the 'squire' of Holborough. He also had his own fireplace (part of which remains under the plaster beneath the 'Dedrick' window at the east end of the north aisle and which was revealed during repairs around 1990.) Another pew for the farmer of Paddlesworth was added to the chancel in 1712, by special permission of the rector.

The nineteenth century saw much restoration of the fabric, first by Henry Dampier Phelps, rector between 1804 and 1865, who moved and added windows, pulled down and re-built the east wall and spent in all some £1644. 5s. of his own money on the church. A singing gallery was added at the rear of the nave in 1824, and Phelps bought a barrel-organ to play the hymns. The most extensive maintenance occurred in 1869-70 under the direction of Rev. Carey, Phelps's successor. The old pews were gradually replaced and new flooring and roofing was installed. It is said that the Baker family, who ran the ferry, paid for the new vestry as a kind of family memorial; certainly it contains memorial stones and tablets to them. Another major renovation took place in 1905. As with all historic buildings. there is constance maintenance and refurbishment. But were Rev, Carey to see the building today, he would be gratified to see that his great labours of 1869-70 have stood the test of time and have helped preserve this marvellous building for those who have come after.

Brasses. 1441: John Brigge; 1486: John Perot; 1487: Edward and Margaret Bischoptre; *c.*1530: man and two ladies; 1541: William, Isabel and Joan Tylghman.

Memorials. Martha Manley, 1682: recent scholarly opinion is that this memorial came from the workshop of the famous London sculptor Grinling Gibbons and is probably the work of his partner Artus Quellin III; John Walwyn, 1713; Arthur Elton Bingley and Frederick Mildred Bingley, 1902; Thomas Fletcher Waghorn, 1850 and Harriet Waghorn, 1857; Samuel Lee, 1852: William Lee, 1881; Charles de Rocfort Wall, 1932; Frederick Rookhurst Roberts, 1959; War Memorial 1914-18.

Furnishings include brass lectern in memory of Ernest Dalby Finch-Smith, 1909; railings in memory of Harry and William Greenstreet, 1954.

Windows. Only fragments of the mediaeval windows survived the land mine which fell nearby in 1942. They have been re-instated in mosaic style (with other later fragments) in three windows. The former 'Palmer' window of 1407, but substantially altered in later times, is now in the west wall nearest the tower. Others include some windows given by Rev. Phelps (above the chancel arch and in the vestry); 'An angel offering incense' and 'The Good Shepherd', given by Mrs. Eustace Hook, 1870; a window of the 'six acts of mercy', in memory of Mrs. Ann Roberts, 1881; 'Crucifixion and Resurrection', in memory of Rev. Carey, 1885; figures of St. Peter and St. Paul (origin unknown; probably *c.*1900); The East window and another in the chancel showing 'Emblems of the Saints' (1953) by Hugh Easton; 'The Annunciation' (1957) and 'Visitation of the Shepherds' (1962) by Hugh Easton; window in memory of Willie Emerson Dedrick by Moira Forsyth, 1963.

CHRIST CHURCH, LOWER BIRLING

In his book on Snodland's history (1928), Rev. Charles de Rocfort Wall tells us that 'When houses began to be built on the Brook, Sunday School and occasional Services were held in an iron room in Oxford Street.' During the day it was used as a private school and later by the Salvation Army. The land had been given for this purpose on 16 October 1873 by Rev. Canon Coulson (or Colson), M.A., of Guildford. (Canon Coulson came from Bramley, Yorkshire, and owned a great deal of land here. Bramley Road takes its name from this connection.) With the growth in population at Ham Hill and in Malling Road (both in Birling parish), it was decided to build a chapel of ease at St Catherine's Bank. The £2000 needed to build the church was raised by voluntary subscriptions. 'Operations were commenced on the 1st of March' and the foundation stone was laid by Hon. Mrs. Ralph Nevill of Birling on 30 April 1892. Christ Church is in Early English style and was built by the firm of Robert Langridge of Ham Hill to a design by Percy Monckton M.R.I.B.A. Materials are Kentish rag stone, with Bath stone dressings. The original design included a bell-tower at a further cost of £600, but this was never built: some say because of fears that the ground would be too unstable to support it, although Woolmer in his *Historical Jottings of the Parish of Snodland* (1894) says 'A suitable tower will probably be added to the building as soon as the necessary funds are procured.'

The church and churchyard was consecrated by the Bishop of Dover at a service on 10 October 1893. To begin with clergy were supplied by the mother church of Birling, principally Rev. A. Cochrane (to September 1902), J. R. Burton (1902-1904) and A. P.

Ronald (1904-1908). The first Vestry Meeting took place on 24 April 1895. A year later more land was acquired as a site for a church room and this was opened in April 1897, the year of Queen Victoria's Diamond Jubilee, and naturally was called the 'Victoria Room'. That same year the East Window was installed in the church: 'To the Glory of God & in memory of the Rev. Jacob Marsham this window was erected by his niece Louisa [i.e. Mrs. Ralph] Nevill & other relations & friends, 1897'. Following a petition, the churchyard was enlarged and was consecrated by the Bishop of Dover on 6 November 1899. The earliest burials date from 1894.

On 8 November 1908, Rev. A. Pollok Williams, a Scotsman, was made assistant priest with particular responsibility for Christ Church. At the end of 1910 there were moves to surrender the Patronage of the living to the Church Pastoral Aid Society and on 23 January 1911 the King's Order in Council forming Christ Church into a separate Chapelry and Parish was signed. The CPAS immediately offered the living to Rev. A. P. Williams. His Institution and Induction by the Bishop of Rochester took place on 12 May 1911.

At the first Vestry Meeting (7 February 1911) the Church Council was elected: Messrs Ashdown, Barnden, Butcher, Goringe, Hucks, Jefferys, Langridge, Mason, Sabine, Weire, Weaver and Champion. Mr. Brattle and Mr. Dabner were churchwardens. Miss Bishop was the organist and Mr. Dale the choirmaster. Later Mr. Gordon Russell became choirmaster for a time.

The church seems to have had a harmonium for the first few years, but a one manual organ by Forster and Andrews was installed in 1906. A gate and path were made from the Victoria Room to the Church. In 1915 additional seating for the choir was placed in the chancel as the gift of Mr. Walter Gates, churchwarden. A vicarage was sorely needed and the original plan was to site it behind the Victoria Room. There seem to have been difficulties in arranging this, however, and the present fine building was erected in 1916.

At the end of the First World War it was proposed to build a War Memorial and subscriptions were invited. Plans were made (a) for a cement moulded panel at the West end of the church, (b) for a pair of iron gates at the entrance and (c) for a Lych-gate. These schemes proved too ambitious, however, and the present brass on a marble surround was preferred. Those commemorated are Percy Abnett, Alfred Bailey, Harold Bounds, Arthur R. Burt, Albert Goble, Frederick Goble, Herbert Goodchild, Robert N.A. Langridge, Charles Maynard, Herbert Maynard, Percy Maytum, Herbert H. Roots, Percy J. Sweetser, Frank Terry, Frederick Wimsett.

In 1921 the Mothers Meeting presented a brass jug for the font and a brass altar book-rest is in memory of 'Thomas Lingham, Sept 29th 1922'. At the beginning of 1925, following the resignation of Miss Bishop, Mr. C.F. Butcher became organist. He also took over the duties of choirmaster, a post which had been vacant for a couple of years. Steps were soon put in hand to repair and enlarge the organ. In 1927 a new heating system was installed at a cost of £96. Rev. A. P. Williams resigned on 6 October and moved to All Hallows, Hoo. On 26 October the Opening and Dedication of the reconstructed and enlarged organ took place with a service conducted by Rev. C. H.

Daniel, Vicar of Birling. It included a recital by Percy Whitlock, then assistant organist at Rochester Cathedral, and an address by the archdeacon of Tonbridge. The work on the organ cost £260, which was raised by voluntary subscriptions. (Further improvements were made to the instrument in 1937). Rev. Harold James Howden, M.A. was Inducted on 27 November. He moved on after five years and the Rev, James Butler was Inducted in turn on 27 March 1933. Two memorials of different kinds commemorated church wardens: one is the stained glass window by William Aikman in memory of Harry and Sarah Ann Phyall, 1935; the other was a special service on 8 August 1937 to commemorate F. C. Butcher (also the church treasurer). The font cover is in memory of James Cramp, Christmas Day, 1935. (A 'William Cramp' was buried on 18 June 1934.)

Rev. Butler moved to Cobham and Rev. Charles Rascen Pridmore was Inducted on 25 February 1938. The service registers record a number of special services such as the Day of National Prayer in 1940 and a Thanksgiving for Victory in 1945. In spite of the war years, the Bishop of Rochester conducted a Confirmation Service in June 1943 and returned on 10 October that year for a Jubilee service celebrating the fiftieth anniversary of the first service held in the church. Mr Cecil F. Butcher (son of F.C.) resigned as organist/choirmaster in 1948 and was replaced by Mrs Smith.

Throughout the church's life special services have marked the deaths and accessions of the English monarchs. To commemorate the coronation of Queen Elizabeth II, the parishioners of Ham Hill presented an Alms dish and this was dedicated on 18 December 1955. Andrew Ashbee became organist and choirmaster in January 1957. Gas lighting was replaced by electric lighting in 1962. In 1968 it was decided to join the parishes of All Saints and Christ Church. Rev. Pridmore and his successors have since had the responsibility for both churches. Following Rev. Pridmore's retirement, Rev. Paul Charles Delight was Inducted on 2 January 1975. War damage and the underfloor heating system had caused the chancel floor to be cracked and uneven for many years. In 1977 the whole of the chancel floor was removed and relaid, a major operation which cost £7000. Although it was sad to lose the Victorian tiles, the new floor (lacking fixed furniture) has proved to be an asset for presenting concerts, dance and dramatic presentations alongside traditional services.

Rev. Delight moved to the Channel Islands and Rev. James Edward Tipp was Inducted on 13 January 1982. In recent years parishioners have continued to play a major part in the upkeep and refurbishment of the church, church room and churchyard. A Garden of Remembrance was made in 1983. The whole church has been re-decorated and re-arranged. Beautiful red curtains now hang behind the altar; new books and kneelers have appeared; the font has been moved to the front of the nave; new lighting and heating has been installed; the bell has been cleaned; a book of remembrance (made by Valerie Hearn) is kept in a wooden display case (made by Owen Lambert). Another holds gifts from the church in Moyeuvre Grande, a twinning which has brought great joy to the christian communities of both towns. Most striking of all is the Parish Room at the rear of the church (constructed by Mr. Bertie Taylor).

A special centenary service was held on Sunday, 26 April 1992, led by several clergy who had been associated with the church; the congregation included a party from Snodland's twin church at Moyeuvre Grande. The new digital organ was also dedicated and first heard at this service. Other associated events included a Flower Festival (18-20 April) and a concert.

THE NON-CONFORMIST CHURCHES

Among the archives of the United Church is a book headed *Church Book of the Independents, Snodland, Kent*, part-register and part memorandum-book, which opens with an account (apparently dating from 1836) of the beginnings of non-conformist worship in Snodland:

> The gospel was introduced into Snodland by agents of the Chatham Itinerant Society about the year 1822. At first worship was conducted in a cottage, and afterwards a chapel, capable of accommodating about 200 persons, was fitted up, chiefly at the expense of Mr William Joynson, who occupied the paper-mill. Mr. J. was not only the honoured instrument of providing a chapel without any charge for rent, but also of inducing many to attend. Twelve persons from this village were received into the church at Chatham, under the pastoral care of the Rev. J. Slatterie. About the year 1832 Mr Joynson removed to St Mary Cray, and the paper-mill was shut up: several of his workmen also, who had received the gospel, accompanied him. This occurrence proved a severe trial to the friends of the gospels, and caused its enemies to rejoice. At length, however, this dark cloud was removed by the arrival of Mr. John Clarke, a member of an Independent Church in Buckinghamshire, who, having enjoyed the paper-mill, became a resident in the village, and espoused with all his heart the infant cause. Mr C. (having enjoyed the benefits of a regular ministry) became anxious that efforts might be made, in order, if possible, to obtain a minister to reside among the people, who might visit the numerous villages in the vicinity. In furtherance of this object, application was made to a gentleman connected with the Home Missionary Society, who came over to confer with the people on the subject of obtaining and supporting a Missionary. A subscription was immediately entered into, and in November 1835, a Missionary was sent down from London. Those persons who had joined the church at Chatham, now became desirous of forming themselves into a separate church. Accordingly steps were taken to bring this about and on the 8th of March 1836, a church, comprising 12 members, was formed on the principal of Congregational or Independent Dissenters. The Revd. G. Evans, of Mile End, London, and the Rev. P. Thomson of Ebenezer Chapel, Chatham, together with the Missionary, assisted on this interesting occasion. 'May the little one become a thousand, and the small one a strong nation'.

Later in the book is a list of members with the dates of their admission. The twelve who subscribed on 8 March 1836 were:

John Clarke	John Butler	Sarah Higgins
James Clarke	Elizabeth Butler	Elizabeth Dartnell
Thomas Kidwell	Richard Peters	Frances Hadlow

James Peters   William Bristello   Mary Norris

In fact there is evidence that these meetings had begun even before Joynson came to Snodland. The first of three surviving certificates 'for a meeting house' in Snodland is dated 16 April 1816. Given by Joseph Slatterie of Chatham, Dissenting Minister, it confirms that a 'Dwelling house and Barn of Anthony Hunt of Snodland ... is intended forthwith to be used as a place of Religious Worship by an Assembly or Congregation of Protestants'. Hunt was a tenant of William Gorham between 1815 and 1818 and may have lived in one of the two houses formerly on the present site of the New Jerusalem church. Slatterie was minister at the Ebenezer Chapel of Chatham and the early registers from that chapel (now at the Public Record Office) include eight baptisms of Snodland parishioners between 1817 and 1833, the first of which is for Edward, son of Anthony and Sarah Hunt. The others were for children of William Joynson, James Peters and John Butler (all listed above) and of William Fryer and George Harding, papermakers. It would appear that all these baptisms were held at Snodland. The second certificate, dated 7 June 1824, is for the house of Thomas Kidwell. The third, of 28 March 1828, states: 'I, William Higgins of Chatham ... Woollen Draper, do hereby certify that a certain Building ... in Snodland ... in the occupation of Wm. Joynson, Paper Manufacturer, is intended forthwith to be used as a Place of Religious Worship by an Assembly or Congregation of Protestants'. This building (Kidwell's house) is clearly marked as the 'Independent Chapel' on the 1844 tithe commutation map, and was situated at 'Snodland Wharf'. Kidwell was a paper-maker from Maidstone, who lived here until his death, aged 85, in August 1860. Although it had long ceased to be used as such, in the 1891 census it is still referred to as 'The Old Chapel House'. There is a picture of it [PLATE   ] in use as the mill's time office, but it must have been completely destroyed in the 1906 mill fire.

With continual comings and goings, particularly of the paper-makers, the congregation had grown little and numbered just seventeen when a new list was made on 9 November 1851. But there was a considerable increase in membership during ensuing years, no doubt encouraged by the building of a new Chapel on the Holborough Road (and today still within the complex of buildings at the Clock Tower). This was begun in the autumn of 1854 and consecrated on 6 April 1855, being Good Friday.

At length this building was sold to the Misses Hook to become the Infant department of the British Schools and the church book notes:

> The Congregational Church hitherto meeting in Holborough Road has removed to the more commodious building erected in High Street Snodland and opened for public worship by a service conducted by the Revd. Chas. Spurgeon of Greenwich, November 28th 1888.

> The cost of the New Church & Schools is £1521. 15s. 0d. of which sum £1050 was realized by the sale of premises in Holborough Road.

Here it still is, built by Joshua Wilford, but in 1976 the Congregational church and the Primitive Methodist church joined forces and the latter's building in Malling Road was sold.

The foundation stone of the Primitive Methodist Chapel was laid in November 1877. According to Rev. Wall:

> In 1873 preaching was begun in Snodland by members from Maidstone. At first this work was done in the open air, but eventually Mr. James Rand, Brook Street, lent his house. ... The appointment of the Rev. C. Harrison as Minister in 1886 [who had previously preached here] caused such a rapid growth in the membership that the present site was bought and the Church built at an inclusive cost of about £1000.
>
> In 1899 a new School was erected at the back at a further cost of £500; the then Mayor of Maidstone, Alderman Vaughan, laying one of the memorial stones. The building has seating for about 225, and the School accommodates 125 children.

Joshua Wilford of Snodland was the builder [of the school, or both parts?]. In 1976 the church was closed as noted above and has since been used as commercial premises.

In 1894 Woolmer wrote that 'The Baptist denomination which has now been in existence in the village for several years, have no building of their own; but through the liberality of Col. W. H. Roberts they are afforded the use of the Concert Room of the Institute, in which to hold their services.' In 1898 an iron room with a porch was built in Church Fields. Between 1918 and 1931 Mr. Goldsmith travelled from Maidstone by train each Sunday to take the services. The building was acquired by the Lead Wool Company in 1939 and used as a works canteen before being demolished in 1982. The Baptists now hold their services at Halling.

THE CHURCH OF THE NEW JERUSALEM

(This account is much indebted to the researches of Mr. Kenneth Funnell in his book *Snodland Paper Mill*.) During their time in Gloucestershire, the Hook family became acquainted with the Rev. T. Goyder, a retired minister of the New Church of Jerusalem, founded on the teachings of Emanuel Swedenborg (1688-1772). Together they formed and built a chapel in the grounds of Samuel Hook's house. When Mr. Goyder died in 1849, his place as Leader was taken by Charles Townsend Hook. Naturally C.T. Hook established a New Church Society in Snodland on taking up residence. The first meetings were held at the Brook Street house of Joseph Privett, a carpenter and himself from Gloucestershire; was there perhaps some former link between him, the Hooks, or the Society? After two years meetings were transferred to a room in 'Veles'. In 1864 a purpose-built chapel measuring 28' x 18' and seating 70 people was added at the west end of the house, with a separate entrance direct from the High Street. It was dedicated in June of that year by the Rev. D.G. Goyder. The first minister was the Rev. Charles Gladwell, but after two and a half years he resigned and his place was taken by the Rev. Thomas Lewen Marsden, M.R.C.S., a Yorkshireman and a doctor.

On 11th November 1881 the memorial stone of the present church of St. John the Evangelist was laid by Miss Agnes Hook, deputising for her mother who was seriously ill and who died a few days later on 20th of the month. The ceremony was preceded by a service at 'Veles'. The church was consecrated on 27th June 1882, followed by a banquet at 'Veles' and tea and an evening meeting at the Devonshire Rooms, all fully described in newspaper reports. Of the building the 'Kent Messenger' wrote:

> The building ... was erected by Mr. Bridge, Maidstone. ... The style of the building is Gothic, with a slight admixture of the Lancet. The walls are of Kentish ragstone, with Bath stone dressings, chamfered angles, Bath stone plinth, weatherings, strings and copings. The tower is finished with battlemented coping; the octagon staircase leads to the ringers' floor, thence to the battlements. The gables of the nave are finished with crosses. Most of the windows are filled with cathedral glass, diamond-leaded, with amber borders. The chancel window, which consists of painted glass, is very pretty, and on a tablet under it is the following inscription: - "Erected to the loving memory of father, mother, and brother, Henry Hook, died June 16th, 1866; Charles Townsend Hook, died February 11th 1877; Hannah Maria Hook, died Nov. 20th, 1881; by Edith, Maud and Agnes Hook, June 1882." The roofs, which like the seats are open work, are of the best pitch pine, the principals being supported by carved brackets and hammerbeams on stone corbels. The plan of the church is cruciform, having nave, chancel, organ chamber and vestry. The floors of the aisles, nave, chancel and tower are all of handsome tessalated pavement. The building is heated by hot air on the Derby Foundry Company's principle. The interior is lighted by means of a massive brass corona in the nave, the gift of the children of Snodland, and seven full-sized brass standards of seven lights each. The fittings of the church, including the reredos, pulpit, lectern, font, altar table, and reading desk are elegant, and substantial, and greatly enhance the appearance of the interior of the building. The cost of the church [about £5000] has been defrayed entirely by the late Mrs. Hook and the Misses Hook of Veles, conjointly with Colonel Holland, C.B., of Ivymeath, Snodland.

THE CATHOLIC CHURCH

There can be few instances of a cinema becoming a church, but at Snodland this is what happened. When the Wardona Cinema opened its doors on 21 March 1938, the 'Grand Picture Palace' in Holborough Road was redundant. The Roman Catholics, who had previously held occasional services at the Institute, were able to take over the building and convert it to a church.

THE SALVATION ARMY

At first the Salvation Army held their services in a private school in Oxford Street, but in 1928 they took charge of the present building in Malling Road. In 1902 General Booth stopped at Snodland on his way to Chatham and a postcard shows him on the balcony which was formerly on the South side of the Bull, addressing the crowds below.

C. of E. MISSION CHURCH, HOLBOROUGH

The annual Church Paper for 1882 reports that 'The temporary Mission Room, originally opened at this end of the parish through the liberality of Mrs. [Anne] Roberts, of

Holborough Court, is used on Sundays for a Sunday School, morning and afternoon, for occasional Sunday Service in the afternoon, and on Friday evenings regularly. Major Roberts kindly still lends the room' [Anne Roberts having died on 18 May 1881]. It also housed a weekly 'Mothers' Meeting on Monday afternoons. On 17 November 1882 a 'New Mission Room' was opened at Holborough and the 'Old' one, apparently a temporary building, was pulled down two days later. This iron building was given by Col. W.H.Roberts in memory of William Lee and was sited a few yards south of Island cottage.

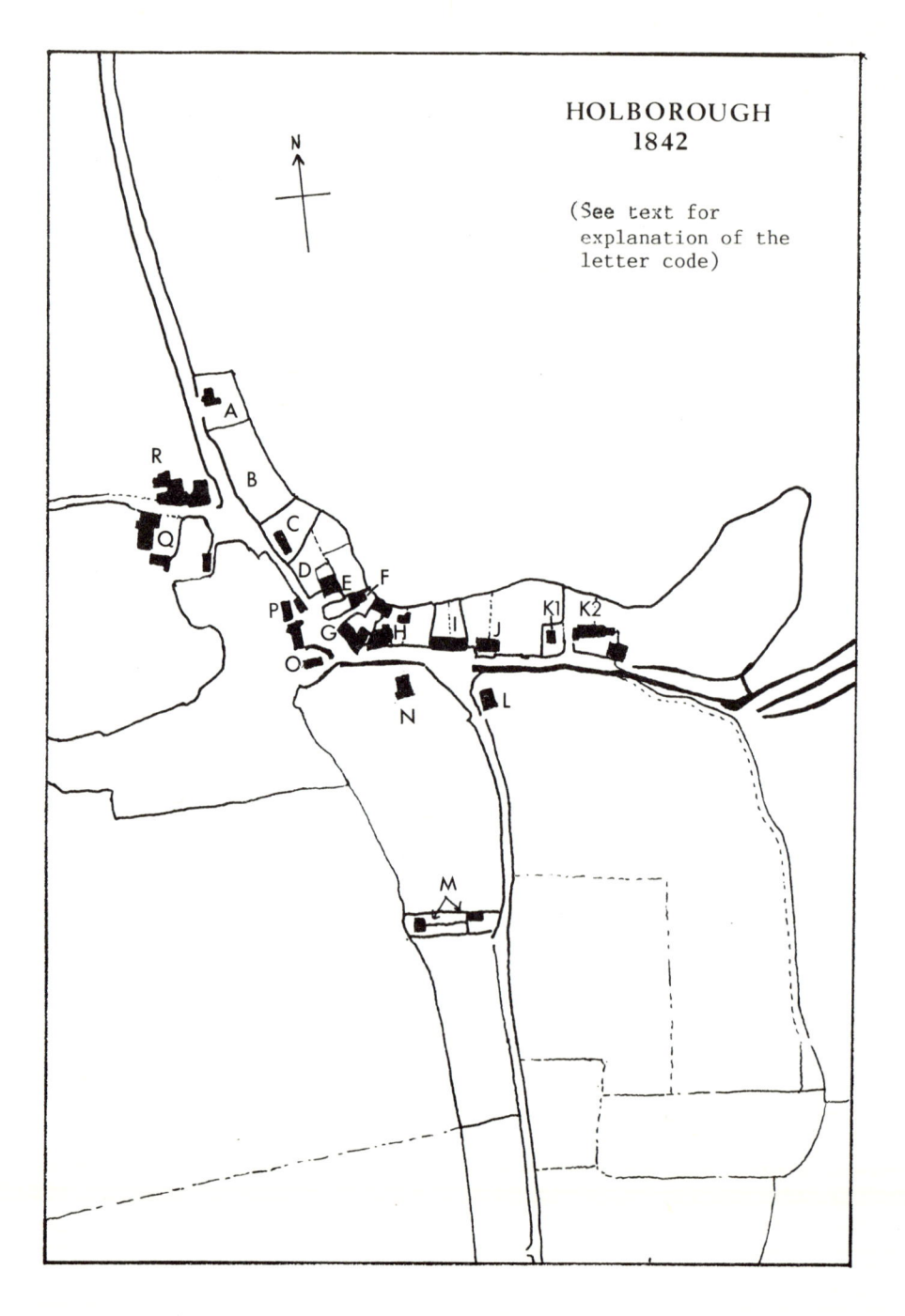

HOLBOROUGH
1842

(See text for explanation of the letter code)

AROUND THE VILLAGE

Those who have lived in Snodland a long time are well aware of the enormous changes to the place, reflected particularly in the growth of new estates, the decline of the cement industry and the coming of the by-pass. Those who have only recently settled here are perhaps unaware of just how much Snodland has grown in recent years. I hope this perambulation will remind older inhabitants of places which are now only a memory and at the same time will provide new parishioners with a guide to how the village/town has changed. This is primarily a survey of Snodland as it was 100 years ago, area by area. Any interesting features or buildings not mentioned elsewhere in the book are noted, including many which have disappeared.

HOLBOROUGH

Until the 1860s Holborough was a separate community with around twenty-five families. Holloway (later Holborough) Court, whose history has already been described, was the principal house in the whole parish. Indeed it could be said that the fate of Holborough became bound to the whims and decisions made by those living in the big house and its ultimate decline tied in closely with the sale of the estate by the Roberts family. The hamlet had mainly an east-west axis, parallel to the mill stream, which was forded, steering the main road past the mill and Holloway Court. It must have been very picturesque in its heyday, for all the houses seem to have been very old. Maybe that was their downfall, for the nineteenth century was not 'conservation conscious' in the way that we are today, and one after one the properties were demolished. Let me quote from Woolmer's description, made in 1894, but recalling earlier times. (The labels in [ ] refer to the map):

> At Holborough the flour mill [P] formed the most conspicuous feature in the hamlet ... Close by this ancient structure, and round the back of Holborough Court [R], formerly ran the high road, which eventually joined the Strood Road near to the meadow which was afterwards known as Holborough Park. Near to the mill was an old residence [G?] which, undoubtedly, had at one time served the purposes of a better residence than the mere tenements into which it has of late years been converted. Adjoining were a couple of shops [F] which were added later on. The water springs, by whose force the working gear of the old mill were kept in motion, were too powerful for the demand of power they were called upon to perform, and hence their silvery waters fell over a waterfall, which formed an exceedingly pretty sight. ... Within a few yards of the mill were some farm buildings, adjacent to which was a large old thatched house [K1], for many years occupied by the late Mr. Thomas Peters; and about fifty yards south-east of this were three weather-boarded cottages [M?], in front of which were well-kept gardens. Close by stood the forge and oast-house [L], both of which are now used for the business of a house-furnisher. An old general shop [J], for a great number of years kept by the late Mr. Richard Peters, with cow-sheds and orchard adjoining, were also

in existence; the shop still remains. A few yards below was the farmyard [K2] for several years owned by the late Mr. George Pierson, of 'The Cedars'.

With the increasing growth of the cement works, several rows of houses were built in the 1870s to house the workmen at that end of the parish. At the railway end of Holborough were (14) Victoria Cottages, (4) Walgrave Place (also called Hayman's Cottages), (14) Orchard Cottages, with (7) Dorking Place (also called Lee's Row) on the east side of Holborough Road towards Snodland. All have now gone.

The Water Mill.

[R] There has been a water mill at Holborough since before 838 A.D., when it is mentioned in the earliest surviving Snodland charter. In 1323 it is recorded that the then Bishop of Rochester, Hamo of Hethe, rebuilt it with wood from Persted [Bearsted] at a cost of £10. Although the Bishop leased the mill to others ' ... with the Custome of grinding att the said Mill, and all ways, paths, waterponds and other rights and app[ur]ten[a]nces w[ha]tsoever to the said Mill belongeinge', he always retained many rights over its use and profits. Leasing was controlled by one of the Bishop's stewards who was responsible for running the Manor of Halling.

The names of some millers are known from surviving documents, the earliest being Robert Fisher in 1516. With some conjecture, it is possible to trace most of them after 1600. William Giles (*d.*1614) is mentioned in a lease of 1606 and it seems that his sons William (*d.*1616) and John (*d.*1620) succeeded him. John's widow Ann married John Amiss, widower, on 25 February 1628, two years after the death of his wife, and it is probable that Amiss had run the mill since 1620. His lease was scheduled to expire in 1648, but evidence is lacking as to when he died or moved on. An undated note, perhaps from the 1630s, records that 'Rumney of Snodland would have Holborough mill & give 14 or 15 [£s] p. an. [rent]'. (The rent was previously £8 a year.) This is probably Richard Rumney, two of whose children were baptised in 1628 and 1634 respectively, but no other reference to him has come to light. By 1661 John Lambe was miller and, following his death in 1667, it passed to Stephen Roberts (*d.*1693) with Daniel Richards the younger. It is interesting to note that a Daniel Richeards was a miller at East Malling some time prior to 1678. John Curd (*bur.* 19 December 1720) may have been the next miller, together with his son Robert (*bur.* 25 March 1721). Mary Curd, either widow or daughter of Robert, married George Courthop at St. Margaret's, Rochester, on 13 April, and by a deed dated 15 July that year the mill was said to be occupied by Peter Curthorpe. But it is George who is named as miller until at least 1735 (and perhaps later), and although he eventually moved to Wouldham he retained ownership of some property in Snodland. The next known millers probably belonged to a Wrotham family: by 1755 William Crispe seems to have taken over, and was succeeded by his son Thomas Crispe around 1779. After him the first half of the nineteenth century saw a West Malling family in charge: James Martin (1802-36) and Edward Martin (1837-51). Later millers included Robert Whitby (1851-5); George Steadman (1857-61-); James Field (-1867-); Anne Field (-1874-); Edward Wood (1887-91-); Walter Henry Cooke (-1894-9-).

What of the building itself? A schedule of 1684 includes:

> 'In and aboute the wheghte mill part of the Tenem[en]t [...] One French Stone being Nine Inches thick, one Waterwheele being Eleavenfoote and Two Inches high and in breadth Two Foote and three Inches being neare worne, One cogg neare worne; One trunde neare worne. One Tunn and one Trough.
>
> In & aboute the Malt Mill other part of the Tenem[en]ts [...] One paire of peake stones wherof one is three Inches thick and the other two Inches thick. One wallower One Tunn and one trough.

As to its appearance before William Lee undertook the present restoration in 1880, we have to rely on a remarkable set of circumstances. A few years ago a series of pictures by an amateur artist, Mr. A. Wells came up for sale in a Maidstone bookshop. The pictures are all of Kentish mills, but technically are quite poorly drawn. Before they were sold, photocopies were made. Two depict Snodland Paper Mill and two portray the mill at Holborough, all drawn by Mr. Wells in 1933. But three of the four pictures are themselves copies of others which Mr Wells must have seen in the village, but which have since disappeared. Those of the paper mill and ferry were first made 'about 1870' and one of Holborough Mill is dated '1873', leading one to suspect that the lost originals were the work of Agnes Hook. At any rate Holborough mill then was much smaller than the present brick pile, two rather than three storeys, with a weather-boarded upper floor and a central hoist. A note on the front of a seventeenth-century deed reads: 'It was rebuilt in 1880 by old Mr Lee of Holdborough Court who laid out £2000 on it and got an extension of 30 years' lease of it - he died in Sept. 1881 when it went to the holder, his grandson Henry Roberts Esq.'. In spite of William Lee's desire to resuscitate the mill, it never really thrived after the rebuilding and after the 1890s was only used occasionally for a few years to produce animal foods.

Island Cottage

[O]. Island cottage, so named because the mill stream runs each side, was certainly in existence as early as 1631 when it formed part of the bequest from Thomas Clottery to his nephew Thomas Williams. Since Clottery purchased from the Tilghman family, the property is probably more ancient still - perhaps the one mentioned by William Tilghman in his will of 9 February 1594?:

> Item: my minde and desire ys that the litle mesuage and garden at Holberth in the parishe of Snodland nowe devided into twoe dwellinges, wherein widow Blacke and Johane Valentyne do nowe inhabit and dwell, shall allwayes be ymployed as an Almeshouse to the use of the poore for ever by my ... wife [Susan] or such myne heir as shall from tyme to tyme inherit my mansion house wherein I nowe dwell, and that she or such heir shall allwayes nominate and appoynte twoe poore persons to have their severall dwellinges therein, paying none other rent to my sayed wife or heir, but only twoe pence yerelie which cometh to a penny a peece for the Lordes rent therof.

No further mention of an almshouse here has been found. Was Island Cottage perhaps the tenement which 'standythe nye unto the myl at holberg wich I laytlie buylded', which was bequeathed by William Ussher to his son John in 1545? At least one sale of land from the Ussher family to William Tilghman has come to light, so the possibility stands. In his turn William Giles, by his will of 1614, left 'all that my lease of the myll at halburough with the two little houses over againt the same' to his children.

The lease or ownership of Island Cottage seems to have been closely attached to that of the water mill. Richard Hamon and Thomas Howlett are named as sometime tenants in the seventeenth century. Possibly this was the property meant by the manorial jury when they recorded on 15 October 1767 that 'We present John Gilder to be admitted a Tenant to two Tenements alienated to him by Geo: Courthope scituate at Holborough'. Courthop was the miller at the time. Although it is not mentioned in his will, the Land Tax assessments make it clear that at his death ownership passed to Gilder's sister Elizabeth, wife of John Fletcher, and at her death in 1803 to John Goodhugh. Residents between 1783 and 1830 were Richard Martin, Thomas Love, Goodhugh himself for a couple of years, then John and Ann Fielder. Thomas Fletcher Waghorn was entrusted with it in 1827 and his mother Ann lived there between 1830 and 1845, succeeded by other members of the family. It was bought by William Lee in 1853.

Holborough Court Farm [Q]

was part of the manor of Halling belonging to the Bishop of Rochester, but was sub-let to the tenant of Holloway/Holborough Court. It was probably the property called 'Nashenden' by Alisander, Tilghman, and later familes, and the yard was situated beside the mill pond, immediately behind the mill. Most of the land was concentrated at the Holborough end of the parish. Eventually it came into the possession of William Lee and his descendants and was acquired from them by the Associated Portland Cement Company as described earlier.

Mill Stream Cottage *or* Little Holborough

[H]. Now the only surviving house in what was once an extended row of ancient properties, 'Mill Stream Cottage' was always among the finest buildings in the hamlet of Holborough. Like Island cottage it came into possession of the Gilder family and then, if not before, was associated with 'Gilder's Farm', whose yard was further east along the road, near the present railway line. It has not yet proved possible from surviving documents to trace anything of its early history, but a fifteenth century origin seems likely for the building. John Goodhugh, a carpenter, lived there early in the nineteenth century and after his death in 1835 ownership passed to his son James. Later it was the base for one of the village carriers, who delivered to Rochester and elsewhere.

The Cock, Holborough

Edmund Gilder, noted as victualler between 1737 and 1770, was succeeded by his son John (*d.*1783). 'The Cock' was probably what we know as Mill Stream Cottage, which in 1783 became the home of John Goodhugh, a carpenter, and ceased being an alehouse.

The mystery of 'Gassons'

When John May devised his charities in 1800, he specified that a £20 annual rent charge 'issuing out of a ... tenement called Gassons with the lands thereto belonging, containing fifteen acres in the parish of Snodland, payable every 5th day of January' be paid to the churchwardens of Snodland, Halling and Birling 'to the intent that the respective churchwardens should annually lay out sums annually received by them in the purchase of great coats for such poor persons, being inhabitants of the said several parishes but not receiving parish relief, shall deem the fittest. It is mentioned again in his will, with its 'barns, stables, outhouses, edifices, buildings, yards, gardens, lands and appurtenances lying ... in ... Snodland ... and late in the several tenures or occupations of Thomas Beech, John Goodhew, William Gorham, John Loft, John Hawkes and James Bowyer ... or ... their assigns or undertenants.' Together with the Holloway Court estate, ownership of 'Gassons' descended first to Edward and Elizabeth Wickham before being purchased by Poynder and Hobson in 1817. In 1846 it came to William Lee and the schedule gives more details:

> A house, two barns, stables, garden and orchard;
> 3 pieces of land together adjoining Barrow Hill: about 5½ acres;
> 1 piece called Lads: 3 yards;
> 1 piece called Cat's Brains: ½ acre;
> 1 piece called Care Croft: 4 acres, 1 yard;
> 1 piece in a field called Mill Field: 3 yards;
> 1 piece of meadow land in the Marsh: 1½ acres;
> 1 piece of meadow land in Northmead;
> 'together with the usual carrying way there from a place called Hulburrough through the place called Barrow Hill as the same has heretofore used unto the said three pieces of land adjoining to Barrow Hill';
> 1 piece in a field called the Underwotten: 2½ rods;
> 2 acres in Stony Field, afterwards divided and fenced off.

The tenants are named as formerly William Huggins and James (probably a mistake for 'Thomas') Parsons, afterwards Robert Widgeon and J. Gaskin, then Thomas Beech and the others detailed in May's 1805 will, since Edward Wickham, James Bowyer and John Loft, then after Edward Wickham, John Loft, James Martin and John Goodhugh (with the last two pieces formerly Thomas Parsons, then Robert Vigeon, then Henry Robins, then John May, then Edward Wickham. In fact the list enables us to trace a duplicate in a deed of 1710, when the tenants are again named as William Huggins and Thomas Parsons (*bur.* 1694). Ownership at that time was transferred from Richard Parker of Snodland, joiner, to William Pound of Snodland, yeoman.

It is usually the case that a name like 'Gassons' derives from one of the tenants. The clue in the above lists would appear to be 'J. Gaskin' - experience shows that lists of this kind are notoriously inaccurate regarding spellings and correct Christian names - who can probably be identified as the Thomas Gason/Garson, a labourer 'of Holborrow' named in the manorial records from 1716 onwards and who was buried at All Saints on 16 June 1754. (Robert Vigeon had died in 1723.)

'Gassons', then, was a small holding with several pieces of land near Holborough, but it has never been clear which house was involved. By a process of elimination, we can narrow the choice down to two properties, either Court Cottage (mentioned below) or a house adjoining 'Mill Stream Cottage' on the west side, but unless further evidence comes to light, there the case must rest. John Loft, incidentally, was kindly treated by John May, who in his will left him a pension of two shillings weekly and allowed him to 'live in the house in which he now resides rent free for and during his life'. Loft died in 1819 at the great age of 89. His wife Ann lived on until 1836, but it is not clear whether or not she moved house after her husband's death. If she did not, then 'Gassons' is likely to be 'Court Cottage' where William Peters had taken up residence in 1822/3.

Court Cottage

[A]. Court Cottage, whose earlier history remains uncharted, has a curious position facing away from the main road and surrounded by open ground. This is due to the fact that it was situated on the east side of the old road to Strood. James Luckford lived there, perhaps following his married in 1795, but between 1822 and 1847 it was the home of William Peters, manager of the lime works.

Demolished Buildings

[B]. The map shows a curious 'garden' plot, which, we can be reasonably certain, was the 'land whereon a Messuage, Barn, Stable, and Outhouses were formerly standing and burnt down by fire and was formerly called the Buck's Head', mentioned in the schedule of William Lee's 1846 purchase. No record of the fire has been found, but 'the Bucks head at halbergh with garden and c.3 acres of land in Halling in the tenure of Richard Hills' was among properties formerly belonging to Thomas Clottery in 1631 and sold by Humphrey, Elizabeth and Thomas Williams in 1650.

[C]. A 'House with stables, outhouses, gardens, backsides, etc.' can be traced as early as the 1660s, when it belonged to Nicholas Paine (*d*.1678). Between 1754 and 1837 it belonged to two carpenters: Edward Jupp and his son William. Then it became a beershop, where Richard Gowar was victualler in 1844.

[D]. By an exchange of land William Lee acquired from Constantine Wood three cottages at Holborough. These may have been built in the 1820s, but documentation is imprecise. Certainly they were in place by 1828, when they were shared between members of the Efford, Capon and Fielder families.

[F]. This seems to have been the home of John and Ann Loft from around the time of their marriage in 1774 to her death in 1836. In those days it was quite normal for more than one family to occupy one house, and the elderly and widowed Ann may have shared her home with others, glad of a rent to maintain her. By 1844 Edward Hawks had his shop here, while the house had passed to John Fielder the younger; both were carpenters.

[G]. A blacksmith's forge is recorded here from the later seventeenth century, but with a change of ownership in 1838 it was joined by a grocer's shop. In 1878 it was described as a 'Smith's forge, forge and ground fronting Holborough Road with shop, parlour, bakehouse and oven; 4 rooms over, with shed and outbuildings.'

[I]. Here was another forge, run by at least five generations of the Phillips family from the 1680s to the 1830s. By 1838 'a new blacksmith's forge' [E] was positioned behind the carpenter's shop of Edward Hawks [see D above] and business was transferred there. Around 1850 the new road to Rochester was built through the site of the old forge.

About 1847 the house adjoining became 'The Rising Sun'. The proprietor was Richard Gowar (who evidently had moved from his beershop at 'B'). Although ownership passed to his son Ambrose in 1862, Ambrose was actually a shoemaker living in the High Street, and the business was run by Henry Hawks (who had married into the Gowar family in 1851). Hawks was serving as assistant to Richard then and himself acquired the property in 1868. A familiar landmark on the way to Rochester, 'The Rising Sun' had to make way for the by-pass in 1984.

[J]. These two houses are already in place by the time the earliest surviving manorial records appear in 1702. Possibly they (rather than Island Cottage) were the ones which John Gilder acquired from George Courthop (documentation is poor in the mid-1700s). Gilder certainly had ownership and left them to his housekeeper Sarah Wood for her life, and then they were to descend to 'John Pankhurst, son of Edward Pankhurst who now lives with me'. In the late 1700s one was occupied by Thomas Hubble (*d.*1797), a shoemaker, and the other by David Smith (succeeding his father, William) and Edward Pankhurst. In the 1820s Richard Peters arrived in Snodland with others of his family to take up work as a lime-burner, but by 1838 he had changed occupations, joining the two cottages into a house and grocer's shop, where he remained until his death, aged 90, in 1881. The shop continued to be used at least until the 1930s, but was demolished along with the rows of Victorian cottages which had grown up to the east of it.

Gilder's Farm [K]

Next door was 'Gilder's Farm' and it seems Richard worked some of this since he is described as a 'dairy farmer' at one time. Part of the farm land was swallowed up by the South Eastern Railway and part was sold to George Pierson, who in 1857 had become the principal farmer at Holborough. He lived at 'The Cedars'. [K1] was the house of Richard Peters' son, Thomas William, who later became the village coal merchant and who built Anchor Place and Hope Terrace in the High Street.

To trace the history of this farm presently depends as much on conjecture as on fact. 'Gilder's Farm', comprising a farm house, buildings and about 22 acres of land, was sold to John Goodhugh by the Earl of Romney in 1808. Goodhugh paid £2120 for it. The name 'Gilder' must refer to Edmund and John Gilder who (as already shown) lived at Holborough from around 1718 to 1783 and owned several properties there. Edmund Gilder is also recorded as a tenant of the Earls of Romney on a rent roll of 1741, paying £10. 10s. rent. - presumably for 'Gilder's Farm'. Among the archives of the Earls of Romney is a series of deeds for a house, kitchen, barn, stable, edifices, buildings, backside garden and orchard and 22 acres (in seven parcels of land) - which fits the precise description of the property when it was sold in 1808. The deeds show that this property was owned and occupied by the Taylor family between 1569 to some time after 1636, after which it passed briefly to James Mercer, a grocer of Frindsbury, and then to Robert Cart, a shipwright of Rochester, who sold it to Sir John Marsham in 1674. Early wills enable us to construct a tentative family tree which indicates that the Taylor family had probably held 'Gilder's Farm' as far back as the fifteenth century. Alice Taylor, widow, died there in 1581. Among seventeenth-century tenants were Robert Golding (*c.*1625-30), John Hickmot (*c.*1630-40), Nicholas Paine and John Lander (by 1663) and Thomas Osborne (-1668-1674-). James Goodhugh, son of John, farmed it for his father and took possession following John's death in 1835. During the later nineteenth century 25 houses were built here, but one of the old houses on the farm remained as a companion until all were demolished around 1940.

[L]. On this corner the tithe commutation map of 1844 shows an oast house. By 1894 it had become a house furnishers. Later the building was used as offices by the cement company and it was demolished prior to the building of the by-pass.

[N]. Opposite was a cherry orchard with two cottages and with associated land elsewhere. In 1634 this ground was rented by John Amis, but no house is shown on the map. Robert Austin from Westerham and some of his descendants (who were tailors) lived there from the 1730s onwards, as for a time did John Couche, a shoemaker. He fell on hard times in 1775 and was supported from the poor rate. A trip to the hospital in July of that year cost 10s. 8d. (53p), but he died in April 1777. John Orpin, senior and junior, held it for around thirty years to 1854, when it passed to William Peters.

[M]. Of the three houses further south on Holborough Road, part of what was once called Sawpit Field, the two at the rear were old. Before demolition a few years ago they were known as 'Nightingale Cottages', but the 1891 census refers to them as 'Sawpit Cottages'. The one fronting the road was built by John Goodhugh, who described it as 'newly erected' when he made his will in 1831. It too was a casualty of the by-pass.

SNODLAND
(West)
1842

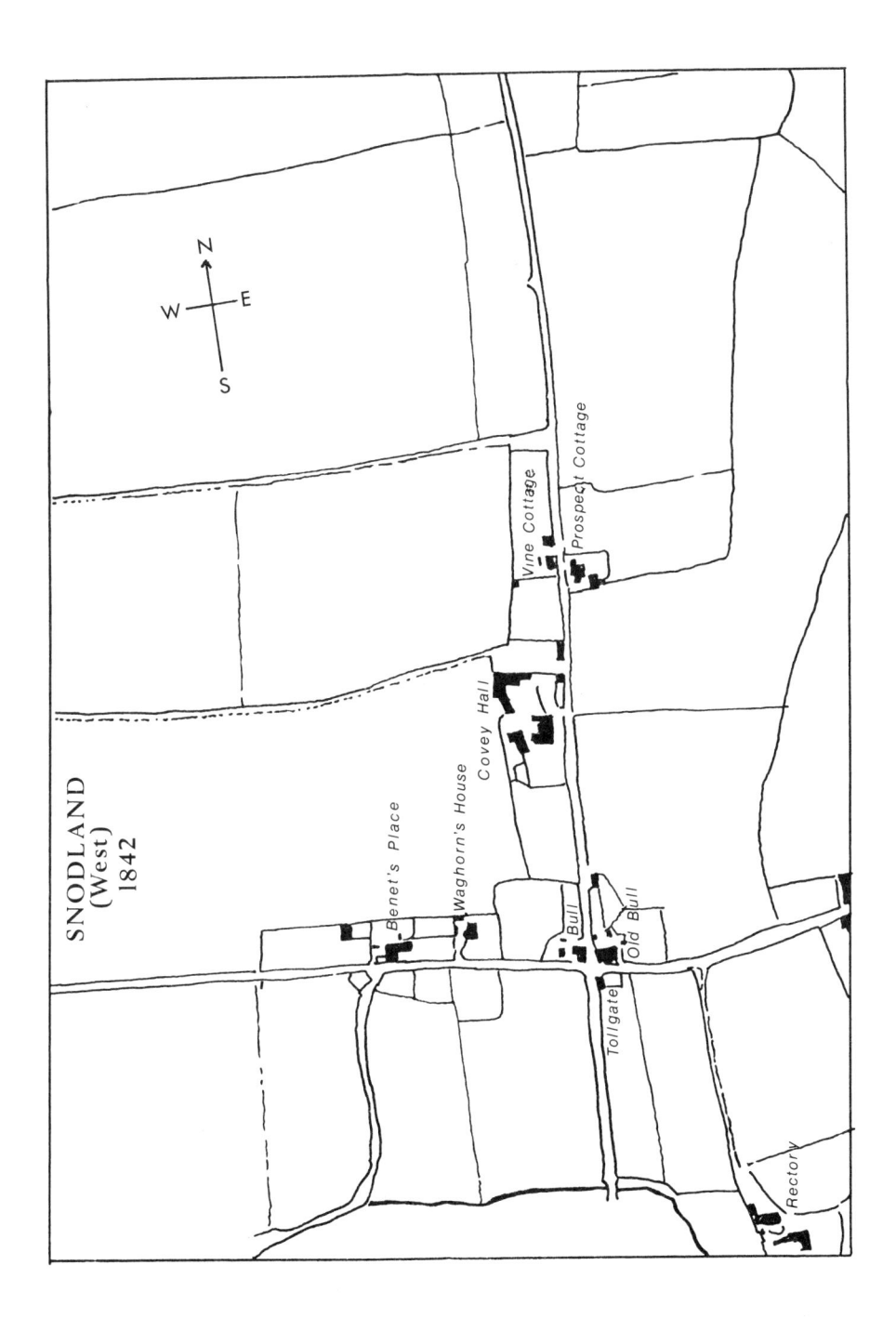

SNODLAND 1842

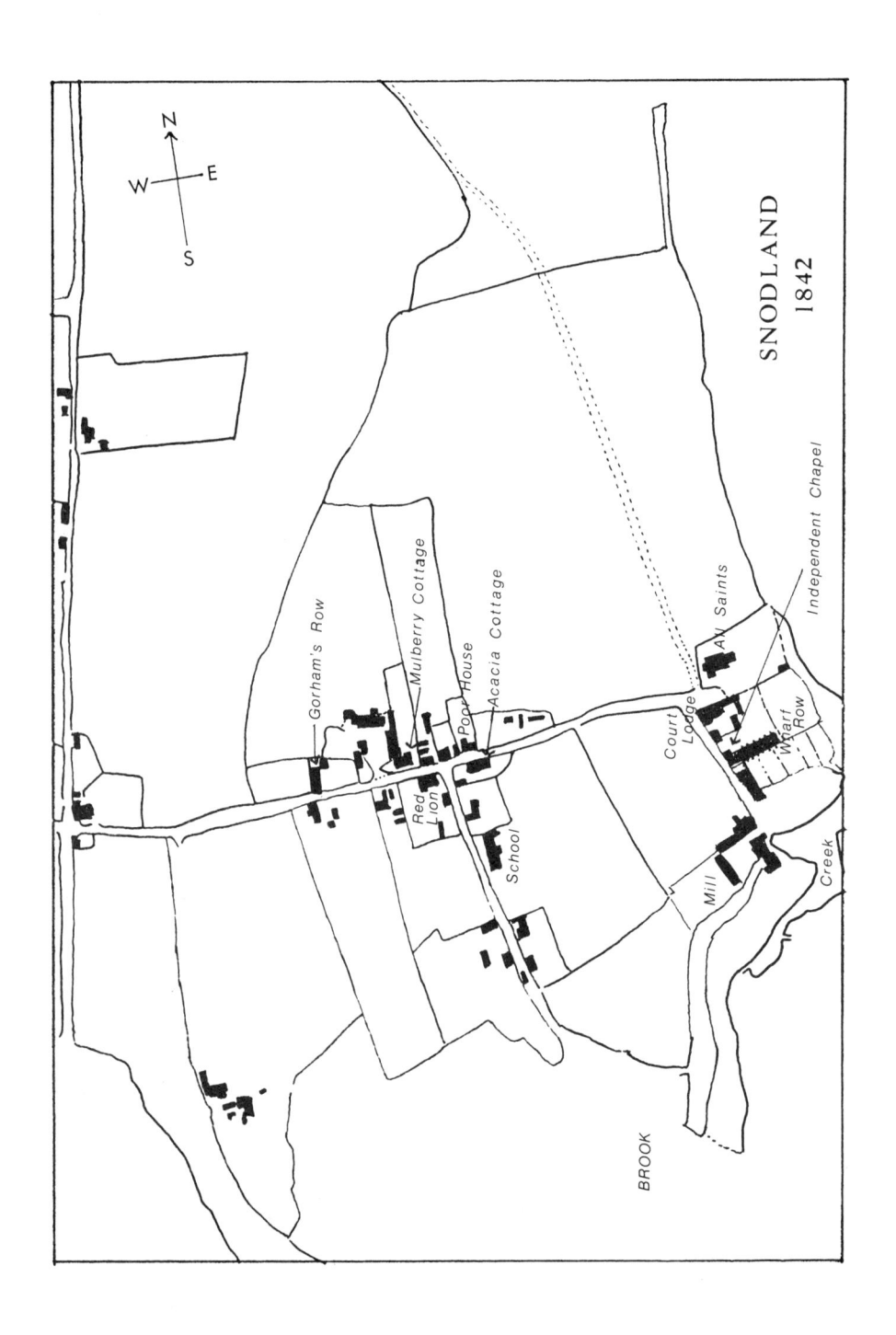

HOLBOROUGH ROAD

In early times this road was known as 'North Street'. Travelling north along it from the 'Bull corner' one would see few houses.

The Bull

In 1730 the property is described as the 'Bull', with barn, stable yard, garden, orchard and about 5 acres, then formerly occupied by Thomas Vousden and since by Elizabeth Vousden, John Goffe [senior] and John Goffe [junior]. John Goffe senior had bought the property from Abraham Clarke of Aylesford, carpenter, in 1714. Thomas Vousden, a tailor 'from Strood', was perhaps the son of Micah Vousden, a farmer, baptised at All Saints on 1 December 1678. He is noted as a tenant of George Costen (the farmer of Covey Hall) at the latter's death in 1704 and he married Elizabeth Husband on 1 May 1705. Presumably then Costen was the previous owner of the Bull, which was sold by his son and heir William Costen (1686-1734) to Abraham Clarke in 1708. Its earlier history is unclear owing to the lack of manorial records prior to 1702. John Goffe the younger died in 1769, and by 1775 the property was 'new built', owned by Richard Wray from East Malling and with William Squibs (1739-1786) as tenant. Squibs' widow Elizabeth remained for one more year. Later landlords were James Bowyer (1787-1801), William Hills (1802-1811), Robert Hills (1812-1822), Frances Brown (1823-1829), Thomas Blackford (1830), John Marden (1831-1841), Stephen Phillips (1841-1874+), Richard Gowar (1880s-1890s). The present building was built in 1881 - to judge by maps in front of, rather than behind, the former inn, but still allowing for the road to be widened.

On the east side was the 'Old Bull' (fronting the High Street) and next door were two small houses which were part of the same plot of land. In the 1840s these belonged to members of the Moore family, who were bricklayers. They expanded their interests first into a grocer's shop and later became beer retailers; what more natural than for their pub to be named 'The Bricklayer's Arms'? In time the grocer's shop was replaced by the present building [Drews]. The remainder were demolished in the 1980s to make way for 'Ostler's Court'.

Prospect Cottage

Further along was a fifteenth-century hall house (called 'Prospect Cottage' in the nineteenth century). It seems likely that for much of its history, as now, it served two families. Few early records of the property have been discovered, but it may have been the 'two tenements together in Northstreete in Snodland now or late occupied by Thomas Watts and Richard Hamon/Hamm', together with 1 barn, 2 gardens, 2 orchards and 1 acre, which was among property shared between his children by Thomas Godden, farmer at Paddlesworth, in 1632. A Paddlesworth connection runs through later owners: Robert Chambers was the last known rector of the place (but seems to have lived at Malling) and it was purchased from his heirs by Nicholas Wray, farmer there, in 1727. Ownership passed in turn to his son and grandson. Residence by Micah Vowsden, Shinton/Shelton and William/Nicholas Stimpson in the early eighteenth century is mentioned but not precisely documented. By 1748 it had passed to Jasper Crothall, the manager of the paper mill, and he rebuilt it extensively around 1780, adding the present brick portion. Note the insurance mark still present high on the South facade. Crothall's nephew and successor at the mill, Isaac Wenman, held it from 1781 to 1792. It then passed to the Brain family and became a butcher's shop and slaughterhouse - remaining so until within living memory. There was a period between 1819 and 1840 when it seems to have housed a succession of millers who worked the windmill on the bank where Jessamine Cottages now stand. This windmill was dismantled by John Steadman in 1839, transported to the wharf and ferried to Gillingham where it was re-erected near another mill. Both eventually burned down, one in 1883 and one in 1893. One wonders whether the George Steadman, miller at Holborough for a time around 1860, was a relation of this John. From 1840 onwards the butcher's shop was owned by George Gorham...Now extensively restored and cleaned, and hemmed in by other houses, Prospect Cottage has lost its land which once set it in splendid isolation amid the fields.

Covey Hall

Quite where the name 'Covey Hall' comes from has not been discovered; it may be a corruption of 'Coney Hall', which was a house on the estate, formerly situated alongside Whitedyke Road immediately north of the cemetery. From the later sixteenth to the early eighteenth centuries the Costen family were farmers here. Thomas Whittaker bought it in 1729. A map of 1741 shows its extent of some 108 acres, with a wide strip of land running west of the farm buildings as far as the Pilgrim's Way, and with several other fields on the east of Holborough Road. John (*d.*1752), William (*d.*1792) and John Wingate (*d.*1831) were the farmers during the eighteenth century, replaced by Thomas Matthews in 1818 and William Peters in 1855. The old building (Plate   ) was converted into its present form around 1880 by Joseph Champion, who also modernised some of the outbuildings, although the old granary and oasts remained. Champion moved there temporarily while extensive alterations were made to 'Woodlands' farm-house. In 1897 Alexander Thomson rented the farm, remaining there until his death in 1939. As a tenant of the Roberts family of Holborough, he was helpless when the land was sold to the A.P.C.M. for quarrying, and little by little it disappeared!

To the north of Covey Hall farmhouse was a small-holding with an orchard, for many years the home of William Wilson, fruiterer. In the 1850s it was demolished by James Brown, a builder, who erected a new house there called 'Belle Vue Villa'. Vine Terrace and Dover Terrace occupy the site today. The Institute (opposite the Working Mens' Club) and the Clock Tower buildings are noted elsewhere. Most of the nineteenth-century housing was concentrated on the west side of the road, apart from Prospect Place (10), Covey Hall Place (6) and, at the Holborough end, Victoria Cottages (12). The latter were demolished to make way for the by-pass, as was the 'Prince of Wales' public house and other properties near Holborough on the west side.

HIGH STREET: NORTH SIDE
The Old Bull

The 'Old Bull' faced 'The Bull' on the opposite side of Holborough Road on the corner of the High Street. When Richard Everest made his will on 5 September 1727, he gave the property 'commonly called by the name or sign of the Old Bull ... in Snodland, together with the stable, orchard and all lands ... now in the tenure of Stephen Obey, to my son Richard'. Confusingly it is sometimes called simply 'The Bull', making identification difficult, but it is possible that Richard Eason the elder owned it jointly with Francis Aldridge. Aldridge had married Elizabeth Eason on 4 January 1747, perhaps a sister of Richard. Between at least 1757 and 1760 Aldridge was licensed as publican at 'The Hoy' and it would appear that he had temporarily changed the name. Eason himself was a shipwright and Aldridge had been a hoyman, so the choice was apt. It reverted to its former name when William Knight took over. From the 1830s it served as a grocer's and butcher's shop, and also, for a time, as the Post Office. Older parishioners will remember it as the 'World Stores', with its little garden and tree jutting into the High Street. Traffic demands caused the tree to be felled and the garden removed and later the whole corner was redeveloped to make way for the present buildings. Also demolished was 'Nepthalite Villa', built by the ferryman Edward Baker from the proceeds of his service, and which in its last years was Stedman's the chemists.

The next house (now the Bank) came later. In the 1880s Albert Norman, a butcher, built 'Deengaar' for himself to live in, with a row of three cottages to the east. The Congregation church was erected in 1888. Also built at this time were some of the houses opposite the cricket meadow: Hope Villa, Trefoy House, and Lyndale House. According to a note inked on the back of an old photograph of All Saints church, Thomas William Peters, the village coal merchant, built Anchor Place for himself and Hope Terrace for his family to live in as they grew up and were married; all are shown on the 1868 map of the village. However the censuses indicate that his plans came to nothing and Hope Terrace had other occupants. To the east of them was a row of cottages, known as 'Gorham's Row'. William Gorham purchased the house and land of John and Elizabeth Fletcher, following their deaths in 1803. He built (or rebuilt) three houses soon after; a fourth was added in the 1830s by converting a stable. They were aligned at right angles to the High Street and, with one end jutting into the road, again became something of a traffic hazard, so were demolished in the 1960s. Gorham himself lived directly opposite on the south side of the High Street, presumably in the Fletchers' own house. A second house on the site was occupied by his brother Alexander, a tallow chandler and butcher. Their brother George was the butcher at Prospect Cottage in Holborough Road. William himself was the Relieving Officer and ran the first Post Office in the village. Alexander's house was demolished when the New Jerusalem church and Ivymeath were built, but the maps seem to indicate that part of the Post Office building survived at least to the end of the century, abutting the east of the church.

By the 1890s parts of Waghorn Road and Queens Road had houses lining them, together with the Devonshire Rooms (1895), a group of almshouses and the technical school (1893), all built by the Misses Hook. Formerly this area had been the farmyard of 'Mulberry Cottage'; it contained an oast house and other outbuildings, including, according to Rev. Wall, 'a very picturesque old cottage [which] had unfortunately to be destroyed to make room for this school'.

Mulberry Cottage

One of the major landmarks in the village and one of its most striking buildings, this house was largely rebuilt (but using the old timbers) in the 1930s. Prior to its restoration, it had accumulated shop fronts and other accretions and its present form comes much closer to how it would have appeared in the 16th century. It is not recorded as having much land attached to it - the earliest surviving deeds mention 6 acres or thereabouts - probably because it was primarily concerned with malting and producing ale rather than with general farming. The earliest tenants' names we have are Vincent Coaste (-1626-), Mark Parker (-1641). William May and William Manley, this last a tenant of William Pound (*d.* November 1710). A month later Manley too was dead; his widow Amy married William Turner on 9 October following, but he died in January 1714, although his estate was valued at £150, a very considerable sum for the time. When Amy herself died around 1725, her son Stephen inherited the property. His memorial outside the vestry of All Saints church is now virtually illegible, but fortunately was noted 150 years ago:

> Here lieth the Body of Stephen Manley of this ph; he died Oct. ye 8th 1763 aged 62 - Here Also lieth the Body of Elizh Manley wife of Stephen Manley. She died Jan ye 1 1769 aged 65 years; left Issue one Son John Manley. Here also lieth four of their children who died in their Infancy viz. - Stephen - Thomas - Amy - and Elizh - William their son died Aug 7 1762 Aged 29 years.
>
> Farewell vain world I know enough of thee
> And now am careless what thou say'th of me;
> Thy smiles I court not, nor thy frowne I fear;
> All cares are past, my head lies quiet here.
> What faults you know take care to shun
> And look at home, enough there's to be done.

So John Manley succeeded his father as 'maltster'. John made his will in 1765, but lived on until 1797. Unfortunately he got into serious debt by buying property through loans made with three local tradesmen, but was unable to repay them by the time of his death. So his estate was sold and it was at this time that 'Mulberry Cottage' was divided into two or three dwellings. John's widow Frances lived on there, but shared the house with others. Among the estates which he partly controlled was that of the 'Ferry House or Five Ringers' in Halling [today the 'Five Bells'] leased from William Dalison.

The 1844 map shows fourteen houses to the east of Mulberry Cottage, for this was the centre of the old village, with the market cross outside the Red Lion as its focal point. A grocer's shop stood here from the 1830s, if not earlier, surviving until the by-pass was built. Next door, in earlier times, were the village 'Poor Houses', where paupers could stay and receive relief payments from the parish overseers. Later, small shops took their place, one of which became a bakery and another 'The Victory'. More old thatched cottages occupied the site later taken up by the garden of 'Delamere' and by 'The Queen's Head'. No picture seems to be known of 'Delamere House', the home of Eustace Hook, but the stables and laundry block survive, much modified, next to the bypass. Houses began to be built in Church Fields from around 1870.

HIGH STREET: SOUTH SIDE

The row of shops which now runs from the Medway Bakery to Durham House dates from around 1890, while the present Post Office was opened in 1909. To reach the Rectory, sited where Rectory Close is today, entailed travelling along the lengthy drive beside the cricket meadow - which itself was formerly part of the glebe land granted to the Rector. The Rectory known to older parishioners dated from the mid 1860s, and was demolished after a hundred years, but there had been an earlier building positioned just east of where Ivymeath is today. Ivymeath itself was the home of Colonel Holland, confidante to the Hook family and manager of the Paper Mill, and newly built for him, but his stay was relatively brief and by 1891 he had moved to Tunbridge Wells. A group of five cottages and gardens was once squeezed on to a small site opposite Waghorn Road, just one of which survives today. These too probably dated from the early years of the nineteenth century, if not earlier. All the rest of the present buildings between the New Jerusalem Church and Red Lion are shown on the 1897 map.

The Red Lion

The earliest known document for what is undoubtedly a much older building is dated 18 October 1738, when the Red Lion was sold by Samuel Duke of Maidstone, surgeon, and his wife Mary, to John May [I]. Proprietors include Hester Cox, who married Richard Waghorn at All Saints, 3 November 1728; Elisha Fallick *bur.* 11 April 1729, and his widow Anne. *d.* Nov. 1748, *bur.* at Cuxton 27 Nov. 1748. All her property was bequeathed to their daughter Elizabeth (*bapt.* at Snodland 16 Jan. 1722), who married Richard Hales at Snodland on 23 Jul. 1751 (his second wife.) He came from Dymchurch, but was in Snodland by 1 June 1740 and is listed as victualler from at least 1744 to his death in 1762. He was buried at Cuxton 16 Sept. 1762 (his first wife Sarah was buried there on 6 Mar. 1750). Hales was succeeded by Jeremiah French (1762-1788), then his widow Mary (1788-1798); William Wood (1798-1809); John Hawks (1809-1815); John Orpin (1816-1842; Anne Orpin (John's widow) (1843); William Kingsnorth (1844-1851); Richard Antrum, Kingsnorth's cousin (1852-1860s); Charles Collier (1871) James Crittenden (1891).

'Veles', the home of the Hook family, has already been described, but it is clear from surviving deeds that there was a house on this site by 1613. The 1851 census calls in 'Acacia Cottage'. 'Veles' itself was built in the 1860s and demolished in 1930, to be replaced by a row of houses in 1932 (and which made way for the by-pass in their turn).

Until the land was sold to enlarge the National School, there were no more houses on this side of the road until the four built next to the railway were reached. But in the 1870s the sale gave rise to May Street and East Street, with many houses lining both roads. 'Carisbrooke House' in May Street was built by the Hook family for their governess, Amelia Drummond, while many of the other properties were occupied by workers from the Paper Mill, which was rapidly expanding in size and production. For a time the Post Office moved to the corner of May Street, later transferring to Bateman's (the 'World Stores') before reaching its present building. May Place and Nyanza House fronted the High Street - the later was the home of Dr White, the first medical practitioner to live in the village, and he named it after a P&O steamship on which he had served.

EAST OF THE RAILWAY LINE

The ancient manor of Veles largely occupied that part of the parish bordering the river. The old house by the church, which was the Court Lodge for the manor, gradually fell into decline during the nineteenth century and disappeared entirely about a hundred years ago. Fortunately the artist William Twopeny drew it and some of its architectural details in the 1820s; clearly it was a magnificent building in its prime [Plate   ]. The family of Veel are recorded in Snodland between 1242 and 1346 and presumably lived here, but it is not until the sixteenth century that it is mentioned in surviving documents. In 1585 John Leeds, a clothier, left the manor to his son Edward. For most of the seventeenth century it appears to have been owned by members of the Whitfield family. John Carnell purchased it from James Whitfield and in 1707 sold it to John Crow the elder. He and his descendants held it until 1732, when it passed to John May the elder and later to May's sons William and then John. At the latter's death in 1805 it was entrusted to Edward Wickham. A clear division between the farm and paper mill areas was established in 1818, after which they were separately assessed. It was the gradual expansion of the paper mill encroaching upon the house and yard, together with a serious fire in 1881, which led to its demise. The 1881 and 1891 censuses simply calls it 'Old Cottage'.

Church Fields remained fields until the 1870s, but nineteen houses had been built there by 1891. Opposite the church was Church Terrace (8 houses) and Church Place (3), with Railway Terrace (5) next to the railway, all now demolished. When the paper mill was still quite small, one could turn right at the bottom of the High Street into Mill Street. Here on the left was the Court Lodge (the real 'Veles') and its yard, while further down on the same side were two more old houses, the first served as a beerhouse ('The Wheatsheaf '), at least at the end of its life, and the second was the old house converted into the first Independent Chapel (as described earlier). Behind them, running towards the river, was a group of houses called 'Wharf Row'. Four of them are mentioned in 1795 as having a right-of-way through the 'Veles' farmyard, but northward expansion of the mill had eaten them up by the 1890s. On the west side of Mill Street was a row of sixteen houses. Following the great fire of 1906, new mill buildings were erected at this end of the site and today just the north end of the Mill Street terrace remains to show where the road once ran.

SOME LOST ALEHOUSES

The Paper Mill

Jane Munt is noted as the victualler (1746-1759). Perhaps this ale-house was near the old mill in the former Mill Street?

The Wheatsheaf

as mentioned above, was in Mill Street, close to the gate of the paper mill. William Mills is named as victualler in the censuses of 1871 and 1881, but by 1891 it had become the 'late Wheatsheaf'.

The King's Head

The position of this alehouse is unknown. Victuallers were Henry Divers (noted in 1706 and 1714) and Margaret Divers (1718). Henry Divers of Strood, fisherman, married Margaret Martain of Snodland, widow, innkeeper, at All Saints of 3 December 1705 (he *bur*. 24-12-1714 & she *bur*. 19-3-1736), so presumably her first husband had previously been innkeeper there.

THE UPPER HIGH STREET AND BIRLING ROAD

The row of shops extending west from the Bull corner was largely in place by 1891, but were among the last properties to have been built in that part of the village. The Lodge was built by Thomas Fletcher Waghorn in 1840. Woolmer records:

> During one of the voyages of that gentleman, he became the possessor of a stone panel, which had served as part of a prison to a lady of high rank abroad. This, Waghorn brought home, and after having had it made to hold glass, it was hung as a door to one of the drawing-rooms in his house. This mansion is situate at the upper end of the High Street, and is now the property of Henry Peters, Esq., of Wouldham Hall.

The Monk's Head, at the junction of the roads to Paddlesworth and Birling, dates from the 1860s. Thomas Barden. was the first publican. East of this was a group of houses known as 'Dodnor Cottages'. These came into being around 1820 when Thomas Stephens, the farmer at Paddlesworth, acquired the large L-shaped house already there and converted it into five cottages as homes for some of his labourers. This had been 'Benet's Place', the home of Thomas Benet (*d*.1461), and later of John and Joan Giles (all of whom have already been mentioned). Following the death of Joan the property came to John's nephew, Henry Hall, and descended through his heirs until it was sold to Thomas Brown in 1773. Around 1700 the estate consisted of a house and outbuildings and 27 acres of land in Snodland, Paddlesworth and Birling, including the 'Cherry Garden' and 'Pondfield'. It seems likely that the land was taken over by Stephens and farmed by him.

A great many houses were built on the Birling Road in the 1860s (many of which still survive). These were sorely needed when the paper and cement industries were rapidly expanding. The Snodland-Birling boundary follows the stream so that most of the houses from Rookery Hill onwards came under Birling's authority, but it touched the road again just once:

Grove Farm

Situated on the border between Snodland and Birling, there was always debate as to which parish should claim the farm. This was officially resolved on 21 November 1693, when Snodland paid Birling £4. 10s. and Birling in turn allowed that Grove Farm should henceforward be a part of Snodland parish. Thomas (*d*.1689) and Hester Pound (*d*.1674) lived there following their marriage in 1663. Hester was the daughter of George and Isobel Savage, whose family seem to have lived in the area from at least 1561. Thomas Pound seems to have been a tenant of the Savage family rather than the owner. George Savage of Luddesdowne (*d.*1683) may have acquired a part-ownership of Groves and certainly Robert Savage (also of Luddesdowne), had purchased a half-share in it in 1697. At his death in 1726 it descended to his three sons Richard, John and George. The whole farm of 30 acres was acquired by Thomas Whittaker in two stages in 1731 and 1733. Hudson was noted as farmer in 1754; Bryant Dartnell in 1761-1818; William Burgess 1818-20; John Knell 1821-1840s; Laurence Knell 1840s-1854; Elizabeth Knell 1854-70; Robert Knell. 1870-. In her book *Birling - a backward glance*, Margaret Collins records an early nineteenth century account of the old house being pulled down and illustrates an old fireplace beam from it. The replacement house was pulled down in the late 1950s.

THE PADDLESWORTH ROAD

Woodlands *or* Cox's farm

As with 'Covey Hall', the name appears without reason, for no-one called Cox seems to have farmed anywhere in Snodland! A seventeenth-century list of 'Evidences concerning Newhouse' (which then was its name), begins on 1 September 1468, when it belonged to John Holloway (*d.*1477), and shows that Thomas Godden, farmer at Paddlesworth, took possession of it and other property in 1589. His descendants eventually sold it to the Earl of Romney in 1665, who held it until 1808, when William Gorham paid £4000 for the farm of 136 acres. Among the Earl's farmers were Nicholas Newman (1760s-1780) and Thomas Beech the elder (1781-1808). Following Gorham's death in 1820, it was sold to Thomas Luck of West Malling who remained the owner until the 1870s. Joseph Champion then held it and in 1903 David Thomson, brother of Alexander, who was already resident at Covey Hall, rented it.

The three old cottages, built I believe in 1733, were attached to Woodlands as homes for the farm labourers.

Mark Farm

The names of several parishioners called 'de Merke' are known from the period 1300-1350, implying that the site of Mark Farm, currently in a sorry state, is of great antiquity. In his will of 20 May 1442, William Bereman bequeathed 13s. 4d. (67p) to repair the highway called 'merkestrete'. Around 1500, according to a seventeenth-century list of deeds, Thomas Watts 'of Paddlesworth' (*d.*1521) acquired a house and one acre of land here and his heirs remained tenants until 1654, when they sold it to the Earl of Romney. Thomas Brown worked it for about twenty years until 1785. By 1786 Bryant Dartnell was farming it together with Grove Farm (the lands were adjacent to each other) and his successors seem to have continued to do so.

Punish Farm

This farm, high on the downs, is also of great antiquity. The name stems from the family of Povenashe, documented here between 1242/3 and 1346. On 11 June 1562 Thomas Browne leased the estate to Robert Deane for 21 years, but soon after it was divided into three parts shared between Roger, Alexander and Jasper Browne. Roger sold his part to 'Silvester Deane, widdowe' on 24 February 1564. The famous brass in Halling church indicates that this Silvester cannot have been the wife of Robert, nor his daughter:

> Silvestre, the daughter of Robert Dene, Gent and of Margaret hys wife was borne 18th December 1554, Maryed to William Dalyson, Esquire, the 29th June 1573. After that maryed to William Lambarde, Gent the 28th July 1583 and died the 1st Sept. 1587, leaving on lyve by William Dalyson, Sylvestre, a daughter and Maximillian a son; and by William Lambarde, Multon, a son, Margaret a daughter and Gore and Fane sonnes and twins.

Nevertheless, Punish farm did descend to Sir Maximillian Dalison (the Maximillian on the brass) who had acquired a third part from Sir Henry Fane in 1627, and who came to an arrangement with his step-brother Sir Multon Lambarde that the estate would descend to Maximillian's daughter, Theodosia, wife of Dixy Longe. They in turn granted it to Sir John Marsham of Whorne's Place, Cuxton, in 1653, whose descendants owned it until 1808. It was described as a house, two barns, a stable, 106 acres of land, 66 acres of pasture and 95 acres of wood in Snodland, Birling, Paddlesworth, Ryarsh and Luddesdown. Later farmers included Thomas Sanders (-1782), George Brook Cork (1783-1796) and Thomas Beech (1797-1808). Punish was bought from the Earl of Romney by William Tidd for £3600 in 1808, his farmers included Henry Reeve (1808-1818), George Kebble (1819-1828) and Richard Postans (1829-).

Pomfrey Castle

Finally, because of the curious name, it is worth mentioning 'Pomfrey Castle' - a group of half-a-dozen cottages formerly on the hill further to the north of Punish/Holly Hill House, overlooking the valley of Dode and Buckland. Although they were still inhabited 100 years ago, they were gradually abandoned thereafter and today all that is left are a few remnants of the foundations.

SNODLAND CHARITIES

Godden's Charity

By his will of 8 February 1662, Edward Godden, son of the farmer at Paddlesworth, a Citizen and Haberdasher of London, gave "20 acres in Ivychurch to Brett Netter and his heirs to the intent that they should pay yearly to the churchwardens and overseers of Snodland £10 on trust with £5 thereof to put forth one poor child male or female apprentice to some honest trade or calling'. Income from this farmland has increased. Young people who are apprenticed may apply to the trustees of either Snodland or Birling. The participation is based on ecclesiastical parish boundaries. The trustees are able to make grants as long as funds are available, to assist genuine young apprentices.

John May's Great Coat Charity

In 1800 John May, who lived at Holborough Court, granted a yearly rent charge of £20 'issuing out of a messuage or tenement called Gassons, with the lands thereto belonging, containing 15 acres in the Parish of Snodland, payable every January, without any deduction, on trust, to divide the same between the Parishes of Snodland, Halling and Birling, one third part to each ... for the ourchase of great coats for poor persons, being inhabitants of the said several parishes.' The money is now give, on application, for the purchase of warm clothing.

William Hodgson Trust

William Hodgson lived in Snodland for many years and bequeathed £300 to Snodland so that pound notes could be given annually to five elderly men and five elderly women.

The Clock Tower Trust

The Clock Tower was erected by Mrs Hook, Miss Maude Midsummer Hook and Miss Agnes Darlington Hook, in memory of Charles Townsend Hook who died onFebruary 11th 1877. It was made by Messrs. Cooks of York. The dials are six feet in diameter and the striking bell weighs 4 cwt. The clock was endowed by means of a gift of ground rents in Shirley, Southampton.

Ivy M. Rich Trust

Mrs Ivy M. Rich was clerk to Snodland Parish Council for many years. Her voluntary work for the older members of the village was very extensive and will long be remembered. By her will she gave £1000 to Snodland Parish Council 'upon trust, to invest the same ... and to distribute the income arising therefrom at Christmas to such old age pensioners resident in the parish of Snodland as such council shall in its abslute wisdom think fit ... I direct and especially desire that the income be used for no other purpose whatever.'

William Lee Roberts Memorial Fund

This was founded by deed dated March 8th 1932. It derives its income from investments resulting in the sale of Little Holborough, which was bequeathed to the parish by John Hollingworth Roberts, a descendant of the builder of Lee's Cement and Lime Works. Yearly income from this fund is distributed annually at Christmas time to the old and needy of the parish.

Mary Gorham Charity

In 1921 Miss Mary Gorham gave £100 towards the restoration of the churchyard of All Saints and £500 for a Charity to be invested by the Parochial Church Council: 'the interest to be distributed through the Council to deserving cases in the Parish of Snodland and Lower Birling'.

William Alisander Charity

Although recorded on a charity board in All Saints church, this bequest by William Alisander [died 1470] of a 'weekly stipend of bread to the poor for ever' is not documented.

John May School Foundation

By a deed dated 10 October 1800, John May provided for the establishment and maintenance of a school in the parish of Snodland, at which 20 poor children of the parish of Snodland, and 10 poor children each of the parishes of Halling and Birling would be allocated places. (That is to say those would be 'free' places, paid from the endowment; paid places were available to other pupils). With continual changes to the provision of education, free places for all, and ultimate responsibility for the school and its buildings being taken by the Kent Education Committee, the scheme became redundant. Remaining monies were transferred by the Charity Commissioners to the Rochester Diocesan Board of Education. Income from this investment is available for disbursement for religious education in accord with the Church of England in the Parish of Snodland.

ROAD NAMES IN 1994

Where the meaning of names is obvious I have not explained them.

Annie Road	Ham Hill. It is said that both Annie Road and Cooper Road were named by a former vicar of Birling: Annie after his mother and Cooper after his car - a Mini Cooper!
Apple Close	Ham Hill
Ashbee Close	Mildred Ashbee, former chairman, Parish Council
Benedict Road	St Benedict's Church at Paddlesworth.
Bingley Close	John George Bingley, Rector 1874-1895
Birling Road	Formerly the route to Malling as well as to Birling
Bramley Road	Named after Bramley in Yorkshire, the birthplace of Rev. Coulson/Colson (Rector of Cuxton, 1875-1901) who owned this and other land in Snodland and Birling.
Brook Lane	Ham Hill. An ancient roadway.
Brook Street	The ancient road to the common land.
Bull Fields	Formerly fields, but associated with Benet's Place rather than the Bull inn.
Busbridge Road	A. John Busbridge, former chairman, Parish Council
Cemetery Road	Part of Whitedyke Road
Chapel Road	Beside the Primitive Methodist Chapel, now a car showroom
Charles Close	Charles Townsend Hook.
Church Field	An ancient footpath always ran this way, modified when the railway was built and in the 1870s enlarged at the south end for the houses.
Constitution Hill	
Cooper Road	(See Annie Road above)
Covey Hall Road	Land formerly belonging to Covey Hall farm
Cox's Close	Part of the farmland formerly belonging to Cox's farm.
Dowling Close	Jeremiah Dowling, former doctor; his wife, Mrs A. F. Dowling, former Parish Councillor
Dryland Road	Wynand de Dryland, Rector 1295-1319
East Street	Built, like May Street, in the 1860s
Freelands Road	A corruption of 'Fryland's'. In the 18th century Samuel and Thomas Fryland farmed an estate of about 23 acres in Halling and Snodland.
Gassons Road	In 1800 John May directed that rent from a house called 'Gasson's' be used for charitable purposes.
Godden Road	Edward Godden established a charity in 1662.
Gorham Close	Mary Gorham established a charity in 1921
High Street	At first called 'Burgate Street' (from 'Burgh' a town and 'gate', a street = 'town street').
Hodgson Crescent	William Hodgson, a former parishioner, established a charity

Holborough Road	Formerly called North Street.
Hollow Lane	Birling. The old road to Malling went this way.
Hook Road	Charles Townsend Hook and family
Kent Road	
Lad's Lane	Parishioners usually call this 'New Road', recalling that the road to Lad's farm was diverted from its previous route between the mill and Holborough Court.
Lakeside View	
Lakeside Close	
Lee Road	William Lee, owner of the cement works
Lucas Road	A former local agent for a political party.
Malling Road	Built and opened in 1825 as a toll road to Malling.
May Street	The sale of this land provided funds to sustain the school established by John May.
Medway Walk	
Midsummer Road	Maud Midsummer Hook
Moorhen Close	?
Nevill Place	The Earls of Abergavenny, Lords of the Manor of Birling
Nevill Road	
Norman Road	Basil H. Norman, former Parish Councillor
Orchard Way	
Oxford Street	
Paddlesworth Road	
Portland Place	Portland cement helped build the houses
Pout Road	James F. Pout, former Parish and District Councillor
Pridmore Road	Rev. Charles Rascen Pridmore, vicar of Christ Church and later also rector of All Saints
Queen's Avenue	Queen Victoria
Queen's Road	
Recreation Avenue	
Rectory Close	Site of former rectory was here
Rich Road	Ivy M. Rich, former Clerk to the Parish Council, established a charity
Roberts Road	William Lee Roberts of Holborough Court established a memorial fund
Rocfort Road	Rev. Charles de Rocfort Wall, Rector 1909-1930
Roman Road	Roman remains have often been found in the Parish.
St Katherine's Lane	Formerly called Bedlam Lane, Birling
Saltings Road	Former salt marsh
Sandy Lane	Formerly Horn Street, Birling
Sharnall Lane	Henry de Sharnale and others may have lived here in mediaeval times; Margaret Collins discovered that as a place-name Sharnal means 'Dung-Spring' or 'place near a dung heap or midden'.
Simpson Road	A former councillor from Ham Hill.

Snodland Road	
Stevens Close	Thomas Stevens, father and son, were farmers at Paddlesworth.
Taylor Road	Norman R.J.Taylor, former chairman, Parish Council
The Bullrushes	
The Groves	Beside the former Grove farm.
Thomson Close	Covey Hall (and Woodlands) were farmed by sons of Charles Thomson, all of whom came to Kent from Scotland.
Tomlin Road	Near here, running parallel to the Paddlesworth Road, was a row of 14 cottages called 'Tomlin's/Tomlyn's Cottages', built during the 1860s. Usually such names derive from the builder or from a resident in the row. Also called Back Row.
Townsend Road	Charles Townsend Hook, Owner of the paper mill.
Vauxhall Crescent	Another car?
Veles Road	Veles was an ancient manor in the east of the parish
Waghorn Road	Thomas Fletcher Waghorn, founder of the overland route to India via Egypt.
Whitedyke Road	An ancient way to the west
Woodlands Avenue	'Woodlands' or Cox's farm
Wyvern Close	Named after the car owned by the builder!

EXTRACTS FROM THE 1891 SNODLAND CENSUS

Since this book is, in part, a centenary celebration, it is fitting to conclude with a document which tells us most about Snodland 100 years ago. The Parish is divided into two halves for the census: first the dwellings east of the Malling/Holborough Roads (and on the east side of those roads), and second those on the west side, including the outlying farms. Spellings are as in the original, and are not entirely reliable or consistent: Wallace/Wallis; Beadle/Bedell; Hawks/Hawkes; Feaver (not Fever), and so on.

Column 1: the address, travelling logically round the village, beginning in the east and concluding at Holborough. This shows exactly which buildings were present in April 1891; the names are interesting, but sometimes vary from previous lists. The second section begins with houses on the west side of Malling Road, proceeds to the upper High Street and surrounding roads, then Holborough Road and Holborough, ending with the outlying farms. The 'Head' of household listed first is given in column 2 as the prime resident at the address. Where two families share the same house is shown by '[same]'. Where persons with other surnames are resident in the house I have coded the reason for their presence: 'L' for Lodger; 'S' for servant (including shop assistants); 'R' for relations of the principal occupier. The latter are varied: grandparents to grandchildren, including 'in-laws', uncles and aunts, nieces and nephews.

Column 2: the surname of the Head of the household. All other surnames resident in the house are given, except in the case of step-children.

Column 3: Christian name of the male Head of household. Here and in Column 5, second names and initials are omitted.

Column 4: Age of male head of household; Column 6: Age of female listed. There are many difficulties in reading these ages because the enumerator or later inspector of the volumes crossed them through with heavy pencil. Again they are not entirely reliable.

Column 5: Christian name of the wife; of unmarried or widowed heads of households; of female servants, etc.

Columns 7: Occupation of the head of household. The census rarely records an occupation for wives. Widows and women who need to earn a living because their husbands are incapacitated or away are often an exception to this rule. 'On the Parish' or similar entry indicates that the person is receiving financial or other assistance from the Parish officers.

Column 8: Place of birth of the head of household. I have corrected spellings as far as possible, but one or two places (not in Kent) have not been traced.

Column 9: To have included names of all the children would have made this list three times as long. In due course a complete list will be deposited in the Snodland Library. This column shows the number of people sharing a house. Examples: '10' etc., means that ten people share the house, all members of a single family (perhaps including relations as mentioned in Column 1 above); '12(6)', etc., means that 12 people live in the house, six of whom are lodgers, servants or other strangers. '2+' [next row] '2', etc., means that two separate households, each of two people, share the house.

EAST SIDE

Address	Surname	Head	Age	Wife	Age	Occupation of Head	Head born at	Persons in House
1 Riverside	Browning	Frederick	54			General Labourer	East Malling	1
2 Riverside	Hawkes	William	36	Caroline	30	Waterman	Snodland	4
1 Church Fields	Wooding	Isaac	71	Elizabeth	70	General Labourer	East Malling	3(1)
[same] L	Russell	Daniel	45			General Labourer	High Wycombe	
2 Church Fields	Gooding	Kenneth	32	Emily	38	General Labourer	Snodland	6
3 Church Fields	Austen	William	32	Amelia	30	General Labourer	Tenterden	6+
[same]	Moody	William	33	Agnes	30	Cooper	Essex	2
4 Church Fields	Rand	James	47	Phoebe	45	Cement burner	Oakley, Essex	7
5 Church Fields	Gooding	William	29	Ellen	29	Prudential Agent	Snodland	7(1)
[same] S	Tutchener			Ellen	16	Domestic servant	Snodland	
6 Church Fields	King			Mary	42		Snodland	5
7 Church Fields	Woodruff	Frederick	29	Isabel	32	Engine Driver	Halling	3(1)
[same] L	Woodburn	Archibald	32			Assistant Manager; mill	Bombay	
8 Church Fields	Chantler	William	43	Esther	53	Stone Mason	Tudely	3(1)
[same] S	Feaver			Florence		Domestic Servant	Wouldham	
9 Church Fields	Smith	Robert	26	Harriet	25	Clerk in Paper Mill	London	3(1)
10 Church Fields	Hilder	Tom	46	Ellen	46	Assistant Overseer	Tonbridge	10
11 Church Fields	Mason	John	45	Jane	45	Clerk of Works	Coxheath	7(1)
[same] S	Homewood			Agnes	16	General Servant	Halling	
12 Church Fields	Netherton	John	46	Annie	32	Medical Assistant	Ireland	3
13 Church Fields	Bird	John	48	Mary	40	General Labourer	London	13
14 Church Fields	Blunt	Thomas	66	Mary	56	Coal Dealer	Moulsoe, Bucks.	5(1)
[same] L	Brett	Henry	34			Cooper	Sheppey	
15 Church Fields	Banks	William	44	Elizabeth	44	Labourer: Paper Mill	Maidstone	6
16 Church Fields	Hammond	Harry	29	Annie	24	Cement Labourer	West Peckham	3
[same] R	Plummer			Alice	7	Scholar	Snodland	
17 Church Fields	Parker	James	36	Sarah	34	Bargeman	Ramsgate	6
18 Church Fields	Gilliard	John	69	Jane	66	Waterman: barge	Maidstone	2
19 Church Fields	Wooding	Thomas	57	Hannah	55	Bricklayer	East Malling	4
1 Church Place	Weaver	William	60	Adelaide	55	General Labourer	Sevenoaks	4
[same] R	Sweetser			Kate	11	Scholar	Snodland	
2 Church Place	Craddock	William	37	Caroline	31	Platelayer: railway	Maidstone	6
3 Church Place	Wells	John	39	Emma	33	Waterman: barge	Rochester	7

124

1 Church Terrace	Beck	Albert	41	Mary	42	Bargeman	Maidstone	10
2 Church Terrace	Greenstreet	Harry	36	Susan	38	Signalman: railway	Wye	7(2)
3 Church Terrace	Monk	Albert	43	Louisa	45	Cement miller	Snodland	9
4 Church Terrace	Hucks	Harry	33	Elizabeth	29	Waterman	Mereworth	4
5 Church Terrace	Chantler	Alfred	40	Sarah	36	Bargeman	Tudely	9
6 Church Terrace	Green	Joseph	30	Alice	25	Paper maker	Ireland	4
[same] R	Foster			Emma	12	Scholar	Rodmersham	
7 Church Terrace	Longley	Albert	33	Annie	31	Chalk Labourer	Ryarsh	3
8 Church Terrace	Gibbons	George	30	Emma	33	Coal Carter	West Malling	5(2)
[same] R	Pankhurst	George	28			Farm Labourer	Addington	
[same] L	Sparkes	William	18			Wharfman	Addington	
Ferry House	Kidwell	Henry	48	Elizabeth	48	Ferry man; bargeman	East Malling	6
[same] R	Phillips	Edward	8			Scholar	Luton, Kent	
2 Ferry House	Gorham	John	67			Ferry man	Snodland	1
Old Cott.: Mill Road	Chittenden	George	76	Mary	78	General Labourer	Malling	2
1 Late 'Wheatsheaf'	Saunders	Henry	24	Eliza	23	General Labourer	Snodland	6(1)
[same] RS	Capon			Ellen	18	Domestic servant	Snodland	
2 Late 'Wheatsheaf'	Mills	William	59	Emma	55	General Labourer	Cuxton	8(1)
Old Chapel House	Penny	William	59	Charlotte	57	Storekeeper at mill	Canterbury	5
1 Mill Row	Murry	Thomas	42	Annie	39	Paper maker	Scotland	5
2 Mill Row	Stapley	Frederick	29			General Labourer	Chartham	1
3 Mill Row	Parker	Alfred	32	Rhoda	40	Police Constable	Ashurst	6
4 Mill Row	Saunders	John	27	Mary	25	Paper maker	Catteshal	4
5 Mill Row	Moore	Richard	29	Emma	23	Paper maker	Snodland	5
6 Mill Row	Hazel	William	38	Elizabeth	37	Paper maker	Snodland	5
7 Mill Row	Still	Frederick	56	Matilda	55	General Labourer	Trossley	3
8 Mill Row	Brooker	George	53	Mary	52	Brick Labourer	Boughton	3
9 Mill Row	Taylor	Frederick	45	Eliza	41	General Labourer	Higham	8
10 Mill Row	Stevens	John	39	Elizabeth	39	Fitter's Labourer	Strood	4
11 Mill Row	Penny			Rebecca	57	Dress maker	Chartham	2
12 Mill Row	Still	William	37	Amy	33	General Labourer	Ditton	4
13 Mill Row	Leaver	Stephen	35	Kate	34	Paper finisher	Henley	7
14 Mill Row	Wingate	William	25	Ann	24	General Labourer	Snodland	5
15 Mill Row	Hunt	William	51	Eleanor	47	General Labourer	Borden	4
16 Mill Row	Pett	John	61	Ann	62	Gas Stoker	Walmer	2
1 Railway Terrace	Kelvie			Fanny	53	Lodging House Keeper	East Malling	1(3)+
[same]	Oben	William	38			General Labourer	East Malling	2

Address	Surname	Forename		Age		Occupation	Birthplace	
[same] L	Paine	Charles		34		General Labourer	Chatham	
[same] L	Corke	George		67		General Labourer	Bearsted	
2 Railway Terrace	Saunders	William	Elizabeth	31	30	Barge Captain	Snodland	6
3 Railway Terrace	Burton	Thomas	Annie	39	41	Gardener	Preston/Middlesex	9(2)
[same] L	Goldfinch	Stephen		42		Bricklayer	Margate	
[same] L	Parkes	George		26		Carter, horse	Peckham, Kent	
4 Railway Terrace	Wooding	William	Eliza	69	59	General Labourer	East Malling	6
5 Railway Terrace	Stevens	Charles	Alice	28	21	Cooper	London	3+
[same]	Pointer	William	Lucy	27	23	Stoker: Paper Mill	Stone	2
Railway Gatehouse	Austin	John	Mary	72	53	Signalman; Porter	Belvedere	4
Railway Station	Young	James	Emily	38	34	Station Master	Scotland	8
1 Railway Place	Reynolds	William	Mary	34	32	Bricklayer	Staffordshire	2
2 Railway Place	Burt	Francis	Mary	33	29	Bargeman	Padstow	4(1)
3 Railway Place	Larkin		Martha		30	Milliner	Burham	1(1)
[same] S	Powell		Emma		14	Domestic servant	not known	
4 Railway Place	Dartnall	William	Ann	76	63	Grocer	Halling	2
5 Railway Place	Hammond	Walter	Florence	23	22	Cement miller	Snodland	2
Meadow Villa	Woodard	Walter	Ida	28	20	Cement Labourer	Kelsale: Suffolk	5(1)
[same] S	Church		Emma		15	Domestic servant	Snodland	
1 May Place	Garratt	John	Ellen	42	45	Life Insurance agent	Wooburn	6(2)
[same] L	Saville	William		20		Carpenter	Clavering Newport	
[same] L	Field	Harry		24		Butcher	High Halden	
2 May Place	Palmer	John		39		Doctor	Long Sutton	3(2)
[same] S	Appleton		Emma		31	Cook; housekeeper	Ryarsh	
[same] S	Filmer	Jesse		15		Surgery boy	Wouldham	
3 May Place	Sweetser		Mary		49	Tobacconist	Birling	1+
[same]	Capon	Thomas	Emma	40	39	Cement Labourer	Malling	5
4 May Place	Phillips	Henry	Matilda	44	45	Grocer, etc.	Snodland	4(1)
[same] L	Wisbey	Herbert		26		Assistant schoolmaster	Boreham, Essex	
Queen's Hotel	Reeve	Arthur	Sarah	36	36	Licensed Victualler	Margate	10(4)
[same] S	Vokes		Alice		20	Barmaid	Rochester	
[same] S	Cassey		Lillie		23	Domestic servant	Standford	
[same] S	Hodges		Kathleen		14	Nursemaid	Leybourne	
[same] S	Drury	Thomas		26		Ostler; groom	Maidstone	
Post Office	Rumble	Walter	Lucy	32	20	Postmaster	Snodland	4(2)
[same] S	Coast		Mary		25	Postal assistant	Newcastle	
[same] S	Mires		Emily		18	Domestic servant	East Farleigh	

126

Address	Surname	Forename	Age	Occupation	Birthplace	Col
1 May Cottages	Gordon	Daniel	30	Hairdresser	Scotland	5
2 May Cottages	Baker	Elias	50	Carpenter & Joiner	Tonbridge	4
[same] R	Latter		83		Mereworth	
3 May Cottages	Brattle	William	27	Plumber, etc.	Maidstone	5
1 Gladstone Place	Saunders	George	52	Mariner; seas	Chatham	5
2 Gladstone Place	Wingate	Henry	42	Ferry man; barge	Snodland	9
3 Gladstone Place	Rankin	William	48	General Labourer	Maidstone	4
1 Portland Place	Kemsley	John	42	Stat. Engine Driver	Snodland	7
2 Portland Place	Chapman	George	45	Cement Labourer	West Farleigh	11
3 Portland Place	Wilford	Joshua	35	Builder, etc.	Dudley Port	8
[same] R	Young	William	20	Carpenter	Cowes, IoW	
Carisbrooke House	Vaughan	Charlotte		Housekeeper	Chartham	1
1 Springvale Place	Baker	Maria	45	Paper maker	Exeter	7(3)
[same] L	Colbert	Henry	24	Joiner	Chatham	
[same] L	Hubble	George	26	Limeburner	Wrotham	
[same] L	Denston	John	47	Nightwatchman; mill	Little Downham	
2 Springvale Place	Paddick	John	81	Cowkeeper	Tufton, Hants.	5(1)
[same] L	Bramley	Kesia	24	General Labourer	Birling	
Mons House	Gash	Thomas	28	Physician	Ireland	1+
[same]	Banks	Ellen	47	General Labourer	Birling	3
[same] R	Beach	Ellen	8	Scholar	Birling	
1 Faith Place	Brooker	Henry	54	Nightwatchman; port	London	3(1)
[same] L	Relf	Sarah	24	Paper sorter	Maidstone	
2 Faith Place	Brooker	Henry	31	General Labourer	London	6(1)
3 Faith Place	Eslor	George	36	Paper maker	Ireland	3
1 Western Cottages	Mills	William	28	Paper maker	Snodland	3
2 Western Cottages	Beach	John	31	Engine Driver: P. Mill	Birling	6
3 Western Cottages	Green	John	38	Paper maker	Ireland	7
38 May Street	Siddall	Mary	70	Private Schoolmistress	Shorne	2
39 May Street	Gray	Joseph	27	Engine Fitter	Camer, Dorset	2
42 May Street	Groombridge	Thomas	29	Millwright	Aylesford	5(1)
[same] L	Neal	William	45	Millwright	Sussex; not known	
41 May Street	Clayton	Tom	35	Engine Fitter	Huddersfield	3
Coffee Palace	Hasburgh	James	55	Cement Labourer	Scotland	8(4)
[same] L	Sykes	Robert	27	General Labourer	Cranbrook	
[same] L	Steadman	Sidney	40	Weighman; cement wks	London	
44 May Street	Mayatt	Joseph	41	General Labourer	St Mary Cray	8
45 May Street	West	James	56	Straw boiler at mill	Tunbridge Wells	2

127

Address	Surname	Forename	Age		Occupation	Birthplace	
46 May Street	Randell	William	66		Chemical Lab. at mill	Fisherton	4
47 May Street	Stevens	John	43	Ellen	Paper Finisher	Guildford	5
19 May Street	Edgeler	James	38	Fanny	Gardener	Godalming	4
18 May Street	Martin	Henry	50	Eliza	Paper maker	Wooburn	7
17 May Street	Bax	John	35	Sarah	Paper Mill Labourer	Minster	5
16 May Street	White	John	67	Sarah	General Labourer	Sittingbourne	3
[same] R	Bates	Freedom	18		Paper cutter in mill	Malling	
15 May Street	Ashbee	William	34	Elizabeth	Gas Stoker	Aylesford	8(2)
[same] L	Wakeman	William	15		Butcher's assistant	Burham	
[same] L	Mackenzie	Henry	19		Butcher's assistant	London	
14 May Street	Whitehouse	Robert	43	Mary	Paper maker'	St Mary Cray	9
13 May Street	Andrews	Christophr	30	Mary	Fitter's Labourer	East Peckham	6
12 May Street	Bristow	Charles	28	Edith	Paper Mill Labourer	Dartford	2+
[same]	Miller	John	21	Ada	Fitter's Labourer	Bloomsbury	3
11 May Street	Day	Robert	41	Elizabeth	General Labourer	London	10(2)
10 May Street	Penny	John	22	Emily	Straw cutter; mill	Farnham	3
[same] R	Crowhurst			Alice	Sister's help	East Malling	
9 May Street	Russell	Stephen	56	Sarah	Paper maker	Teston	8
[same] R	Smith	Joseph	34		Stoker; Paper mill	Northbourne	
8 May Street	Mayatt	Edward	43	Ellen	Machine man; mill	St Mary Cray	10
7 May Street	Fowle	Thomas	27	Sarah	Cutter man; mill	Dartford	4
6 May Street	Maynard	George	37	Sarah	Paper Mill Labourer	Old Brompton	9
5 May Street	Piper	Edward	34	Emily	Cement Labourer	London	7
[same] R	Whybrow	Albert	19		Cement Labourer	Maidstone	
4 May Street	Law	George	24	Rose	Paper Mill Labourer	Maidstone	4
3 May Street	Dodd	Alexander	52	Margaret	Paper maker	Sunderland	3
2 May Street	Lee	William	27	Jane	Paper Mill Labourer	Birling	3
Millbrook House	Hyde	Jesse	50	Emma	Engine Foreman; mill	Predbury	4
May Villa	Bates	John	48	Harriet	Paper maker	Wooburn	9
1 East Street	Cohen	Thomas	68		Paper Mill Labourer	Maidstone	8
2 East Street	Goodsell			Elizabeth	Laundress	Ryarsh	6(1)
[same] L	Steer	Clifford	30		Paper maker	Woking	
3 East Street	Mecoy	Alfred	42	Emily	Paper Mill Labourer	Snodland	7
4 East Stree	unoccupied						
5 East Street	Hope			Ellen	Rag Cutter; mill	Maidstone	5
6 East Street	Golding	John	40	Emma	Mill Fitter	Maidstone	9
7 East Street	Fowle	Jabez	57	Mary	Railway Inspector	Brenchley	7

Address	Surname	Forename		Age	Forename2	Occupation	Birthplace	
8 East Street	Randell	Charles		38	Drusilla	General Labourer	Fisherton	5
9 East Street	Robinson	George		42	Amelia	Engine Driver, mill	Strawbridge	9
10 East Street	Patey	John		48	Louisa	Paper Finisher	Colnbrooke	10(2)
11 East Street	Prescott	George		29	Frances	Stoker; Paper Mill	Ewell	5
[same] R	Hyden				Jane	Scholar	London	
[same] R	Hodges				Ann	Kept by family	Wrotham	
12 East Street	Wheeler	William		26		General Labourer	Wooburn	6(3)
[same] LL	Taylor	Mary		57	Emma	Paper mill hands	Maidstone/N.Hythe	
13 East Street	Bennett	Henry		52	Caroline	Paper maker	Meopham	12(6)
[same] LLLLL	Bristow	Hannah		48	&4 daugh.	Paper mill hand	Meopham	
1 Garden Cottages	Lucas	Edward		46	Mary	General Labourer	Maidstone	7
2 Garden Cottages	Finn	William		42	Eleanor	General Labourer	Lenham	8
3 Garden Cottages	Morrison	William		45		General Labourer	Scotland	6
1 Vine Cottage	Plater	Edward		35	Louis	Painter	Stony Stratford	6(1)
[same] L	Orpin	John		35		Bricklayer	Sutton Vallence	
2 Vine Cottage	Bampton	William		43	Mary	Paper maker	Iffley, Oxford	5(2)
[same] L	Flaherty	James		20		Paper maker	Norwich	
[same] L	Miles	James		22		Paper maker	New Hythe	
14 Brook Street	Thompson	Edward		32	Charlotte	Engine Driver, mill	Ireland	7
15 Brook Street	Bailey	Frederick		38	Emily	General Labourer	Maidstone	10
16 Brook Street	Purton	Edward		29	Emily	Paper Mill Labourer	Dartford	8(3)
[same] L	Humphery	Stephen		28		Paper Mill Labourer	Dartford	
[same] L	Humphery	Alfred		18		Paper Mill Labourer	Dartford	
	Murphy	Caroline		36		Mill worker	Dartford	
17 Brook Street	Semark	William		40	Eliza	General Labourer	Tunbridge	5
[same] R	Jenner	Alfred		19		General Labourer	Ditton	
1 Brook Side	Gough	John		57		Paper Cutter Man	London	1+
[same]	Brown	Thomas		31	Rachel	Bricklayer	Maidstone	2
2 Brook Side	Hood	Thomas		48	Maria	General Labourer	Ryarsh	7
[same] R	Hooten				Emma	Paper mill hand	Snodland	
3 Brook Side	Mayatt	Charles		68		Paper maker	Snodland	12
4 Brook Side	Baker	Henry		36	Mary	General Labourer	Wandsworth	6
1 Wray's Cottages	Fowler	John		20	Lillie	Cooper	Faversham	2+
[same]	Fowler	William		21	Annie	Cooper	Faversham	2
2 Wray's Cottages	Judges	Ernest		21	Rosetta	General Labourer	Plaxtol	3
3 Wray's Cottages	Wray			65	Amelia	Cowkeeper	Halling	7
[same] R	Francis	William		14		Cow boy	Halling	

129

Address	Surname	First name		Middle name	Age	Occupation	Birthplace	Col
[same] R	Francis			Eva	15	Scholar	Snodland	3(2)
Shephard's Cottage	Saxby	Richard		Emma		Agricultural Labourer	Beneneden	3
[same] S	Gowar		42			Domestic servant	Ightham	
National School	Judges	Charles	31	Edith	30	Schoolmaster	New Windsor	3
1 Alma Place	Trowell	Henry	37	Maria	36	General Labourer	Maidstone	7
2 Alma Place	Gladwell	Charles	25	Emily	32	Bricklayer	Thurnham	6
3 Alma Place	Bush	Alfred	55	Jane	48	General Labourer	Fobbing, Essex	8
4 Alma Place	Arnold	Albert	22	Mary	25	General Labourer	Snodland	3
5 Alma Place	Stroud	Arthur	49	Rose	52	Cement Labourer	Herts.	2
6 Alma Place	Jeffrey	James	34	Elizabeth	33	Cement Labourer	Chatham	8
7 Alma Place	Kemsley	John	41	Jane	34	General Labourer	Malling	6
8 Alma Place	Mew	William		Kate		Cement Labourer	Snodland	4(1)
[same] S	Burgess			Mary	40	Housekeeper	Malling	
9 Alma Place	Deen			Mildred	70		Birling	2
[same] R	Shayes	Alfred	60	Catherine	35		Snodland	
Ivymeath: Gardener					52	Blacksmith	Strood	5
Delamere House	Burgess	Thomas	66			Gardener	Snodland	3(2)
[same] S	Crosswell			Anne	20	Cook	Snodland	
[same] S	Moon			Alice	16	Housemaid	Wouldham	
Ivymeath	unoccupied							
Coachman's House	unoccupied							
9 Brook Street	Knell	James	44	Emily	45	Blacksmith	Langley	2
[same]	not returned							
8 Brook Street	Long	John	50			Stoker in mill	Borden	4(1)
7 Brook Street	Hazel	Thomas	44	Emma	40	Paper Mill Labourer	Chislehurst	6
6 Brook Street	Walker	Alfred	62	Charlotte	57	Cooper's Labourer	Charing	7
[same] R	Johnson			Ethel	2		Snodland	
5 Brook Street	Dorrell	Alfred	43	Sarah	42	Bargeman	Milton	6(1)
[same] L	Dedrick	Stanley	21			Clerk	Milton	
4 Brook Street	Leman	John	50	Mary	49	Gardener	Snodland	10
3 Brook Street	Fairburn	William	60	Lucy	55	Paper maker	Scotland	2
2 Brook Street	Chapman	George	40	Mary	36	Bricklayer	Wateringbury	4
1 Brook Street	Crane	Robert	54	Olive	50	Paper maker	St Mary Cray	2
Brooklyn House	not returned							
4 The Causeway	Penny			Caroline	59		Farnham	5
3 The Causeway	Russell	Henry	35	Emily	39	Tailor	Trossley	5
2 The Causeway	Cripps	John	38	Eliza	37	General Labourer	Wrotham	9

[same] R	Feaver	Edward	58		General Labourer	Boughton	
1 The Causeway	Clark	Edward	31	Elizabeth	General Labourer	Wrotham	2
Curtis House	Watts	George	34		General Labourer	Grays	7
[same] RRRRR	Lee	William	26		Bricklayer's Labourer	Snodland	
Thatched Cottage	Viney	George	55	Margaret	44 General Labourer	Dymchurch	7
next to Camb. Villa	West	Frederick	38	Emily	37 Gardener	Tunbridge	8
Cambridge Villa	Greenhalgh	William	48	Eliza	58 Paper maker	Lancashire	6
[same] R	Smith			Mary	59 Retired dressmaker	Bishops Lideard	
The Veles	Drummond			Amelia	70 Companion	Newport, IoW	0(3)
[same] S	Taylor			Eliza	35 Housekeeper	Rochester	
[same] S	Griffin			Jane	19 Housemaid	Maidstone	
Veles Cottage	Newman			Mary	26?	Addington	8
Baker & Seed Shop	Cook	William	36	Alice	38 Baker	Chatham	5(1)
[same] S	Hopkins			Beatrice	13 Domestic servant	Snodland	
Victory Bar House	Langridge	John	38	Alice	28 Beer retailer	Birling	2
Grocer's Shop	Deacon	Joseph	50	Ann	62 Grocer	St Paul's Cray	7(2)
[same] S	Metcalf	Frank	20		Grocer's porter	Halling	
1 Delamere Road	Dunn	George	32	Ellen	36 Baker	Eddington	3
2 Delamere Road	Crowhurst	Jesse	40	Matilda	35 General Labourer	Halling	7(1)
[same] L	Judges	Edwin	26		General Labourer	Snodland	
3 Delamere Road	Saul	Daniel	37	Mary	34 Paper Labourer	Surrey	8
Sweep's House	Bradley	John	46	Carry	40 Chimney Sweep	Romford	4
Sweet Shop	Adkins			Emma	42 Paper mill hand	Detling	6
Blacksmith's House	Tong	Matthew	59	Harriet	58 Blacksmith	Stalisfield	4
Red Lion	Crittenden	James	48	Maria	47 Publican	East Malling	6
Corn Shop	Wood	Henry	37	Marion	37 Seedsman	High Halden	9
Chemist's Shop	Morgan	Samuel	27		Chemist's assistant	Llandovery	1+
[same]	Tong	Charles	32	Jane	33 Blacksmith	Snodland	6
[same] R	Partridge			May	1	London	
Shoe Shop	Mills	Arthur	48	Emily	46 Boot maker	Halling	7
Coal Office	Tomlin	George	40	Eliza	40 Manager: Coal Office	East Malling	3
next to Coal Office	Thomas			Eliza	69	Snodland	2
1 Grapevine Villa	Wallis	Thomas	52	Ellen	49 General Labourer	New Hythe	2
2 Grapevine Villa	Church	Henry	36	Annie	37 General Labourer	Shoreham	2
Greengrocer's Shop	Glover	Edward	36	Maria	34 General Labourer	Frindsbury	8
[same] R	Crick	Ambrose	59		Greengrocer	Norfolk; unknown	
[same] R	Simmonds			Alma	14 Domestic servant	Snodland	
Hairdresser's Shop	Gotham	Frederick	37	Bessie	37 Hairdresser	Faversham	5

Draper's Shop	Ayers	William	45	Jane	38	Draper, etc.	New Romney	7
Butcher's Shop	Reeves	John	41	Harriet	37	Butcher	Old Brompton	2
Waterworks Office	Settatree	Albert	38	Sarah	40	Plumber, etc.	Westwell	10
1 Tanner's Terrace	Roots	Frederick	34	Edith	32	Cement Labourer	Trossley	4
2 Tanner's Terrace	Day	William	56	Ann	46	Farm Labourer	Otford	10(1)
[same] L	Goldsmith	Thomas	29			General Labourer	Surrey; unknown	
3 Tanner's Terrace	Masters	Philip	53	Emma	59	Thatcher	Birling	6(1)
4 Tanner's Terrace	Gash	William	32	Helen	26	Mariner; sea	Halling	2
5 Tanner's Terrace	Burke	James	34	Emily	32	Cement Cooper	Ireland	4
6 Tanner's Terrace	Bassett	Frederick	31	Emily	30	Cement Labourer	Snodland	'6(2)
[same] L	Mills	Henry	45			Hoopmaker; cooper	Capel, Surrey	
[same] L	Fairfield	James	28			Hoopmaker; cooper	Guildford	
7 Tanner's Terrace	Tanner	James	38	Isabel	26	Instructor; artillery	Maidstone	6
2 buildings	uninhabited							
1 Gorham's Row	Wingate	Thomas	46	Charlotte	46	General Labourer	Wouldham	5(1)
[same] L	Healey	James	42			Bricklayer's Labourer	not known	1
2 Gorham's Row	Phillips	William	71			Gen. Labourer (Deaf)	West Hoathly	1
3 Gorham's Row	Foreman	William	34	Kate	27	General Labourer	Chatham	7
4 Gorham's Row	Young	Charles	26	Harriet	34	Baker	Snodland	4
8 Hope Terrace	Alldridge			Rhoda	44		Brenchley	4(1)
	Holland	Robert	30			Cooper	Ireland	
7 Hope Terrace	Tremlett	John	60	Eliza	50	Platelayer; railway	Exeter	5
6 Hope Terrace	Wooding	Thomas	34	Mary	27	Engine Driver; cement	East Malling	5
5 Hope Terrace	Jeffrey	John	52	Mary	55	Bricklayer	Aylesford	5
4 Hope Terrace	Dracon	Rowland	25	Mary	24	Carpenter	Snodland	2
3 Hope Terrace	Wingate	William	37	Martha	31	Blacksmith's Labourer	Snodland	3+
[same]	Field			Mary	53	Laundress	Barling,Essex	3
2 Hope Terrace	Martin	Alfred	42	Mary	50	Chalk Labourer	Peckham	2
1 Hope Terrace	Beadle	Edward	40	Frances	43	Sailmaker	Halling	5
Anchor Place	Peters	Thomas	74	Emily	56	Living on own means	Dorking	4
Lyndale House	Winchester	Henry	30	Laura	28	Physician; surgeon	Milborne port	6(3)
[same] S	Ratcliffe			Rhoda	30	Nurse; dom. servant	Homewood	
[same] S	Tutheridge			Mary	23	Cook	Ditton	
[same] S	Collins			Anne	17	Housemaid	London	
Trefoy House	Mannel	John	20			Steam Crane Driver	Illogan,Cornwall	3
Hope Villa	Archer	Thomas	31	Rebecca	32	Congregatnl.Minister	Camberwell	5

The Rectory	Bingley	John	57	Mary	48	Rector of Snodland	Middlesex	12(6)
[same] S	Hucks			Mary	25	Cook	Strood	
[same] S	Seers			Alice	17	Housemaid	Snodland	
[same] S	Chittenden			Mahala	20	Parlourmaid	East Malling	
[same] S	Hunt	Arthur	16			Groom	Snodland	
1 Norman Cottages	Butler	Thomas	36	Eliza	32	Bricklayer	Hendon	3
2 Norman Cottages	Sheedy	Peter	43	Henrietta	35	Living on own means	Greenwich	5
3 Norman Cottages	Fletcher	John	27	Charlotte	22	Bricklayer	Halling	4
[same] R	Bond	William	10			Scholar	Dover	
Deengaar	Norman	Albert	40	Elizabeth	40	Butcher	Halling	3
Nepthalite Villa	Baker	Edward	80	Frances	80	Living on own means	Snodland	3
[same] R	Bateman			Edith	24	Companion	Snodland	
Butcher's Shop	Bateman	William	49	Mary	46	Butcher and Baker	St Mary Cray	8
Grocer's Shop	Honess	Frederick	30	Lily	30	Grocer, etc.	Wateringbury	4
Tobacconist's Shop	Lambert	Benjamin	41	Emma	38	Engineer	Greatbridge	7
Confectioner's Shop	Daley	John	34	Mary	30	Cooper	London	7(1)
[same] S	Bonning			Grace	14	Domestic servant	Halling	
Printer's Shop	Sprowdon	Charles	25			Printer	Strood	1+
[same]	Mullard	William	36	Jane	43	Police Constable	Penshurst	3(1)
[same] S	Bates			Anne	13	Domestic servant	Snodland	
Baker's Shop	Horton	John	35	Mahala	33	Baker	Leeds	3
Grocer's Shop	not returned							
[same]	Wolfe	John	32	Hannah	35	Miller's Carter	Mereworth	5(1)
Butcher's Shop	no residents							
1 Malling Road	Vallins	Herbert	46	Elizabeth	45	Cement miller	Greenhithe	3+
[same] R	Simmonds	Arthur	24	Clara	22	Blacksmith	Swanscombe	4(1)
[same] L	Simmonds	James	22			General Labourer	Sittingbourne	
2 Malling Road	Wellard	Thomas	64	Sarah	60	General Labourer	East Malling	7(1)
[same] L	Steel	William	55			General Labourer	East Malling	
3 Malling Road	Weaver	William	29	Annie	29	Cement Labourer	Snodland	2+
[same]	Davis	George	41	Harriet	27	Carpenter	Sturry	3
4 Malling Road	Weller	William	43	Angelina	38	Watchmaker	West Hoathly	5
5 Malling Road	Bailey	Thomas	51	Louisa	44	Butcher	New Hythe	6(1)
[same] L	Clegg	William	28			Assistant schoolmaster	Accrington	
6 Malling Road	Lambert	William	29	Jane	27	Engine Fitter	Darlington	5
7 Malling Road	Gay	George	52	Emma	47	Printer	Watford	3(2)
[same] L	Beadle	Richard	18			Printer	London	

Address	Surname	First name	Age	Spouse	Occupation	Birthplace	Col
8 Malling Road	Spice	Edwin	30	Charlotte	26 Printer's Foreman	Kennington	6(1)
[same] L	Collison	Stephen	19		Butcher	Headcorn	
9 Malling Road	Norman			Lucy	44 Laundress	Birling	7(5)
[same] R	Pankhurst			Ethel	6 Scholar	Aylesford	
[same] L	Dicker	Arthur	20		Butcher	London	
[same] LL	Godwin	Harold	32		Fitter, labourer	London	
[same] L	Fuller	Thomas	23		Bricklayer's Labourer	Fulham	
[same] L	Pries	Christian	20		Cement Labourer	Bloomsbury	
10 Malling Road	Payne	Henry	41	Hannah	37 Cooper	Chatham	11
11 Malling Road	Lambert	Benjamin	66	Elizabeth	55 Horse manager	Cradley, Worcs.	3
12 Malling Road	Dale	George	37	Phoebe	30 Hoop maker	Warnham	10(3)
[same] RR	Skinner	Victor	4 mo.	Frances	24	Malling/London	
[same] L	Mills	John	72		Hoopmaker	Albury, Surrey	
[same] LL	Ansell	Robert	43		Hoopmaker	Abingdon	
13 Malling Road	Gomer	John	43	Fanny	41 Cooper	Isle of Wight	7
14 Malling Road	Brasier	Edwin	60	Emma	53 Insurance Agent	Lenham	2
15 Malling Road	Barden	George	72	Harriet	67 Living on own means	Ditton	3
16 Malling Road	Quarrington	Edward	37	Eliza	34 General Labourer	Luton	7(1)
[same] L	Marshal	John	79		Living on own means	Portsmouth	
17 Malling Road	Williams	William	54	Louisa	50 Carter, Paper Mill	Plaxtol	4
18 Malling Road	Growes	Thomas	32	Ellen	30 Stoker	Maidstone	3
19 Malling Road	Boorman	John	58	Jane	52 Engine Driver; mill	Snodland	5(1)
[same] L	May	Thomas	45		General Labourer	Wooburn	
20 Malling Road	Bennett	John	46	Caroline	50 General Labourer	Plaxtol	5
Grocer's Shop	Moore	Thomas	59	Ann	57 Grocer	Snodland	3
1 Moore's Cottages	Phyall	John	51		General Labourer	Snodland	5
2 Moore's Cottages	Moore	John	50		Bricklayer	Snodland	4
Butcher's Shop	Moore	Arthur	30	Nellie	26 Butcher	Snodland	4(4)
[same] S	Hope	George	30		Butcher's assistant	Birling	
[same] S	Simmonds	Charles	17		Butcher's assistant	Snodland	
[same] SS	Tilley			Kate/Eliza	15 Domestic servants	Snodland	
Orchard Cottage	Gorham	William	70		Retired butcher	Snodland	3
1 Prospect Place	Norman	Daniel	60	Sarah	61 Straw dealer	Halling	6
2 Prospect Place	Wenham	James	40	Elizabeth	39 Cement Labourer	Loose	10
3 Prospect Place	Hensman	David	35	Clara	39 Stoker; Cement Works	Kingswalden	5
[same] R	Sharp			Eliza	19 Dressmaker	Kingswalden	
4 Prospect Place	Acott	Henry	38	Eliza	38 General Labourer	East Peckham	6(1)

[same] R	Brook	Peter		36		General Labourer	Mayfield	
[same] R	Brook	Jesse		32		General Labourer	Mayfield	
[same] L	Rawling		Elizabeth		28	Schoolteacher	Scarborough	
5 Prospect Place	Gurr	William	Mary	65	54	General Labourer	Winchelsea	8(3)
[same] L	Brant	William		16		Grocer	London	
[same] LL	Branser?	Annie	Florence	13	10	Scholars	Wouldham	
6 Prospect Place	Beadle	John	Ellen	31	28	Stoker at Paper Mill	Birling	4
7 Prospect Place	Simmonds	Henry	Annie	45	38	General Labourer	Maidstone	9
8 Prospect Place	Holt	James	Emily	51	42	General Labourer	High Wycombe	4(1)
[same] R	Butler		Mary		10	Scholar	Malling	
9 Prospect Place	May	William	Eliza	40	37	Cement Labourer	East Peckham	10
10 Prospect Place.	May	Charles		27		General Labourer	Snodland	2
[same] R	Lamb	Jesse	Maria	28	36	Waterman	Snodland	6
6 Covey Hall Place	Hammond		Sarah		32	Dressmaker; deaf/dumb	Strood	
5 Covey Hall Place	Gunner	William	Sarah	40	39	Cement Labourer	Ightham	8
4 Covey Hall Place	Bolton	James	Sarah	55	48	General Labourer	India	5
3 Covey Hall Place	Fletcher	William	Charlotte	40	37	General Labourer	Seal	7
[same] R	Jessup	Samuel		84		Living on sons	Sevenoaks	
2 Covey Hall Place	Over	Edward	Emily	51	50	General Labourer	East Malling	4(1)
[same] L	Knight	Arthur		28		General Labourer	Larkfield	
1 Covey Hall Place	Eyles	Sidney	Bertha	40	38	Cement miller	Chute, Wilts	8
12 Victoria Cottages	Baldwin	George	Frances	29	32	General Labourer	Maidstone	3
[same] R	Tutchener	William		10		Scholar	Snodland	
11 Victoria Cottages	Parker	William		49		Mechanical Engineer	Greenwich	4
10 Victoria Cottages	Beadle	William	Mary	34	28	Chalk Labourer	Halling	5
9 Victoria Cottages	Wallace	Richard	Sarah	45	45	General Labourer	Snodland	6(1)
[same] R	Woodhams		Florence		13	Scholar	Halling	
8 Victoria Cottages	Efford	Thomas	Maria	36	36	General Labourer	Snodland	5
[same] R	Freeman		Emily		10	Scholar	Maidstone	
7 Victoria Cottages	Ashdown	William	Emily	26	26	Cement Labourer	Leybourne	5
6 Victoria Cottages	Crowhurst	Benjamin		27		General Labourer	Snodland	2
5 Victoria Cottages	Woollett	Joseph	Mary	44	42	Blacksmith	Maidstone	5
4 Victoria Cottages	Waller	John	Emma	46	41	Cement Labourer	Kingswalden	9
3 Victoria Cottages	Tilley	George	Elizabeth	59	63	General Labourer	Tonbridge	5(2)
[same] L	Neil		Matilda		67	Living on own means	Maidstone	
[same] L	Eves	James		56		General Labourer	Borough Green	
[same] L	Palmer	George		68		Bricklayer	Malling	
2 Victoria Cottages	Knight	George	Eleanor	59	56	Disabled hip 6 yrs	Wrotham	5

Address	Surname	Forename	Age	Name2	Age2	Occupation	Birthplace	#
1 Victoria Cottages	Raggatt	Stephen	65	Elizabeth	64	General Labourer	Greywell, Hants.	3
Ironmonger's Shop	Dowsett	Thomas	54	Charlotte	41	Ironmonger	Springfield	2
Dairy House	Wells	Richard	32	Jane	31	General Labourer	Hadlow	4(1)
[same] R	May	William	6			Scholar	Bearsted	
[same] L	Ashdown	John	69			General Labourer	Malling	
1 Dorking Place	Curling	Harry	24	Elizabeth	24	Cement Labourer	Birling	2+
[same]	Efford	George	20	Edith	21	General Labourer	Snodland	2
2 Dorking Place	Taylor	Charles	40	May	44	Blacksmith	Luton	4
3 Dorking Place	Wooding	Jesse	30	Emma	26	Painter	Halling	4
4 Dorking Place	Browning	Alfred	32	Elizabeth	31	Coachman; domestic	Haywards Heath	3
5 Dorking Place	Baldwin	Frederick	43	Sarah	54	Cement Labourer	Meopham	2
6 Dorking Place	Perrott	Richard	58	Ellen	44	Carpenter	Paignton, Devon	10
7 Dorking Place	Mayhew			Mary	31	Charwoman	Tonbridge	4
1 Walgrave Place	Eves	Edward	25	Esther	24	General Labourer	Maidstone	4
2 Walgrave Place	Howard	John	50	Eliza	51	Paper maker	Lynn, Norfolk	4
[same] R	Bromley	Augustus	6			Scholar	Maidstone	
3 Walgrave Place	Bridgland	Henry	35	Ellen	34	Cement Labourer	Goudhurst	7
4 Walgrave Place	Buss	George	26	Minnie	25	General Labourer	Staplehurst	4
Orchard Cottage	Buxton	Charles	51	Mary	42	Blacksmith	Rattleston	3(1)
[same] L	Nelson	John	23			Hammerman	Chatham	
1 Orchard Cottages	Woodruff	James	59	Harriet	55	Cement miller	Margate	6
2 Orchard Cottages	Peters	Thomas	53	Harriet	55	Lime burner	Halling	7
3 Orchard Cottages	Daniel			Emily	42		Strood	5
4 Orchard Cottages	Thorndycraft	Edward	39	Frances	37	Cement Labourer	Sutton Valence	6
5 Orchard Cottages	Wallace	Richard	74	Jemima	74	Cement Labourer	Aylesford	4
[same] R	Stewart	Louis	13			Scholar	Snodland	
6 Orchard Cottages	Garniss	John	37	Mary	32	Coachman; domestic	Barrow, Humber	7
7 Orchard Cottages	Judges	Alfred	51	Matilda	47	Limeburner	Yalding	11
8 Orchard Cottages	Curling	Robert	51	Catherine	55	General Labourer	Iwade	4
[same] R	Whitmore	James	16			General Labourer	Gravesend	
9 Orchard Cottages	Lock	Henry	34	Louisa	33	Millwright, etc.	Thetford, Norfk.	6
10 Orchard Cottages	Evans	Charles	34	Sara	31	Bargebuilder	Stockbury	6
11 Orchard Cottages	Peters	Thomas	34	Mary	33	Steam Crane Driver	Halling	7
12 Orchard Cottages	Gower	Jonathan	60	Susan	54	Cement Labourer	Meopham	5
13 Orchard Cottages	Judges	George	36	Ellen	38	General Labourer	Maidstone	6
[same] R	Hale			Harriet	79	Living on sons	Henley on Thames	
14 Orchard Cottages	Hilder			Sarah	63	Living on own means	Cuxton	2

			WEST		SIDE		
1 Malling Road	Bishop	Harry	38	Sarah	38	Bricklayer	Birling	9
2 Malling Road	Durling	Joseph	26	Sarah	24	Tailor	Chatham	4
3 Malling Road	Kite	William	34	Emma	33	Shipwright	Bapchild	3
4 Malling Road	Hedgecock	Charles	30	Floremce	24	Cooper	Faversham	3
5 Malling Road	Pemble			Isabel	38	Dressmaker	Halling	3
6 Malling Road	Ashburner	James	55			Paper finisher	Grampound, Corn.	2
7 Malling Road	Moore	Charles	25	Lily	25	Dairyman	Snodland	3
8 Malling Road	Moore	John	30	Mary	30	Grocer	Snodland	2
9 Malling Road	Johnson	James	31	Sophia	29	Cooper	Strood	6
10 Malling Road	Beadle	Henry	39	Catherine	34	Insurance Agent	Halling	6
11 Malling Road	Norrington	Thomas	43	Martha	45	Cooperage supervisor	Borden	3
12 Malling Road	Tremaine	Jesse	39	Elizabeth	34	Cement Labourer	Cutham [Cudham?]	4+
[same] L	Foreman	Edward	23			Cement Labourer	Hythe	
13 Malling Road	Davis	Willie	28	Fanny	28	Paper maker	Sutton Courtney	4
14 Malling Road	Rust	John	47	Sarah	65	Cooper	Limehouse	2
15 Malling Road	Mayger	Joseph	46	Martha	48	General Labourer	Leeds, Kent	6
16 Malling Road	Mason	Robert	29	Clara	30	Oil and Soap Merchant	Scotland	6(1)
[same] S	Knott	Walter	16			Domestic servant	Snodland	
17 Malling Road	Woolmer	Alexander	54	Jane	48	Waterman; barge	Rochester	4+
[same] R	Walls			Jane	5	Scholar	Snodland	
[same] L	Letchford	Elias	22			Steam Crane Driver	Halling	1
18 Malling Road	Draycon	Alfred	51	Abigail	52	Plumber, Glazier, Painter	Chatham	4
19 Malling Road	Elliott	Harry	25	Alice	24	Plasterer	Maidstone	3
20 Malling Road	Davis	Stephen	57	Ellen	60	Paper finisher	Sutton Courtney	2
21 Malling Road	Stunt	William	57	Catherine	55	C. Clerk	Brighton	3
22 Malling Road	Spice	Arthur	26	Clara	26	Paper dresser	Kennington	5(1)
[same] R	Gay			Florrie	23		Snodland	
23 Malling Road	Masters			Harriet	61	Laundress	[not given]	2(1)
[same] L	Goldsmith	Albert	23			Labourer at Coal Wharf	Little Peckham	
24 Malling Road	Peck	William	24	Clara	22	Carpenter	West Malling	2
25: Brook House	Smith	Joseph	65			Surgeon; G.P.	Horsley, Gloucs.	2(1)+
[same] S	Bartlett			Emma	38	Housekeeper	Maidstone	
[same]	Faraday	Alfred	50	Emily	44	New Church Minister	Fenton, Staffs.	2
1 Bull Field	Baker	James	76	Jane	70	Living on own means	Snodland	2
2 Bull Field	Beadle	Walter	34	Maria	34	Engine Driver	Snodland	2

Address	Surname	Forename	Age		Occupation	Birthplace	
3 Bull Field	Sears	John	54	Esther	48	Bricklayer	Birling	5
4 Bull Field	Phyall	Henry	45	Eliza	44	Bricklayer	Boughton Monch.	7
5 Bull Field	Russell	William	64	Sophia	59	Bricklayer	Charing	2
6 Bull Field	Walburton	Robert	41	Ann	35	Paper maker	Stone Clough, Lan.	7
7 Bull Field	Halford	Henry	49	Emily	45	Cooper; cement works	Bourne, Lincs.	7
8 Bull Field	Finch	Frederick	35	Julia	26	Chalk Labourer	Harrietsham	4
9 Bull Field	Hucks	Henry	56	Elizabeth	56	Lime Labourer	Plaxtol	5
10 Bull Field	Jenner	William	29	Annie	26	General Labourer	Malling	5+
[same]	Abnett	Frederick	23			Engine Driver	Maidstone	1
11 Bull Field	Foreman	Jesse	30	Jane	28	General Labourer	Rochester	6
12 Bull Field	Barnden	Thomas	44	Eliza	43	Lime Labourer	Ryarsh	5
13 Bull Field	Wells			Sarah	50	Living on own means	Staplehurst	
14 Bull Field	Woodger	William	51	Louisa	42	Labourer	East Malling	5
15 Bull Field	Wellard	George	29	Mercy	31	Cement Labourer	Ryarsh	3
16 Bull Field	Seagull	William	61	Sarah	61	Bargeman	Strood	3(1)
1 Portland Place	May	William	28	Mildred	28	Paper maker	Alan Wood, Cumb.	6
2 Portland Place	West	William	33	Mary	32	Bricklayer	Ryarsh	8
3 Portland Place	Barker	James	56	Mary	56	Cooper	Maidstone	3
4 Portland Place	Wickham	Theodore	35	Hannah	35	Blacksmith	Rotherfield	8
5 Portland Place	Barker	Robert	25			Cooper	Stepney	4
[same] R	Tunbridge			Emily	56		Chadwell	
6 Portland Place	Chantler	Peter	39	Elizabeth	29	Cement tester	Tudley	5
7 Portland Place	Wells	George	37	Fanny	35	Cement Labourer	Brenchley	9(1)
[same] L	Shoobridge	James	19			General Labourer	Tudely	
8 Portland Place	Williams	John	40	Rose	37	Bargeman	Sittingbourne	8
9 Portland Place	Gibson	Benjamin	36	Florence	21	Cooper	Limehouse	3
10 Portland Place	Walters			Elizabeth	57	Living on own means	Cork, Ireland	5(4)
[same] LLLL	George			Millicent	15		Wingham	
11 Portland Place	Giles	Caleb	35	Mary	39	General Labourer	Sutton Valence	9
[same] R	Rhodes	Harry	31			Bricklayer's Labourer	Headcorn	
12 Portland Place	Wibley	Frederick	49	Julia	49	Lime Labourer	Trottiscliffe	3
13 Portland Place	Mitchell	Josia	46	Mary	60	General Labourer	Ditton	3
14 Portland Place	Swan	Edward	26	Eliza	26	Bargeman	Milton	4
[same] R	Bridger			Clara	16		West Farleigh	
1 Mayatt's Cottages	Fowler	John	43	Eliza	42	Cooper	Faversham	7
2 Mayatt's Cottages	Longhurst			Annie	42		Snodland	7
3 Mayatt's Cottages	Garrett	Ernest	44	Sarah	44	Blacksmith	Strood	4
4 Mayatt's Cottages	Peck	James	46	Lucy	45	Carpenter	Thorndon, Suffolk	9

1 Mole's Cottages	Russell	George	47	Mary	46	Bricklayer	Charing	5
2 Mole's Cottages	Mole	Walter	60	Catherine	59	Bricklayer	not known	4
1 Martin's Cottages	Knott	George	48	Emily	35	Labourer	Wouldham	2
[same] R	Austen	George	14				Stone	
2 Martin's Cottages	Hopper	William	42	Sarah	39	Signalman; port	Margate	7
1 Moore's Cottages	Mills	William	22	Sarah	28	Cooper; machine hand	Halling	4
2 Moore's Cottages	Newman	Charles	55	Anne	53	General Labourer	Plaxtol	5(1)
[same] RR	Woollett			Mary	76	Seamstress	Maidstone	
[same] L	Faucett	Henry	45			Cement Labourer	Peckham, Kent	
3 Moore's Cottages	Blackman	William	25	Anne	20	Cement Labourer	Halling	2
4 Moore's Cottages	Peters	Henry	40	Catherine	57	Shoemaker	Snodland	2(1)
[same] Friend	Taylor			Alice	22		New Hythe	
5 Moore's Cottages	Bailey	Charles	44	Ellen	40	Mill Labourer	Maidstone	8
[same] R	White			Esther	18	Paper Mill hand	Snodland	
[same] RR?	Bailey			Anne	74	On the parish	Maidstone	
6 Moore's Cottages	Adams	William	37	Annie	33	Cement Labourer	Snodland	8
Windham House	Jackson	Robert	65	Sarah	67	Harness maker	Wymondham	3(1)+
[same] S	Woolley			Lydia	18	Domestic servant	Malling	
[same]	Hoysted	Charles	46			Clerk in Holy Orders	Ireland	1
2 High Street	Corney	George	40	Sophia	40	Grocer and Draper	Brighton	9(2)
[same] S	Atkinson	James	25			Grocer's assistant	East Malling	
	Taylor			Eliza	31	Domestic servant	Hadlow	
3 High Street	Millidge	Benjamin	55	Jessie	54	Chemist and Dentist	Newport, IoW	3(1)
[same] S	Bradley			Sarah	16	Domestic servant	Malling	
4 High Street	Stevens	Thomas	59	Eliza	46	Retired ship inspector	Portsea	13
[same] R	Jones			Eliza	73	Living on own means	Liverpool	
5 High Street	Knott	Thomas	47	Annie	49	Shoemaker	Burham	6
6 High Street	Chatfield	Harry	30	Elizabeth	48	Watchmaker	Maresfield, Sussex	3
7 High Street	Fissenden	William	59	Mary	51	Labourer	Birling	5
8 High Street	Bolger	George	34	Elizabeth	35	Shoemaker	London	8
[same] R	Bennett			Jane	70		Hadlow	
	Danells	Alfred	20			Grocer's assistant	Linton	
9 High Street	Stone	Walter	35	Mary	30	Draper and Outfitter	Canterbury	11(4)
[same] S	Peck	Charles	18			Draper's assistant	Malling	
[same] S	Terry			Rose	21	Dressmaker	Maidstone	
[same] S	Weeden			Alice	16	Domestic servant	Snodland	
[same] S	Cook			Florence	15	Domestic servant	Strood	

10 High Street	Standen	George	38	Ann	Baker	Maidstone	8
11 High Street	Judges	John	46	Eliza	Greengrocer	Yalding	5(1)
[same] L	Nye	Edward	28		General Labourer	Rochester	
12 High Street	Hodges	John	40	Hannah	Fireman, cement works	West Malling	8
13 High Street	Figgess	Edgar	32	Edith	Draper, etc.	St Mary Cray	6(1)
[same] S	Chapman		17	Harriett	Domestic servant	Meopham	
The Lodge	Joy	William	44	Eliza	Manager of cement works	Ryarsh	10(2)
[same] S	Bodkin		28	Elizabeth	Domestic servant	Luton, Kent	
[same] S	Hawkes		41	Emma	Domestic servant	West Malling	
1 Constitution Hill	Malt	John	48	Bridget	General Labourer	Hockwold, Norf.	5
2 Constitution Hill	Crowhurst		67	Elizabeth		Luddesdown	2
3 Constitution Hill	Hawks	Henry	39		Coal Heaver	Snodland	7
4 Constitution Hill	Master		66	Mary		Birling	5
same] RRRR	Huggett	Henry	31	Clara	Cement Labourer	Aylesford	
5 Constitution Hill	Appleton	Thomas	48	Mary	Bricklayer	Windsor	8
Monk's Head	Burgess	Alban	35	Emma	Licensed Victualler	Halling	5
1 Clara Place	Dulton	William	57		Paper maker	St Pauls Cray	1
2 Clara Place	Baker		62	Harriet		Birling	2
3 Clara Place	Adams		59	Ann		Luddesdown	2
Paper Makers' Arms	Andrews	Thomas	54	Ann	General Labourer	Peckham, Kent	7(3)
[same]	Blanche	John	53		General Labourer	Lewes	
[same]	Pankhurst	Demetrius	28		General Labourer	Hadlow	
[same]	Collins	Richard	43		General Labourer	East Peckham	
1 Kemp's Cottages	Hards	Thomas	57	Hannah	Foreman of Roads	Hull, Yorkshire	4(2)
[same]	Olding	George	35		General Labourer	Maidstone	
[same] S + son	Hayes			Frances	Housekeeper	Snodland	
2 Kemp's Cottages	Chandler	John	46	Emma	Bargeman	Dover	7
3 Kemp's Cottages	Wooding	Richard	29	Mary	Waterman; barge	Snodland	2+
[same]	Wooding	Richard	53	Jane	Labourer	East Malling	4
4 Kemp's Cottages	Adams	Thomas	38	Emma	Cement Labourer	Luddesdown	6
1 Temperance Terr.	Stone	James	46	Louisa	Bricklayer	Maidstone	10
2 Temperance Terr.	Masters	Thomas	38	Hannah	General Labourer	Snodland	9
3 Temperance Terr.	Davis	Frank	36	Sarah	Paper: machine man	Sutton Courtney	9
[same] RR	Hughes		28	Esther		Stuart's Lane, Lon.	
4 Temperance Terr.	Harris	Henry	53	Mary	Chalk Labourer	Snodland	11
Constitution Hill	Rotherham	Henry	48	Cordelia	Cooper	St. George: E Lond.	11
1 Pierson's Cotts.	Hogben	James	58	Anne	General Labourer	Bought. Malherbe	2
2 Pierson's Cotts.	Crowson	Robert	56	Jane	Labourer	Wrotham	2+

140

Address	Surname	Forename	Forename2	Age	Occupation	Birthplace	Col
3 Pierson's Cotts. [same]	McCoy	Charles		56	Labourer	Tovil	1
4 Pierson's Cotts.	Goble	Thomas	Anne	33	General Labourer	Lower Halstow	7
1 Luckford's Cotts.	Harris	Henry	Frances	32	Labourer	Snodland	3
2 Luckford's Cotts.	Knell	Laurence	Sarah	71	Labourer	Brenchley	2
3 Luckford's Cotts.	Judges	Stephen	Fanny	42	General Labourer	Yalding	5
[same] R	Driver	John	Harriet	75	General Labourer	West Malling	6
4 Luckford's Cotts.	Hodges	Edward		20	General Labourer	Ryarsh	
5 Luckford's Cotts.	Hawks		Eliza		On Parish	Snodland	3
6 Luckford's Cotts.	Oates	John	Charlotte	47	Cement Labourer	Dublin	5
1 Victoria Terrace	Dadd	George	Ruth	56	Limeburner	Dallington, Sussex	4
2 Victoria Terrace	Austen	William	Sarah	29	Cement Labourer	Brenchley	4
3 Victoria Terrace	Digby	George	Eliza	40	Paper Mill Labourer	Black Notley, Essex	8
4 Victoria Terrace	Godden	John	Maria	41	Cement Labourer	Stansted	10
[same] L	Pankhurst	Tom		47	Gamekeeper	Birling	6(3)
[same]	Capon	Harry		23	Paper Mill Labourer	Snodland	
[same]	Brown	Alick		56	Cooper	Felling, Durham	
Constitution Hill	Dadson		Rose		Housekeeper	Peckham, Kent	
Birling Road	Gammon	John	Jane	49	Baker	Canterbury	9
[same] R	Weaire	Frederick	Emily	33	Manager; Grocer/ Draper	East Grinstead	6(3)
[same] L	Goodwin	William		18	Draper's assistant	East Grinstead	
[same] S	Moon	Frederick		21	Grocer's assistant	Wouldham	
Birling Road	Taylor	William		17	Grocer's assistant	Hadlow	
[same] R	Bennett		Edith		Domestic servant	Snodland	
1 Tomlyn's Cotts.	Russell		Amy		Shopkeeper	Ash	2
[same] RRR	Lane		Amy	61	Shop assistant	Swanscombe	
2 Tomlyn's Cotts.	Bedell	John	Harriett	65	General Labourer	Mereworth	6
3 Tomlyn's Cotts.	Tomlin	Away on barge		16	Housekeeper	Offham	
4 Tomlyn's Cotts.	Simmon	George		51	Plumber	Maidstone	1
5 Tomlyn's Cotts.	Hook		Jane	56	Laundress	Ryarsh	3
6 Tomlyn's Cotts.	Hills	James	Jane	52	General Labourer	Brasted	2
7 Tomlyn's Cotts.	Hayler	Thomas	Susan	31	Cement miller	Snodland	4
[same] L	Holman	Henry	Clara	34	Plumber	Tovil	4(1)
8 Tomlyn's Cotts.	Bran	William	Isabel	54	General Labourer	Snodland	4
9 Tomlyn's Cotts.	Sales	Charles		35	General Labourer	Westerham	3
10 Tomlyn's Cotts.	Wisking	George		39	Cooper	London	6
11 Tomlyn's Cotts.	Austen	Harry	Eleanor	33	General Labourer	Riverbridge, Suss.	5
	Dearing	John	Mary	56	Chalk Labourer	Wrotham	

141

12 Tomlyn's Cotts.	Turner	Thomas	47	Sophia	44	General Labourer	Grendon, Bucks.	8(1)
[same]	Dyke	William	27			General Labourer	Kemsing	
13 Tomlyn's Cotts.	Lamb	Jesse	73			Parish and other help	Halling	1
14 Tomlyn's Cotts.	May	Walter	23	Marriane	25	Milkman	Hadlow	
[same]	Andrews	Harry	23			Cement Labourer	Snodland	
1 Birling Road	Chalklin	Daniel	27	Rose	28	Stationary engine driver	Burham	3
2 Birling Road	Hodges	William	43	Diana	33	Cement Labourer	Leybourne	7
3 Birling Road	Sykes	Thomas	39	Amy	35	General Labourer	Dorking	8
4 Birling Road	Mortimer	James	31	Mary	40	Farm Labourer	Wendover, Bucks	6+
[same]	Lovell	John	72	Eliza	65	Post work	Seal	2
5 Birling Road	Coomber	Richard	34	Rose	28	Bricklayer	Southborough	9
[same]	Coomber	Arthur	21			Blacksmith	Hadlow	
6 Birling Road	Plummer	Harry	46	Sarah	48	Lime burner	North Cray	11(1)
[same] L	Hawks	James	45			[none given]	Snodland	
7 Birling Road	Wheeler	Edward	37	Susan	42	Shoemaker	Maidstone	9(3)
[same] L	Stevens	John	46			Parish and other help	Hawkhurst	[imbecile]
8 Birling Road	Spice			Sarah	58	Dressmaker	Strood	1+
[same] R	Durling	James	23			Labourer	Chatham	1
9 Birling Road	Phillips	Stephen	78			Retired	Snodland	2
10 Birling Road	Wallis	William	30	Rosa	33	Plumber and Painter	East Malling	5+
[same]	Brixey			Isabella	62	Charwoman	Caithness	1
11 Birling Road	Herrington	Ambrose	50	Eliza	48	Cement Labourer	Strood	8
12 Birling Road	Bran			Mary	54	Mangling; wash	Meopham	6
[same] R [son]	Stevens	Tom	36			Labourer	Meopham	
[same] R [son]	Stevens	Henry	20			Labourer	Snodland	
13 Birling Road	Patton	Charles	60			Lime Labourer	Wakes Colne	4
[same] L	Knight			Lucy	17	Paper Mill hand	Cuxton	
14 Birling Road	Bishop	William	50	Harriett	50	Chalk Labourer	East Peckham	5
[same] R	Capon	James	60			Farm Labourer	Ryarsh	
15 Birling Road	Collins	Henry	40	Eliza	36	General Carrier	Plaxtol	8
16 Birling Road	Oliver	Charles	38	Eliza	38	General Labourer	Maidstone	9
17 Birling Road	Fullman	Henry	56			Coal Labourer	Birling	3+
[same] RR	Phillips			Ann	21		Snodland	
[same]	Leman	John	75			Past work; pensioner	Snodland	1
18 Birling Road	Dack	Samuel	38	Eliza	34	General Labourer	Maidstone	8
19 Birling Road	Skinner	Samuel	49	Caroline	50	Chalk Labourer	East Malling	7
20 Birling Road	Sweetser	William	37	Elizabeth	34	Chalk Labourer	Birling	4(1)+
[same]	Brooks	Thomas	49			Foreman; cement works	Rochester	1

21 Birling Road	Langridge	John	37	Sarah	39	Cement Labourer	Hever	9
22 Birling Road	Bardoe	John	51	Agnes	50	Cooper	Northfleet	4
23 Birling Road	Shirley	William	34	Lydia	34	Cooper; cement works	Maidstone	6
24 Birling Road	Coomber	Frederick	34	Caroline	34	Cement Labourer	Loose	8
25 Birling Road	Hayler	William	70	Ann	71	General Labourer	Seal	2
26 Birling Road	Beadle	Frederick	30	Fanny	28	Chalk Labourer	Halling	3
27 Birling Road	Morris	William	26	Charlotte	21	Cement Labourer	Halling	3
28 Birling Road	Banfield	Thomas	34	Elizabeth	33	General Labourer	Wrotham	3
29 Birling Road	Kimber	George	44	Anne	43	General Labourer	Limpsfield, Surrey	8
30 Birling Road	Fullman	George	24	Frances	24	Lime Labourer	Snodland	4
31 Birling Road	Hayes			Susanna	66	Washerwoman	Capel	2
				Cecilia	9	Scholar	Commercial Rd. [London]	
[same] R	Still							
32 Birling Road	Fulcher	Alfred	25	Clara	25	General Labourer	Suffolk, unknown	4
33 Birling Road	Feaver	Thomas	26	Julia	26	Cement Labourer	Capel	5
34 Birling Road	Burt			Eliza	29		Snodland	4
35 Birling Road	Hayward	Thomas	23	Blanche	22	Cement Labourer	Thurnham	2
36 Birling Road	Parks	Walter	38	Eliza	36	General Labourer	London	8
37 Birling Road	Heather	Isaac	59			General Labourer	Graffham, Sussex	3
38 Birling Road	Rotherham	Henry	21	Georgina	20	Cooper	Strood	3
39 Birling Road	Friend			Mercy	49	Paper Mill hand	Rainham	1
40 Birling Road	Cunningham	George	42	Caroline	41	Cement Labourer	Shipborne	5(1)
[same] L	Crocker			Annie	46	Seamstress	Snodland	
Bull Hotel	Gowar	Richard	50	Jane	51	Licensed victualler	Birling	7(1)
[same] S	Waghorn			Rachel	26	Domestic servant	Halling	
Covey Hall Farm	Rayner	William	31	Ellen	30	Farm servant	Stockbury	7
[same]	Gouge	George	39	Rosa	36	Farm servant	Sittingbourne	8
The Institute	Mayger	John	53	Amelia	52	General Labourer	Leeds, Kent	4
1 Dover Terrace	Atkinson	John	55	Ann	51	General Labourer	East Malling	6(2)
[same] L	Moody	John	32			Cooper	Bethnal Green	
2 Dover Terrace	Hughes	George	50	Emma	53	Barge builder	Milton, Sitt.	4
3 Dover Terrace	Beadle	Charles	61	Harriett	57	Chalk Labourer	Hadlow	12
[same] R	Parris			Mary	84		Aylesbury	
4 Dover Terrace	Millum	Charles	54	Alice	43	Coal porter	Yalding	2
5 Dover Terrace	Thomas	William	49	Frances	37	Sail maker	Swansea	6
6 Dover Terrace	Coulter	William	37	Ellen	35	Cement miller	Halling	4
7 Dover Terrace	Woodin	Henry		Eliza	68	Painter	Snodland	4
1 Holboro' Road	Brook						Hawkhurst	2
2 Holboro' Road	Crowhurst			Elizabeth	51		Riverhead	3

143

Address	Surname	Forename	Forename	Age	Occupation	Birthplace	Children
Belle Vue Villa	Brown		Maria	64	Living on own means	Marylebone	2
May Cottage	Goodwin	George	Harriett	60	Agricultural Labourer	Hartley	4
Providence House	Hodgkinson	William	Jane	35	Schoolmaster	Clitheroe, Lancs.	8(2)
[same] R	Clegg		Mary	19	Schoolmistress	Accrington	
[same] S	Vousden		Mary	19	Domestic servant	Goudhurst	
[same] S	Warburton		Hannah	15	Domestic servant	Sutton Courtney	
1 Providence Place	Mannering	William	Mary	31	General Labourer	Maidstoen	4
2 Providence Place	Day		Sarah	73	Seamstress	Burham	1
3 Providence Place	Blunt	Alfred		37	General Labourer	Gravesend	5(1)
[same] S	Brise		Elizabeth	32	Housekeeper	Bucks.	
4 Providence Place	Jackson	Benjamin	Emma	50	Bargeman	Chatham	2
5 Providence Place	Woolmer		Annie	32	Dressmaker	Platt	5(1)
6 Providence Place	Tutchener		Mary	43	Paper sorter	Frant	5+
[same]	Tutchener	Thomas	Fanny	29	General Labourer	Capel	2
7 Providence Place	Lambeth	James	Sophia	71	Lime burner	Rochester	5+
[same]	Shea	Michael		37	Cooper	Ireland	1+
[same]	Barton		Catherine	87	Parish and other help	City of London	1
8 Providence Place	Hammond	George	Sarah	35	Cement Labourer	Brenchley	6(1)
9 Providence Place	Flint	Silas	Charlotte	54	General Labourer	Capel	4
10 Providence Place	Waller	James	Emma	55	Cement Labourer	Kingswalden	2
11 Providence Place	Datner	Edward	Jemima	49	Cutter man; paper	Sutton-at-Hone	5
12 Providence Place	Johnson	John	Elizabeth	57	Jobbing carpenter	Dartford	2
Bryn Cree	Dedrick	William	Minnie	33	Cashier and accountant	Milton, Sittingb.	7(2)
[same] R	Emerson		Julia	67	Living on own means	Norwich	
[same] S	Butler		Grace	16	Domestic servant	Sissinghurst	
[same] S	Penny		Estelle	14	Domestic servant	Snodland	
1 Jessamine Cotts.	Payne	Charles	Louise	45	Machine sawyer	Kingsnorth	5
2 Jessamine Cotts.	Honess	David	Evangeline	30	Carpenter/ wheelwright	Marden	4
3 Jessamine Cotts.	Mitchell	George	Harrietta	46	Labourer	Bush	7
4 Jessamine Cotts.	Fermer	Alfred	Mary	38	Paper maker	Leeds, Kent	5
5 Jessamine Cotts.	Mair	Samuel	Harriett	45	Cement Labourer	Malling	3+
[same] R	Thorp	William		34	Cement Labourer	Mereworth	
[same]	Wheeler		Mary		Needle-woman	Malling	1
6 Jessamine Cotts.	Sutton	John	Emily	34	Bricklayer	Offham	7
7 Jessamine Cotts.	Beasley	William	Lizzie	30	General Labourer	Sandgate	3
8 Jessamine Cotts.	Dunford	George		50	General Labourer	Oxford	1+
[same]	Mansfield		Emily		Domestic nurse	Cranbrook	1
1 Providence Terr.	Peters	Nathan	Annie	38	Tea dealer; grocer	Snodland	8

Address	Surname	Forename		Forename 2	Age	Occupation	Birthplace	
2 Providence Terr.	Fielder	Edwin		Harriett	55 39	Bricklayer	Snodland	6
3 Providence Terr.	Tillbrook	James		Harriett	51 48	Miller; out of work	Gt. Hockham	4
4 Providence Terr.	Efford	Edward		Esther	46 52	Labourer	Snodland	7
5 Providence Terr.	Foreman	Frederick		Georgina	29 28	Cement Labourer	Chatham	5
1 Vine Cottage	Martin			Eliza	71	Living on own means	Ash	1
2 Vine Cottage	Brown	Joe/Jack?		Esther	31 34	General Labourer	Wybaston, Beds.	4
[same] R	Cassel	Joseph			71	Retired pen.; Civil Service	Chatham	
1 Magnolia Terrace	Efford	William		Anne	49 51	Labourer	Snodland	9
[same] L	Efford	Samuel			72		Snodland	
2 Magnolia Terrace	Wright			Sarah	76	General Labourer	Snodland	
[same] R	Platt	Bernard			12		East Malling	4(1)+
[same] L	McCoy	Henry			44	Scholar	London	
3 Magnolia Terr.	Knight	Henry		Dorcas	29 25	Gas fitter	Snodland	1
[same]	Tilbrook	William		Alberta	30 23	General Labourer	Ryarsh	3+
4 Magnolia Terr.	Lambeth	William		Caroline	38 35	Carrier	Carbrook, Norf.	2
Prospect Cottage	Churchill	Henry		Isabella	44 47	Cooper	Snodland	5
Alma Villa	Honess	Edward		Harriett	55 54	Carpenter	Lambeth, London	2
[same]	Efford	William		Alice	23 23	Carpenter	Goudhurst	4+
[same]	Judges	Alfred			28	Bricklayer	Snodland	3+
1 Mount Pleasant	Lambeth	Thomas		Icitt	34 27	Fireman (sick)	Marden	1
[same] S	Attwood			Rose	13	General Labourer	Snodland	8(1)
2 Mount Pleasant	Bolton	Alfred		Harriett	45 40	Domestic servant	Burham	
3 Mount Pleasant	Hawks	Henry		Eliza	66 62	Ag./Chalk Labourer	Charing	5
[same] S	Chapman			Alice	20	Carpenter	Snodland	5(1)
4 Mount Pleasant	Davis			Augusta	38	Domestic servant	Meopham	
5 Mount Pleasant	Bean	Thomas		Sarah	28 29	Living on own means	City of London	4
6 Mount Pleasant	Woodruff	Thomas		Caroline	35 32	Oilman colour	Gipsy Hill	4
7 Mount Pleasant	Cheeseman	George		Ellen	37 32	Sailmaker	Snodland	2
[same] R	Fulcher	Harry			14	General Labourer	Canterbury	3+
[same]	Adams	William			19	General Labourer	Strood	
8 Mount Pleasant	Fuller	George		Emma	44 41	Carpenter	Chatham	1
[same] R	Diprose	William			73	General Labourer	Salehurst, Sussex	6
9 Mount Pleasant	Wallis	James		Martha	29 28	Farm Labourer	Hadlow	
1 Evan's Cottages	Jones	Henry		Caroline	48 47	Dry Cooper	Snodland	5
2 Evan's Cottages	Evans	William		Maria	42 44	Bricklayer	Wickham	7
Reed's Cottage	Towner	George		Emma	48 53	Marine engine driver	Ightham	8
[same] R	Saunders			Florence	7	Chalk Labourer	Capel	4+
[same]	Burgess	Stephen			56	Scholar	Snodland	
						General Labourer	Snodland	2

Rose Cottage	Jessup	Amos	38	Ellen	30	Lime burner	Southfleet	7
1 Holboro' Terrace	Glover	Frederick	45	Sarah	48	Carpenter	Wouldham	6
2 Holboro' Terrace	Wingate	Rayden	53	Sarah	50	Stationary engine driver	Wouldham	6
3 Holboro' Terrace	Freeland	Spencer	33	Sophia	34	Oilman colour	Sedlescombe	2
4 Holboro' Terrace	Bennett	George	41	Isabella	39	General Labourer	Wrotham	8
5 Holboro' Terrace	Knott	James	24	Minnie	22	Chalk Labourer	Halling	4
6 Holboro' Terrace	Wallis	Charles	32	Ellen	23	Cement Labourer	Snodland	5
7 Holboro' Terrace	Jefferys	John	27	Sarah	29	Bricklayer	Maidstone	3
8 Holboro' Terrace	Trowell	Edward	63	Jane	59	General Labourer	Detling	4+
[same]	Lamb	Moses	51			Bricklayer's Labourer	Halling	1
9 Holboro' Terrace	Morris	Robert	19			Butcher	Lenham	1
1 Princes Terrace	Holman	Thomas	34	Agnes Gertrude	30	Grocer & provision mcht	Nettlested	4(1)
[same] S	Knight				16	Domestic servant	Snodland	
2 Princes Terrace	Mannering	William	52	Sarah	54	Wheelwright	Maidstone	4
3 Princes Terrace	Morris	Charles	48	Susan	48	Sawyer	Goudhurst	10(1)
4 Princes Terrace	Drury	Henry	42	Sarah	41	Wheelwright	Luton, Kent	7
5 Princes Terrace	Freeman	James	44	Eliza	44	General Labourer	Loose	6
'Prince of Wales'	Chittenden	William	67	Sarah	71	Licensed victualler	Wrotham	3(1)
[same] S	Drury			Emma	16	Domestic servant	Luton, Kent	
1 Sawpit Cottages	Wallis	William	51	Sarah	54	Dry Cooper	Aylesford	5
2 Sawpit Cottages	Weeden	William	52	Sarah	54	General Labourer	Snodland	6
Princes Cottage	Fletcher	Thomas	51	Mary	48	Foreman; lime works	Seal	8
Island House	Follett	John	42	Jemima	46	Valet; domestic	Rochester	3
Mill & 2 houses	unoccupied							
'Rising Sun'	Hawks	Henry	39	Emma	39	Licensed victualler	Snodland	6(1)
[same] S	Barnden			Amy	16	Domestic servant	Halling	
Lodge House	Owen	Frederick	28	Minnie	27	Cowman	Chilham	4
[same] RR	Pilcher	Thomas	23	Harry	21	Gardener/Joiner	Bromley	
Gardener's Cottage	Roots	John	37	Emily	37	Gardener	Trottiscliffe	5+
[same]	Young	Harry	18			Gardener	Wrotham	1
Holborough Court	Chambers	George	53	Mary	50	Butler	Welbourne, Lincs.	[5]
[same] S	Jones			Mary	27	Housemaid	Carnarvon	
[same] S	Carter			Drusilla	19	Housemaid	Heacham, Norf.	
[same] S	Bailey			Fanny	17	Kitchen maid	Goudhurst	
Coachman's House	Payne	William	33	Mary	31	Coachman; groom	Luton, Beds.	6(1)+
[same]	Honey	Sydney	21			Groom	Maidstone	1
The Cedars	Raven	Henry	61	Katharine	35	Mercantile clerk	Chelsea	7(3)

[same] S	Channer		Emily	24	Domestic servant	West Malling	
[same] S	Woolley		Louisa	17	Domestic servant	Snodland	
[same] S	Kew	George		19	Groom	Rainham, Kent	
Holborough Farm	Terry	William	Jane	45	Farm Bailiff	Wrotham	9
Holborough Farm	Martin	Thomas	Frances	69	Shepherd	Yalding	2+
[same]	Miles	Walter		16	Groom	Bishop Stortford	1+
[same]	Campbell	Harry		20	Groom	London	1+
[same]	Bonner	Edwin		24	Coachman	East Malling	1+
[same]	Aldridge	Robert		29	Coachman	Newbury, Berks.	1
Holborough Farm	Maskell	Samuel	Eliza	45	Labourer	Ware, Herts.	2
Holborough Farm	Weeden		Ainne	53	Housekeeper	Rickmansworth	1
Holborough Cott.	Parrington	Matthew	Edith	38	Estate Agent; Farmer	Chichester	8(4)
[same] S	Waterfall		Charlotte	48	Nurse; domestic	St. Neots	
[same] S	Gardener		Priscilla	34	Parlour maid	Horsham	
[same] S	Ford		Fanny	30	Cook	Bristol	
[same] S	Blundell		Grace	23	Housemaid	Shoreham	
Lad's Farm	Hucks	George	Mary	47	Ag. Labourer	Wrotham	6
Lad's Farm	Kennett	Abraham	Sarah	74	Ag. Labourer	Stalisfield	2
Lad's Farm	Gams?	Edward	Ellen	62	Ag. Labourer	Seal	2
Lad's Farm	Luxford	William	Elizabeth	36	General Labourer	Gravesend	4(2)
[same] L	Wraight		Mercy	7	Scholar	Halling	
[same] L	Russell	William		23	Labourer	Halling	
1 Pomfrey Cottages	Evenden	Aaron		53	Farm Labourer	Mereworth	1
2 Pomfrey Cottages	Jackson	George	Eliza	35	Farm Labourer	Yarmouth, Suffk.	5
3 Pomfrey Cottages	King	William	Bessie	22	Farm Labourer	Hadlow	2
4 Pomfrey Cottages	Petman	John	Mary	50	Farm Labourer	Dover	2
5 Pomfrey Cottages	Evenden	Elon		47	Farm Labourer	Mereworth	2
6 Pomfrey Cottages	West?	Thomas	Kate	43	Farm Labourer	Dover	2
Holly Hill Mansion	Elliss		Elizabeth	41	Housekeeper	Brixham, Devon	[3]
[same] S	Ring	Alfred		42	Coachman	Rotherfield	
[same] S	West?		Catherine	36	Domestic servant	Ightham	
Holly Hill	Harryman	Thomas	Eliza	19	Ag. Labourer	Birling	6
Holly Hill	Baldock	Daniel	Sarah	50	Waggoner	Netlested	6(1)
[same] RR	Vaughan		Emily	30		Birling	
[same] L	Hadlow	William		29	Waggoner	Snodland	
Holly Hill	West	George	Lucy	32	Shepherd	Platt	7
[same] R	Fielder		France	47	Scholar	Plaxtol	
				45			
				6			

Mark Farm	Wickham	William	44	Emily	51	General Labourer	Kemsing	4
[same] R	Weeden	Stephen	72			Carpenter	Wilmington	
[same] R	Godden			Ada	8	Scholar	Malling	
Cox's [Cottages]	Hayward	Charles	54	Ann	52	Ag. Labourer	Headcorn	3
Cox's [Cottages]	Sears	Thomas	30	Jane	27	Farm Labourer	Stockbury	5
Cox's [Cottages]	May	Henry	27	Agnes	26	Ag. Labourer	Hadlow	4
Covey Hall Cottage	May	John	81				Tonbridge	2
Cox's Farm	Champion	Joseph	67	Jane	63	Farmer	Wormshill	8(1)
[same] R	Wilson	Ronald	10			Scholar	Hollingbourne	
[same] S	Godden			Edith	22	Domestic servant	Stansted	
[same] R	Smith	Herbert	12			Scholar	Boughton Monch.	
Cox's Farm.	May	James	67	Anne	59	Ag. Labourer	Hadlow	2

SELECT BIBLIOGRAPHY, SOURCES AND FURTHER READING

Arch. Cant. = *Archaeologica Cantiana,* the Journal of the Kent Archaeological Society
CKS = Centre for Kentish Studies (Maidstone)
P342 = Parish Records for Snodland held at Archives, Council Offices, Strood
BL = British Library; PRO = Public Record Office

General. J. Woolmer, *Historical Jottings of the Parish of Snodland* (Snodland, 1894); Rev. Charles de Rocfort Wall, *Snodland and its History: 55 BC to A.D. 1928* (Snodland, 1928). Wills and administrations are mostly taken from CKS: DRb/Pwr and DRb/Pwa, but a few are among the PCC wills at PRO. Church Registers and Overseers' Accounts: P342; Land Tax Assessments: CKS: Q/RP/346

Beginnings. I.D. Margary, 'The North Downs Main Trackways', *Arch. Cant. LXIV* (1967), pp. 20-3. Patrick, Thornhill: 'The Medway Crossings of the Pilgrims' Way', *Arch. Cant. LXXXIX* (1974), pp. 91-100.

The Romans. N.C.Cook, 'A Roman Site in the Church Field, Snodland', *Arch. Cant. XL* (1928), pp. 79-84; R.F.Jessup, N.C.Cook and J.M.C.Toynbee, 'Excavations of a Roman Barrow at Holborough, Snodland', *Arch. Cant. LXVIII* (1955), pp. 1-61; M.A.Ocock and M.J.G.Syddell, 'The Romano-British Buildings in Church Field, Snodland', *Arch. Cant. LXXXII* (1967), pp.192-217; T.F.C.Blagg, 'Roman Kent' in *Archaeology in Kent to A.D. 1500* (CBA Research Report No. 48, 1982), pp. 51-60; Alec Detsicas, *The Cantiaci* (Gloucester, 1983); See also: *Arch. Cant. XLVI* (1934), pp.202-3; *Arch. Cant. LXXI* (1957), pp.229-30; *Arch. Cant. LXXIX* (1964), pp.225-6

A Saxon Cemetery. Vera I. Evison, 'An Anglo-Saxon Cemetery at Holborough, Kent', *Arch. Cant. LXX* (1956), pp. 84-141

Early Charters/After 1086. P.H.Sawyer, *Anglo-Saxon Charters* (Royal Historical Society, 1968); ed. Philip Morgan, *Domesday Book, 1, Kent* (Chichester, 1983); CKS: CCRb/M6

Fines, etc.: 1193-1450. John Thorpe, *Registrum Roffense* (London, 1769); *Arch. Cant.* [various] I-XVIII *passim;* ed. Charles Johnson, *Register of Hamo of Hythe (Kent Records, Vol. IV ,*(-1946); BL: Harley Charter 76.F.7; BL: Add. Charter 36652

Some fifteenth-century parishioners - the Tilghman family: Beauley grant in *Arch. Cant. X* , pp. 321-3; wills and administrations in CKS: DRb/Pwr, but a few are among PCC wills at PRO; deeds for Holborough mill, etc., are principally in CKS, U522

The sixteenth century. 1524 list = PRO: E179/124/195; Quarter Sessions: CKS: Q/SB; QM/SRc; Q/SR

The seventeenth century. *Calendar of State Papers;* Hearth Tax returns at CKS: Q/RT (1664) and PRO (1662-3); Compton Census returns in *A Seventeenth Century Miscellany* (Kent Records Publications, 1979); *Calendar of the Committee for Compounding*; Edward Hasted: *History of Kent.*

The eighteenth century. Inventories at CKS: DRb/Pi; Manorial records at CKS: CCRb/M1-6; Petty Sessions records at CKS: PS/Ma1-6. John May charities at P342/25/1; registers of alehouse keepers at CKS, Q/RL

The nineteenth century. Census returns; Newspapers (see Andrew Ashbee: *Snodland 1865-1882, A Selection of Newspaper Cuttings* (Snodland, 1991); on Phelps: Esme Wingfield Stratford, *This was a man: the biography of the Honourable Edward Vesey Bligh, Diplomat-Parson-Squire* (London, 1949); on Waghorn: Charles Roach Smith, *Restrospections, Social and Archaeological* (London, 1883), various documents at BL; on the Paper Mill and Hook family: Kenneth Funnell, *Snodland Paper Mill. C. Townsend Hook and Company from 1854* (Snodland, 1979 and 1986); Toll Road: T3; 'Parochialia' = P342/28/20 (published, ed. Andrew Ashbee: *Notes from Snodland Rectory 1865-1882* (Snodland, 1992)); Rollason document: Library of Kent Archaeological Society;

Around the village. Roger Homan, *The Victorian Churches of Kent* (Chichester, 1984); Tithe commutation map and schedule: CKS: CTR; deeds from various collections at CKS, including CCRb, Q/Rdz 3, U30, U47, U522, U787, U838, U1436, U1515, U1644, U1823, U1833, U1882, U2102, U2196, U2685; Manley bankruptcy at PRO: C12/2187/9; See also Margaret Collins, *Birling - A Backward Glance* (Birling, 1982), and Edward Gowers & Derek Church, *Across the Low Meadow: A History of Halling in Kent* (Maidstone, 1979) for numerous family and other connections between Snodland and these neighbouring villages.